Resilient Downtowns

Resilient Downtowns details the innovative and successful approaches that cities have used to revitalize their core downtown areas. Downtowns play an important function despite the problems that city centers have faced in the last couple of decades—deteriorating infrastructures, high vacancy rates, and flight to the suburbs. What most of these communities need is not an enumeration of their problems, but a guide on how to move forward with programs and policies that can help them rejuvenate their downtowns.

While the downtown success stories of large cities have been well touted, those of smaller urban communities where a majority of Americans live, is less well known. With this in mind, Burayidi focuses on small and mid-sized cities. *Resilient Downtowns* explores how small-city downtowns have weathered economic boom and bust, through Burayidi's "en-RICHED" approach, a four-part strategy of residential development, immigration strategy, civic and cultural functionality, heritage tourism, and smart urban design practice.

Key features include:

- fourteen case studies showing how successful communities have redeveloped, and how their success can be replicated in other downtowns;
- information on how to revitalize in periods of austerity and how the recession is affecting revitalization strategies in small cities;
- an alternative model to the Main Street Model with a focus on baby boomers, non-traditional families, new immigrants, cultural tourism, and regional culture.

Resilient Downtowns is an essential guidebook for planning and real estate development professionals, main streets managers, and others involved in redeveloping downtown cores as well as students beginning their careers in these areas.

Michael A. Burayidi is Irving Distinguished Professor and Chair of the Department of Urban Planning at Ball State University, Indiana. He is also author of *Downtowns: Revitalizing the Centers of Small Urban Communities* (Routledge, 2001) and *Urban Planning in a Multicultural Society* (Praeger, 2000).

Resilient Downtowns

A New Approach to Revitalizing Small- and Medium-City Downtowns

Michael A. Burayidi

Routledge
Taylor & Francis Group

NEW YORK AND LONDON

This edition published 2013
by Routledge
711 Third Avenue, New York, NY 10017

Simultaneously published in the UK
by Routledge
2 Park Square, Milton Park, Abingdon, Oxon, OX14 4RN

Routledge is an imprint of the Taylor & Francis Group, an informa business

British Library Cataloguing in Publication Data
A catalogue record for this book is available from the British Library

Library of Congress Cataloging-in-Publication Data
Burayidi, Michael A.
Resilient downtowns : a new approach to revitalizing small and medium city
downtowns / Michael A. Burayidi. -- 1 Edition.
pages cm
Includes bibliographical references and index.
1. Urban renewal. 2. Community development, Urban. I. Title.
HT170.B87 2013
307.3'416--dc23
2012047970

ISBN13: 978-0-415-82765-2 (hbk)
ISBN13: 978-0-415-82766-9 (pbk)
ISBN13: 978-0-203-52219-6 (ebk)

Typeset in Frutiger by
GreenGate Publishing Services, Tonbridge, Kent

Printed and bound in Great Britain by
TJ International Ltd, Padstow, Cornwall

Contents

Acknowledgments

The research for this book was made possible through the generous support of the Irving Distinguished Professorship of the College of Architecture and Planning at Ball State University. The funds provided by such an appointment covered the cost of my travel to the case study cities for site visits and first-hand research. Without this support this book could not have been written. I am thankful to the Irving family for the financial endowment that made this support possible.

I am also grateful for the collegial and moral support I received from the College of Architecture and Planning during the course of my research, particularly the College Leadership Council, which is made up of the Guillermo Vasquez de Velasco (Dean), Michel Mounayar (Associate Dean), Mahesh Daas (Chair of the Department of Architecture), and Jody Rosenblatt-Naderi (Chair of the Department of Landscape Architecture). This is indeed an administrative "dream team" that I was privileged to work with in the course of writing this book.

This book also owes a lot to my research team, starting with Nicole McDermid, my first graduate assistant at Ball State University who got the ball rolling in helping me with research toward the book and then handed over the responsibilities to Abby Wiles upon her graduation from the graduate program. Abby's meticulous research and eye for detail has been of immense help to me during the data gathering and proofreading of the draft manuscript. I am grateful to her for her time and dedicated service to this research project.

People often ask me how I have been able to combine my administrative responsibilities with researching and writing a book. While my duties have been heavy, the administrative coordinators in the Department of Urban Planning have helped lighten the burden for me. This gave me some breathing room between my administrative duties to focus on my research and writing. Barbara Hesselgrave was the department's administrative coordinator when I arrived at Ball State as Chair of the Department of Urban Planning in 2009. Following her retirement, Christine Rhine took over where she left off. I thank both of them for their understanding and support during the course of writing this book.

I thoroughly enjoyed my visit to all of the fourteen case study cities for my field research. I met with wonderful people throughout my stay in these places, people who were very welcoming of my visit, and who in some cases dropped whatever they were doing to provide me with the data and audience that made this book possible. I hope that this book reflects the hard work that each of them is putting in to make their communities, particularly the downtowns, the best places they can possibly be. My thanks to the following community "ambassadors" for their assistance and hospitality:

- City of Charlottesville, VA: William Lucy, Professor of Urban Planning, University of Virginia and past President of the city's Planning Commission; Jim Tolbert, Director of Neighborhood Development Services; and Mary Joy Scala, Preservation and Design Planner.

- City of Chico, CA: Meredith Williams, Associate Planner; Shawn Tillman, Senior Planner, Economic Development/Redevelopment Specialist; Bob Summerville, Senior Planner; and Marci Goulart, Senior Designer, Nantucket Home.

- City of Fort Collins, CO: Jim Clark, President & CEO, City of Fort Collins Convention and Visitors Bureau; and Matt Robenalt, Executive Director of the Downtown Development Authority.

- City of Greenville, SC: Mary Douglas Hirsch, Downtown Development Manager.

- City of Hendersonville, NC: Susan Anderson, Planning Director; Lew Holloway, Main Street Program Director; W. Bowman Ferguson, City Manager; Barbara Hughes, Owner of Narnia Studios; and Richard Crandall, General Manager, Mast General Store.

- City of Holland, MI: Philip L. Meyer, Director of Community and Neighborhood Services; Patty Fitzpatrick, Downtown Development Authority; Dennis Sturtevant, Chief Executive Officer, Dwelling Place; Greg Holcombe, Community Planner, Riverview Group; and Robert Jara, Executive Director, Latin Americans United for Progress.

- City of Lafayette, IN: Dennis Carson, Director, Economic Development Department; and Daniel Walker, Planner/Project Manager, Economic Development Department.

- City of Mansfield, OH: Jennifer Kime, Director, Downtown Mansfield, Inc.; and Jamie Thompson, Co-Director, Downtown Mansfield, Inc.

- City of Middletown, CT: Michiel J. Th. Wackers, Deputy Director of Planning, Conservation, and Development; Quentin Phipps, Executive Director of Downtown Business District.

- City of Nacogdoches, TX: Sarah E. O'Brien, Main Street Manager; Brian Bray, Historic Sites Manager/Historic Preservation Officer; Bruce R. Partain, President and CEO, Nacogdoches County Chamber of Commerce; Melissa Sanford, Convention and Visitors Bureau; Chay Runnels, Assistant Professor, Department of Hospitality Administration, Stephen F. Austin State University; Bill King, President/Chief Executive Officer, Nacogdoches Economic Development Corporation; and Melissa Sanford, Executive Director, Convention and Visitors Bureau.

- City of Ripon, WI: Craig Tebon, Executive Director, Ripon Main Street, Inc.

- Santa Barbara, CA: Bill Collyer, Executive Director, Santa Barbara Downtown Organization; Paul Casey, Assistant City Administrator, City of Santa Barbara;

Michael H. Imwalle, Archaeologist, Santa Fe Trust for Historic Preservation; and Adam Nares, GIS Technician, City of Santa Barbara.

- City of Santa Fe, NM: Matthew O'Reilly, Director, Land Use Department; David Rasch, Historic Preservation Division, City of Santa Fe; Keith Toler, Executive Director, Santa Fe Convention and Visitors Bureau; Leonard Padilla, GIS Analyst; Roy Wroth, Executive Director, Santa Fe Complex; and Sunil S Sakhalkar, Associate, Suby Bowden + Associates.

- City of Wilmington, DE: Mayor James Baker; Carrie W. Gray, Managing Director, Wilmington Renaissance Corporation; Tina Betz, Director of Cultural Affairs and Fund Development; Martin Hageman, Executive Director, Downtown Visions; and Will Minster, Director of Business Development, and Main Street Wilmington Program Manager.

The following colleagues read draft versions of the manuscript and provided me with valuable feedback and I am grateful to them for their time and ideas: William Lucy, Professor of Urban Planning, University of Virginia; David Amborski, School of Urban and Regional Planning, Ryerson University, Toronto, Ontario, Canada; and Susan Bradbury, Associate Professor, Department of Community and Regional Planning, Iowa State University, Ames Iowa.

Finally, and perhaps most important, my wife, Christie, and my children, Dennis, Rodney, and Akiwele, were very patient with me during the time of writing this book. I deserted them for days at a time to focus on my travels and writing and even when I am home I wasn't completely present a lot of the time as my mind was lost in contemplation. I hope that the end product justifies my absences and the lost times we could have spent together.

CHAPTER 1

Bringing Downtowns Back to Life

On March 2, 2012 a devastating EF-4 tornado swept through Southern Indiana, killing forty people in the five states that were in its path. Among the communities affected by the tornado was Marysville, IN, a tiny community of several hundred residents. The town was settled along the railway tracks in 1871, with farming as the community's economic base. Not much had changed since then until the tornado hit. The tornado wiped out the entire community and left no building standing in its aftermath. The question that remained was whether the community would rebuild. Writing on this subject, the Associated Press made this observation:

> When a bigger population center such as Joplin, MO is crippled by tornadoes, there is rarely any question about rebuilding. Larger cities typically have greater resources and defined downtowns to serve as focal points. But this flyspeck village may have suffered a fatal blow.
>
> (Associated Press 2012, p. 18)

The Associated Press' comment underscores the importance of downtowns in uniting a community. Would Marysville, IN, have rebuilt if it had a town center, a downtown that brought the community together? Such a focal point might have provided a gathering place for the community to commiserate about the town's future and to decide together what steps to take to rebuild the community, or not. Without a downtown, there is no gathering spot, no togetherness, and each one is left on their own.

The observation made by the Associated Press also underscores the important role that downtowns play, despite the problems that city centers have faced in the last couple of decades. These problems have been well documented in both the popular press and the academic literature. Among these are the loss of middle-class households to the suburbs, deteriorating infrastructure, high poverty rates, and higher housing vacancy rates. This book is not about the problems of downtowns, but about the innovative and successful approaches that cities have used to revitalize their core areas. What most of these communities need is not an enumeration of their problems, but a guide on how they can move forward with programs and policies that can help them rejuvenate their downtowns. No city is alike in structure and in the problems they face. Nevertheless, there is an opportunity for cities to learn from each other and to adapt successful approaches used in other locations to help remediate their unique situation. That is the quest of this book.

The focus of the book is on small cities. While the downtown success stories of large cities such as Boston and Baltimore have been well touted, those of smaller, urban communities where a majority of Americans live are less well known. A study conducted by the Brookings Institution to determine "Who lives downtown?" examined the downtowns of forty-five sampled cities, but shed no light on the downtowns of small, urban communities. In the same vein, Ann Breen and Dick Rigby, the founders and co-directors of the Waterfront Center in Washington, DC, in their book *Intown Living: A Different American Dream* (2004) sampled mostly large sunbelt cities in making the case that there is a revival in downtown living. The cities studied by the authors were Atlanta, Dallas, Houston, Memphis, Minneapolis, New Orleans, Portland, and Vancouver. The literature on downtown revitalization almost invariably ignores small cities, as though small-city downtowns did not have similar revival stories.

The purpose of this book is therefore to celebrate small-city downtowns and to explain why some downtowns in small cities (defined as settlements of less than 150,000 residents) have been resilient to deindustrialization and boom and bust economic cycles. By doing so, I hope not only to tell the positive stories of downtowns in small cities, but also to provide exemplary cases on which other small communities can model their redevelopment approaches.

Differences between Large- and Small-City Downtowns

Large- and small-city downtowns have similarities, but they also have substantial differences. For example, whether in large or small cities, downtowns were the original sites in which cities were first settled. In many cases, such sites were near a water body such as a river that facilitated the transportation of goods to nearby markets. Later, the railroad influenced the location of settlements, as was the case of Marysville, IN. Also, both large- and small-city downtowns were similarly impacted by decentralization of economic activity to the fringe, starting after World War II and accelerating in the mid-twentieth century following the federal highway program of 1956. But there are also significant differences between large- and small-city downtowns that call for a different approach to their revitalization.

Robertson (2001) enumerated many differences between large- and small-city downtowns. Small-city downtowns have a pedestrian-scale development, such that people are not dwarfed by large high-rise buildings the way they feel they are in large cities. Perceptions of crime and other social vices are more pronounced in large-city downtowns than in small-city downtowns. In addition, large cities have a dominance of corporate presence in their downtowns unlike in small cities. Furthermore, small-city downtowns are less likely than large-city downtowns to be segmented into distinct districts such as retail, residential, entertainment, and historic.

Missing from Robertson's list are other significant differences between large- and small-city downtowns. First, small-city downtowns have less racial and social diversity than large cities. Until recently, most new immigrants to the United States settled in large cities where others from their country of origin had settled. Thus, immigrant entrepôts such as Los Angeles, New York, and Chicago attracted immigrants from Asia, the Middle East, and South America who settled in neighborhoods that already had a large population of Hispanic and Asian immigrants. This made these cities even more diverse. Also, the migration of African Americans in the United States was from rural areas in the south to predominantly large cities, mostly in the north, with a strong manufacturing base and employment prospects for migrants. Smaller cities and their downtowns attracted considerably fewer minorities, making them less diverse than larger cities. In addition to diversity, smaller cities are less likely to have the level of eccentricity that is typically associated with large-city entertainment districts. In small cities where most people are long-term residents and know each other well, there is a social stigma to "standing out" in the crowd.

Second, there is a significant difference in land prices between large-city downtowns and their suburbs. With many corporations in large cities preferring a downtown location, land prices are higher in downtowns than at the fringe. By comparison, the price gradient for land from downtown to the fringe location in small cities is less steep. These cost differences mean that downtown businesses will be less attracted to the outlying locations of small cities, solely on the basis of cost.

Third, small-city downtowns are typically within easy driving distance of all city residents. In many cases, the downtowns of small cities are no farther than ten to fifteen minutes driving distance from all neighborhoods. However, in large cities, the downtown lies much farther out from most residents and, thus, the impedance to visit downtown is much higher for large-city residents than for small-city residents.

Fourth, and perhaps because of the proximity of the downtown, there is a greater affinity of residents in small cities toward their downtown than is the case for large cities. Most large cities are multinucleated with several of these nuclei providing full-service central business districts. This is not the case in small cities. Thus, residents in large cities have more options for shopping, service, and entertainment in other areas of the city besides the downtown. It is not uncommon for some residents in large cities to have never visited the downtown since they can obtain most of their needs from other neighborhood centers.

Finally, while Robertson finds large-city downtowns to be dominated by corporate presence, in small cities one finds a few prominent families that dominate and influence development and redevelopment decisions. Many of these families have established foundations that play a key role in the redevelopment of the community, particularly their downtowns. Examples of such families abound. In Muncie, IN, it is the prominence of the Ball family who relocated their glass manufacturing business to Muncie, IN, in the 1880s, attracted by the availability of cheap natural gas in the area. The family established two foundations: the George and Frances Ball Foundation, with estimated assets of $86 million, and the Ball Brothers Foundation, with estimated assets of $133 million. Together, the assets of the two foundations rank eighth among Indiana foundations in assets (Slabaugh 2012). Both of these foundations leverage public and private sector funds for the community's development.

Similarly, the Blandin Foundation was established in 1941 in Grand Rapids, MN, a town of fewer than 10,000 residents. The foundation was established by Charles K. Blandin, the owner of a paper company, with a goal to build healthy communities with strong economies. The Blandin Foundation has over $100 million in assets and gives away $6 million each year toward its causes. As another example of the prominence of families in small-city development, consider the case of the Orton Family Foundation. Founded in 1995 by Lyman Orton and Noel Fritzinger, it is headquartered in Middlebury, VT. The foundation is supported by profits from the Vermont Country Store, a business owned by the Orton family. The goal of the foundation is to promote grass-roots, bottom-up planning and development and to work with small cities and towns to define and shape the development of communities from the residents' own perspective. Finally, and as we will see later in this book, the Edgar and Elsa Prince Foundation in Holland, MI, is a major contributor to the redevelopment of that city's downtown.

While small-city downtowns share some of the same characteristics as large-city downtowns, major differences still remain. The solutions that work for the problems of large-city downtowns may have limited success in addressing those of small-city downtowns. Given the differences discussed above, it is imperative that small cities have their own, tailored approach for redevelopment.

The National Main Street Program and Downtown Renewal

The story of downtown revitalization cannot be told without reference to the National Main Street program. For over three decades, the National Main Street program has helped communities revitalize their downtown commercial corridors through the four-point approach of organization, promotion, design, and economic restructuring. By all accounts, this program has been a success and has helped hundreds of communities revitalize their Main Streets. In 1997, the National Main Street Center documented the success stories of forty-four such communities in *Main Street Success Stories*. At that time, the program had helped over 1,200 communities to reverse the decline of their downtown commercial districts, generated $5.87 billion in new investment, created 115,000 new jobs and 33,000 new businesses, and rehabilitated 34,000 commercial buildings. Today, over 2,000 communities across the country have certified Main Street programs, leading to the reinvestment of $49 billion in commercial districts since its founding in 1980. In Robertson's (1999) survey of fifty-seven small cities, he found the National Main Street program to be the most successful of the sixteen downtown redevelopment strategies he examined.

Nevertheless, the success stories of the National Main Street program have been on commercial revitalization. Consequently, the redevelopment of residential and other components of downtowns have been largely ignored by the program.

This is understandable, given that the program was designed to reposition downtowns in larger cities to compete with the strip malls springing up on the fringe of these cities. While this formula worked well for cities that already had a stable residential population, it has not been robust enough to tackle the multiplicity of problems that needed to be addressed in downtowns. The program also provides no template for organizing landlords whose property is the subject of rehabilitation, erroneously assuming that downtown retailers own the properties in which they operate. Without the cooperation of property owners, preservation strategies for downtown structures will be futile. As a result of these shortcomings, the program has been of limited benefit to cities that wish to broaden the scope of Main Street revitalization to tackle their declining downtown and near downtown neighborhoods. For example, the City of Mansfield, OH, dismantled their National Main Street program to embrace a broader vision that included revitalization efforts for the city's downtown historic neighborhoods.

As Phil Meyer, the Director of Community and Neighborhood Services for the City of Holland, MI, remarked:

> We were a certified National Main Street program community and gleaned what we could from the four-point approach to Main Street revitalization. However, some of the issues we had were expanding and broadening. We got into housing, traffic and parking issues and we were getting to the level where we were beyond the four-point program so we felt they were not a great resource for dealing with these issues.
>
> (Personal interview with author)

A similar story is told by Michiel Wackers, Deputy Director of Planning, Conservation, and Development for the City of Middletown, CT:

> The National Main Street program is beneficial for communities that are not yet organized and are still in the formative stages of redeveloping their downtown. In such cases, the National Main Street program helps them to get organized. However, the program is not useful to communities with mature downtowns because it doesn't ask the question, "What is next?"
>
> (Personal interview with author)

Despite its success, there is yet another concern with the National Main Street program. The four-point strategy (organization, promotion, design, and economic restructuring) is, in theory, to be pursued by communities in tandem to be effective. As said by Smith (1999), the four-points of the National Main Street program are not four separate categories, but cut across all four areas: "This gives the program balance and ensures that activities in each part of the organization are tightly integrated with the other parts" (p. 2). As Craig Tebon, Executive Director of Ripon Main Street, Inc., observed, the redesign of a window on a historic building to make it visually appealing and energy efficient requires an understanding of economic returns on investment. If the owner of the building is unable to recoup the cost from her investment on the building, she is not likely to pursue it. Businesses must be able to justify the cost of design and investment. Design without an understanding of cash flow is flawed.

Robertson's (2004) survey of 100 communities in fifteen states that implemented the National Main Street program found that cities: i) did not use all four approaches; ii) did not give equal weight to all four strategies; or iii) did not use all strategies simultaneously. Robertson found that the most utilized strategy for Main Street redevelopment in the communities he studied was promotion, perhaps because the backers of the Main Street program have mostly been property owners and local chambers of commerce who owned failing retail spaces. This was the case, even though civic leaders and Main Street managers believed that design is the most effective redevelopment strategy. According to Robertson, "Survey respondents rated the overall effectiveness of design strategies as higher than strategies for promotion and economic restructuring thereby supporting the contention that good design is critical for a successful Main Street" (2004, p. 67).

While the National Main Street program has been widely successful, it provides few guidelines for increasing downtown residential population, building on the traditional civic functions of the downtown, or utilizing the heritage resources of downtowns to leverage tourism development. In addition, the program ignores larger demographic forces that create demand for downtown real estate. Furthermore, it fails to capitalize on other unique qualities downtowns have that can be utilized to support Main Street revitalization. This is unfortunate, because downtowns cannot compete with suburban malls by simply sharpening their commercial qualities. Repositioning Main Street and downtowns in general as mixed-use retail, residential, civic and cultural, and entertainment districts provides downtowns with a better competitive advantage over the suburban mall. This requires that the Main Street tactics rest firmly on new redevelopment strategies to reinforce what has been largely a retail approach. These are: i) capture the growing residential demand of empty nesters, recent immigrants, and non-traditional families to repopulate Main Street and downtown neighborhoods; ii) build on the traditional civic functions of downtowns; and iii) utilize downtown's heritage resources to leverage tourism and increase the daytime population of downtowns. The rationale for these strategies is explained in the next section.

Trends Favoring Small-city Downtowns

Since the turn of the twentieth century, downtowns in both large and small cities have struggled to survive the decentralization of economic activity to the suburbs. Some downtowns have been more successful than others. In my view, four national trends have the potential to positively impact the downtowns of small urban communities. These trends are: i) demographic shifts favoring downtown living, such as the retirement preferences of empty nesters and baby boomers, and the growth of non-traditional families; ii) settlement preferences of recent immigrants to small and medium-size cities; iii) the rise of heritage and cultural tourism; and iv) the comparative cost advantages that small-city downtowns provide for civic and cultural activity location. Downtowns that recognize and seize these opportunities will flourish. Those that fail to proactively use these forces to their advantage will lag behind.

Demographic Shifts Favoring Downtown Living

One trend that has the potential to benefit small-city downtowns is the burgeoning population of baby-boomer retirees and empty nesters. From now until 2030, it is projected that an average of 10,000 baby boomers per day will reach retirement age. In this period, as many as seventy million baby boomers are expected to retire. While most of the baby boomers will retire in the same location, according to the *US News and World Report*, those who move will "no longer flock to seniors-only retirement communities … but are likely to choose walkable communities with lots of amenities, recreational opportunities, and residents from all age groups" (Cochran 2011).

Table 1.1 Proportion of the U.S. population that is 60 years and older, 1990–2010

Age Group	1990	2000	2010
60–64	4.2%	3.8%	5.5%
65–74	7.3%	6.6%	7.0%
75–84	4.0%	4.4%	4.3%
85+	1.2%	1.5%	1.8%
Total	**16.7%**	**16.2%**	**18.5%**

Source: U.S. Census: Profile of General Population and Housing Characteristics, 1990, 2000, 2010.

Table 1.1 shows the growth of the U.S. population cohort that is 60 years and older from 1990 to 2010. The proportion of the population in this age group increased from 16.7 percent in 1990 to 18.5 percent in 2010. In absolute terms, that meant the elderly population increased from about forty-two million to fifty-seven million in the two decades, an increase of almost fifteen million people.

The Brookings Institution's study of downtown living, referenced earlier in this chapter, revealed that the proportion of downtown residents aged 25 to 34 increased from 13 percent in 1970 to 24 percent in 2000. By comparison, the proportion of downtown residents aged 65 years and older declined between 1970 and 2000, from about 17 percent to 13 percent (see Figure 1.1). However, these numbers reflect the pattern of downtown living in large cities, not small cities. Indeed, the same forces that drove out the middle class from the downtown, such as safety and high crime rates, equally influenced decisions by the elderly to move out of large-city downtowns. By contrast, small-city downtowns have relatively lower housing costs and low crime rates. Thus, the exodus of elderly households from small-city downtowns was not as pronounced as it was in large cities.

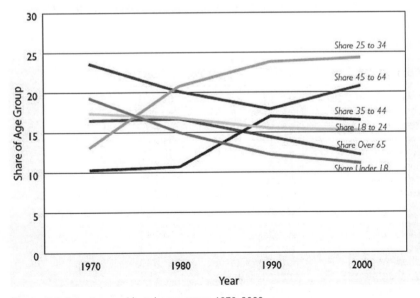

Figure 1.1 Downtown residents by age group, 1970–2000.
Source: Birch (2005).

One notable finding in the Brookings Institution's study is that the share of the downtown population aged 45 to 64 increased from about 17 percent in 1990 to 22 percent in 2000, an upswing (Birch 2005, p. 10). This population cohort represents the baby boomers whose retirement preferences differ from those of the generation before them. It also supports a study by the USDA Economic Research Service that found that an increasing number of baby boomers are seeking to relocate to communities and regions with high amenities such as theaters, museums, and sophisticated restaurants, and to places that provide them with an opportunity for an active lifestyle, including biking, kayaking, and hiking (Cromartie & Nelson 2009). Baby boomers also preferred communities with lower taxes that have a small town feel. Consequently, of the fifteen top places identified by the AARP for baby boomers to retire, ten were small cities and towns (see Table 1.2).

In 2011, an Associated Press–Life Goes Strong poll also revealed that most mid-lifers will retire in the communities in which they live, suggesting that communities that provide the right amenities and conditions for retirees can attract this population group to renew their downtown neighborhoods:

> Many of our parents dreamed of getting that pretty little house in a nice little town somewhere in Florida where mom would play bingo and dad could lounge in his La-Z-Boy chair between rounds of golf. Today very few retirees expect to leave their current home state, with 67% calling that "unlikely" according to the poll and only 13% saying there's even a good chance they'd move across state lines.

> (Cochran 2011)

Small-city downtowns offer the ideal place of residence for the elderly with easy access to entertainment venues, restaurants, shopping, and drug stores. The slower

Table 1.2 Top places for boomers to retire

Community	State	Population
Loveland/Fort Collins	Colorado	62,409
Las Cruces	New Mexico	93,000
Rehoboth Beach	Delaware	1,495
Portland	Oregon	551,226
Greenville	South Carolina	58,799
Sarasota	Florida	50,999
Ann Arbor	Michigan	115,299
Tucson	Arizona	532,288
Montpelier	Vermont	8,035
Honolulu	Hawaii	362,996
Santa Fe	New Mexico	64,040
Atlanta	Georgia	445,709
Charleston	South Carolina	111,980
Northampton	Massachusetts	27,495
San Diego	California	1,251,184

Source: *AARP The Magazine* (2003).

pace of life in small cities also beckons this demographic group. This lends credence to CNN Money's conclusion: "Retirees, empty nesters, and young professionals usually have little in common, but they're all in the vanguard of a recent trend— they're repatriating center cities" (Christie 2006). *The New York Times* also rightly observed thus: "For decades, homebuilders have fed the seemingly endless appetite for the suburban four-bedroom house with the backyard and the picket fence. But increasingly, they are recasting the American dream as a two-bedroom condominium with a gym in the basement and a skyline view from the living room" (Rich 2006).

In Ezell's hortatory book, *Retire Downtown* (2006), he describes downtowns as the "new retirement resorts" and provides several reasons why downtown living is enticing to retirees. He cites, in particular, the opportunities that downtowns provide for retirees, including the opportunity to experience diverse cultures, their exotic nature that provides experiences rivaling that of foreign travels, and chances to interact with different ethnic and racial groups.

The increasing number of retiring baby boomers that seek amenity-rich and walkable neighborhoods in which to retire is precisely the demographic group that needs to be courted for downtown living in small cities. For example, loft and condominium units in downtowns provide a carefree lifestyle for retirees who do not have to worry about snow removal or yard care. This enables retirees to slow down and enjoy their lives with more rewarding activities.

There may already be a shift in living preferences, not just for the baby-boomer generation, but also for the country as a whole, with most people now indicating a preference for walkable neighborhoods. A 2011 community preference survey completed by the National Association of Realtors found 56 percent of those surveyed prefer pedestrian-friendly neighborhoods over neighborhoods that require the use of the automobile. Furthermore, 59 percent are willing to sacrifice more square footage for a smaller house in a walkable neighborhood (National Association of Realtors 2011).

Lucy (2010) noted the turn-around in metropolitan living choices from his research on housing foreclosures:

> By 2000, neighborhoods with housing built before 1940 were no longer the poorest in their metropolitan areas. They were attracting inhabitants with greater means. At the same time, neighborhoods made up of housing that had been built between 1950 and 1970 started to lose their privileged status. Areas developed from 1950 to 1970 were most likely to be dominated by small houses [whose appeal was waning], far from shops and other needs. In other words, both the nature of the houses and their construction and their closeness to, or distance from, everyday needs and services precipitated a profound shift. Urban living gained in popularity.
>
> (p. 35)

Lucy's analysis also showed that in the forty central cities of the thirty-five metropolitan areas ranked as America's largest in 1980, the decline in average per capita income halted. He observed that, "The revival of interest in cities on the part of middle-class whites had a lot to do with a fondness for older homes. In the past, the older the home, the more likely some poor person was living in it. But now that pattern was shifting" (2010, p. 35). These findings led Lucy to conclude that "demand for more mixed use and walkable neighborhoods will increase, and prices in these areas will escalate as supply lags behind demand" (2010, p. 35). He also noted that the suburban housing crisis was due, in part, to a shift in consumer preferences for metropolitan living from the suburbs to the cities. Downtowns appear to be on the rebound because of shifting demographics and taste.

Changing demographics favor downtown living in another important way. There has been an increase in non-traditional and non-family households in the U.S. population in the last three decades. The number of single persons, families without children, and co-habitation has increased. Birch's study of large-city downtowns revealed that in 2000, 71 percent of downtown households were non-family households compared to 41 percent for cities and 29 percent for suburbs and that half of the total downtown households were single person (2005, p. 29). Such demographic changes favor condominium and rental housing markets, most of which in many cities are located in the downtowns or near downtown neighborhoods of central cities. Young professionals who are buying time before settling down in one location often prefer to rent rather than own in order to have the flexibility of moving. Many of these young professionals also value convenience and may choose downtown locations that enable them to walk to places of entertainment, convenient grocery stores, restaurants, as well as civic and cultural amenities. Some may prefer live–work housing units to avoid long commuting distances to work; all of which advantage downtowns over suburbs.

Table 1.3 shows that like the elderly population, non-traditional households have also increased in the U.S. population in the last two decades. In 1990, non-family households made up almost 30 percent of the population, but this increased to about 34 percent in 2010. Such a demographic shift is having an impact not only on the type of housing that is demanded, but also in the location of such housing.

Zimmerman/Volk Associates, a firm that conducted housing assessment studies for several U.S. cities, found 52 percent of downtown residents in Albany, NY, were singles/childless couples, and 39 percent were empty nesters or retirees. The same firm found 38 percent of empty nesters and retirees resided in downtown Toledo, OH, as did 82 percent of the households that live in downtown Bardstown, KY.

Bernard F. Lynch, City Manager for the City of Lowell, MA, credits, downtown living preferences of non-traditional households for helping to rejuvenate the city's downtown. Between 2006 and 2008, $180 million was invested in downtown Lowell, transforming 2.6 million square feet of vacant buildings into condominiums

Table 1.3 Household Types in the U.S., 1990–2010

Type of Household	1990	2000	2010
Non-family households	29.8%	31.9%	33.6%
Family households	70.2%	68.1%	66.4%

Source: U.S. Census: Profile of General Population and Housing Characteristics, 1990, 2000, 2010 Demographic Profile Data. American FactFinder. United States Census Bureau.

and apartments. According to Lynch, such a transformation was made possible by the new demographics of the city that favored downtown living. This demographic group consisted of predominantly non-traditional families.

Immigration

Immigration is another demographic variable that has the potential to shape the fortune of downtowns. The United States has been experiencing an immigration boom since at least the 1980s. According to the Migration Policy Institute (MPI), on average, about one million legal immigrants entered the United States each year since 1980. This does not take into consideration those who entered illegally. The largest immigrant groups are Latinos and Asians. These recent immigrants are no longer settling exclusively in large metropolitan areas such as New York, Los Angeles, Chicago, Houston, Washington, DC, and Boston. They are populating the countryside in Idaho, Iowa, Maine, and the Dakotas. They are drawn to these small cities and towns by employment opportunities on farms, in food-processing and meat-packing plants that do not require fluency in English. They also value the peace and quiet of the countryside and the lower cost of living in these small towns.

Most of the meat-packing plants in the United States today are located in predominantly rural states such as Iowa, Colorado, Nebraska, and Kansas. The world's largest turkey plant, Smithfield-owned Butterball, which processes about 80,000 turkeys a day, is located in Mount Olive, NC, with a population under 4,000. Similarly, JBS, one of the world's largest meat-processing plants, is located in Greeley, CO, a city that is experiencing a significant growth of its Hispanic population. One of the major employers in Beardstown, IL, a town with a population of 6,000 residents, is the Cargill meat-packing plant that slaughters 2,000 hogs a day. These are the communities that offer job openings that immigrants need and the prevailing conditions to attract them.

In Long Prairie, MN, a community originally settled by immigrants of the Nordic stock, African and Hispanic immigrants are now changing the ethnic landscape. In Perry, IA, a community with a population of about 8,000, as much as 40 percent of the population is Hispanic. The majority are employed by IBP, a meat-packing plant. Similarly, Marshalltown, IA, a community with a population under 30,000, attracted a large Hispanic population because of employment opportunities at Swift & Company, a meat-packing plant.

A fifth of the population in Holland, MI, is Hispanic and Hispanics have been a part of the community since the 1950s, attracted by opportunities of farm work on blueberry farms in the area. For over a century, H.J. Heinz of Holland, a pickle-packing plant located on the southern shore of Lake Macatawa, employed Hispanic immigrant workers at its Holland plant. Many local landscaping companies such as Walters Gardens and nurseries have also employed Hispanics to assist with their landscaping business.

African immigrants from Somalia are also settling in small communities in Minnesota and Wisconsin. Recipient cities include Barron, WI, and Rochester, Saint Cloud, Owatonna, and Marshall in Minnesota. Immigrants that were resettled in the United States from Thailand refugee camps now comprise 2 percent of the population of Wausau, WI, a community that has fewer than 40,000 total residents.

As Stephen G. Bloom aptly observed of life in these small towns in the Midwest: "These newcomers arrive in a place where homes still sell for $40,000, a serious crime is toilet-papering a high schooler's front yard, the only smog comes from a late-autumn bonfire, and getting stuck in traffic means being trapped behind a John Deere tractor on Main Street" (Bloom 2006, p.61).

A study by Pyong-gap Min, Director of the Research Center for Korean Community at Queens College, and Chi-gon Kim, Professor at Wright State College in Dayton, OH, showed that since 2000 there has been a drop in the Korean population in the ten so-called "gateway cities for Korean immigrants." Korean immigrants are no longer settling in large metropolitan areas such as New York, Chicago, and Los Angeles, but are now choosing to start their "second lives" in small cities and towns. The authors attribute this shift in behavior to both the financial costs of living in large cities and "the sense of ease Koreans feel in smaller towns" (Min & Kim 2010).

Most recent immigrants in small cities live in or near downtown residential neighborhoods, in part because housing cost is cheaper in these neighborhoods. Close to a thousand Somali immigrants call downtown Lewiston, ME, home. Hispanic immigrants have helped to revitalize the center-city neighborhood in Holland by buying and refurbishing old and historic housing in this near downtown neighborhood. These new immigrants provide an opportunity for cities to repopulate and revitalize their downtowns, as they are the prime demographic for the first-time homebuyer market, typically located in the central city. The lower housing costs, access to retail, and civic and cultural amenities provide a draw and advantage to downtown living for new immigrants.

Immigrants are also very enterprising, creating employment opportunities not only for themselves, but also for others. According to a report published by the Kauffman Foundation, immigrants are about twice as likely as American-born citizens to start their own business (Fairlie 2011). Brazilian immigrants have helped to revitalize the downtowns of Framingham, Marlborough, and Milford in Massachusetts by selling a variety of products from Brazilian pizza to hair products in their shops. Shops owned by Mexican immigrants along the 4th Street commercial district in Santa Ana, CA, are contributing to the city's lively downtown. According to the Orange County Register, "The hustle and bustle of the district is like the heartbeat of the downtown area, which produces $2.6 million in sales tax yearly" (Carcamo 2009).

Many communities are now actively recruiting immigrants as part of their downtown revitalization strategy. In the 1990s, Mayor Jurczynski of the City of Schenectady, NY, sent a bus to round up Guyanese immigrants from Queens to tour his city, so he could showcase the housing potential that the city provides. Often, the mayor would end his tours by treating the immigrants to Italian cookies and wine at his mother-in-law's. These tours convinced the immigrants from Guyana that small-town living offered better prospects than life in the big city. Today, Guyanese make up 10 percent of the city's population. Once desolate downtown streets in Schenectady are back to life.

Schenectady is not alone in recognizing the potential of immigrants for downtown revitalization. In 2009, Philadelphia's mayor, Michael Nutter, announced plans to recruit 75,000 immigrants to the city to help rejuvenate its neighborhoods and the downtown. In Detroit, the New Economy Initiative, the Skillman Foundation, and the Greater Detroit Chamber of Commerce are exploring ways to repopulate the city by attracting immigrants and promoting new intercultural partnerships.

Heritage and Cultural Tourism

A third trend that has potential benefits for downtown renewal in small cities is heritage and cultural tourism. Tourism is a growth industry and a study by Mandala Research, LLC, for Heritage Travel, Inc., a subsidiary of the National Trust for Historic Preservation, found that 118.3 million adults each year participate in cultural tourism, spending an average of $994 per trip, and contributing more than $192 billion annually to the U.S. economy (Mandala Research, LLC 2009). Heritage travelers also stay longer and spend more per trip than other travelers because they seek to enrich their life experiences through travel. According to the National Trust for Historic Preservation, heritage tourism is travel geared toward experiencing authentic places and activities that tell the stories of people's culture and history. These places provide tourists with the opportunity to witness in-situ the wonders of nature, history, and culture.

While heritage and cultural tourism are linked, many cities fail to make the connection and thus, do not capitalize on the benefits their heritage could contribute to the health of their economies. Heritage tourism is intricately linked to historic preservation. As John Nau, then Chairman of the Advisory Council on Historic Preservation, observed in his remarks at a Denver conference in 2004, "historic preservation and heritage tourism are yoked concepts … historic preservation is the key to unlocking the economic engine of heritage tourism" (Nau 2005).

The heritage of most cities is in their downtown. If tourists want to experience authentic history and the culture of a place, it is mostly in downtown that they can have this experience. Downtowns are the only places where buildings have meaning and where there is a sense of place. Downtowns are where a community's story is told, its culture is on display, and its history can be narrated. As Rypkema (2003, p. 12) observed: "Downtown's strength is not homogeneity with everywhere else; the strength of downtown is its differentiation from anywhere else." Small towns have an added advantage in that they provide affordable tourism destinations. Thus, historic preservation can be used to enhance a community's heritage tourism potential.

Santa Fe, NM, is a city that has used historic preservation as a catalyst for the development of its downtown. The city has successfully capitalized on its 400-year-old history and unique architecture to promote heritage tourism. To ensure the preservation of the city's historic assets, Santa Fe has one of the oldest and most strict historic preservation ordinances in the country. As a result, heritage tourism is the driving force behind the health of the city's downtown.

This opportunity has not been lost in the minds of other community boosters. Many communities have sought to portray their uniqueness through destination branding. In 2007, city officials in Santa Rosa, CA, hired North Star to assess the city's tourism potential. The outcome of the study was a new tagline for Santa Rosa. "Place of Plenty" was created to highlight the city's "agricultural heritage and abundance of food and wine." Dayton, OH, is branding itself as a place of innovation with the slogan, "Dayton Patented. Originals Wanted."

In Florida, the state marketing organization, Visit Florida, launched a program to work with 1,000 Friends of Florida to promote a tourism marketing theme "Downtown and Small Towns" (D&S), in part to highlight the attractive qualities of small-city downtowns to tourists but also to manage urban sprawl in the state. The D&S initiative is "intended to reinforce urban revitalization efforts currently taking place, in addition to serving as a legitimate new tourism product promoting the arts, historical and cultural districts" (Hiller and Pennington n.d.).

The Town of Apex, NC, developed around a small railroad station which initially attracted tobacco farmers and became a preferred shipping point for products such as lumber and turpentine. After several decades of population decline, the establishment of the Research Triangle Park in North Carolina in the 1960s attracted high-technology workers and contributed to the town's growth. To preserve the historic character of the downtown and the surrounding residential neighborhoods, the Town of Apex enacted an overlay zoning district in 2006. Apex renovated its Town Hall into the Halle Cultural Center that now draws many visitors to the city. Apex's downtown neighborhoods are listed on the National Register of Historic Places and serve as an example of an intact turn-of-the-century railroad town in North Carolina, an attraction for heritage tourists.

Of course, not all communities are cognizant of, nor have they made efforts, to preserve their historic heritage to capitalize on its potential for tourism. Davis (2004) wrote of how the Maple Ash Neighborhood in Tempe, AZ, with pre-1940 houses in a variety of architectural styles is being torn down and replaced by modern buildings similar to that of the Pueblo Grande development. Like other communities, she came to the conclusion that short-term economic motives appeared to hold sway over preservation:

> The downtown was an outdoor mall; the new housing which replaced the cottages was utilitarian and uncomplimentary. But the prevailing sentiment was that the development was good for the city and good for the people. In Arizona, itself such a new state, newness is what sells. The Maple Ash Neighborhood Association (MANA) and other preservation groups will likely find it difficult to convince people that, for long-term economic success, and to preserve a sense of place, Tempe needs to hold on to its architectural history as it ventures into the future.
>
> (Davis 2004, p. 9)

The unique heritage of downtowns, in addition to the opportunities for walking, biking, and chance encounters, are all appealing assets of small-city downtowns. There is one more advantage to heritage tourism for cities: people approaching retirement often travel to many interesting locations before forming a decision about the most desirable place to relocate after retirement. Thus, heritage and cultural tourism can be used as a recruiting tool for attracting retiring baby boomers who now seek small-town living.

Retention and Expansion of Civic and Cultural Amenities in Downtowns

The extent to which a community is able to retain civic and cultural activity in its downtown has a direct correlation to the health of the downtown. Both centripetal and centrifugal forces contributed to the decentralization of economic activity and population from central cities. The centrifugal forces that repelled economic activity from downtowns, especially in large cities, were high land costs, fragmented land ownership that made it cumbersome to assemble land for development, and higher crime rates. However, lower land costs and property taxes, preferential insurance rates, and easy access to customers near the interstate highways were the centripetal forces that drew business to the fringe.

For a long time, civic buildings such as courthouses, municipal offices, police stations, and jails, as well as newspaper offices, stadiums, and ballparks seemed immune from such centripetal forces. However, in recent years such activities are facing increasing pressure to relocate to the fringe. Built at the turn of the nineteenth century, many of these civic buildings have become functionally obsolete as their size is no longer able to accommodate the volume of services that they are now required to provide. Others are in violation of building codes, due to the difficulty of retrofitting them to meet current building standards. For example, a dispute arose in Columbus, OH, over whether the Sheriff's office should be allowed to relocate outside the city's boundaries. Athens County Sheriff, Patrick Kelly, argued that his office long outgrew its downtown Athens location and that there were no inner-city lots large enough to accommodate a new operations and offices facility.

California's SB 1407, which will be discussed in Chapter 5, also has the potential to undermine downtown revitalization efforts in the state. Enacted in 2008, the law allows the state of California to charge court fees for the renovation or rebuilding of courthouses that are deemed in need of repair. Forty-one courthouses in thirty-four counties have been identified as needing renovations and many central cities are at risk of losing their courthouses to suburban locations.

One such community affected by SB 1407 is Nevada City. The State Judicial Council has earmarked the city's courthouse as one that needs to be rebuilt. The new courthouse of 83,000 square feet will cost $108 million to rebuild and provide parking for 210 vehicles. Due to its size, the Judicial Council decided there was not enough land in the downtown to rebuild the courthouse. Hence the decision was made to relocate it at highway 49. This led residents to mobilize to form the "Save the Courthouse" group to protest the relocation of the courthouse outside the downtown. Residents expressed concern that relocating the building outside the downtown will hurt merchants who will lose the 800 customers and workers that frequent the courthouse every day.

The *Nevada City Advocate* cited Gary Tintle, a member of the State Judicial Committee, as saying, "The committee was informed that state officials had not even analyzed whether it was worth remodeling or renovating the courthouse and that they were opposed to the idea of moving workers during construction." Abiding by strict criteria in the renovation of the forty-one courthouses throughout California will certainly mean many of them will be relocated outside the downtown, hurting downtown business and redevelopment efforts.

Unlike large cities where the cost of land downtown is high, small-city downtowns continue to provide a competitive advantage in the location of civic and cultural buildings. In addition, public leaders in small cities are acutely aware of the impact of such buildings on the health of their downtowns and are sensitive to their relocation outside of the central city. As Langdon (2003) narrated, Amherst, MA, a city with a population under 40,000, fought to retain the Post Office building downtown in the 1980s after the U.S. Postal Service floated the idea of moving from the downtown to an outside location. Once retained, the city built a community center and a new police headquarters in the downtown to complement the Post Office building. These projects resulted in an increase in population in the city's downtown. By contrast, the high cost of operating the offices of the *Atlanta Journal Constitution* (AJC) was cited as the reason for moving the paper's offices from downtown Atlanta to a former Macy's distribution center in Dunwoody along I-285, a location dubbed O.T.P. or outside the perimeter by Atlantans.

Public buildings are a stronger and more significant presence in the downtowns of small urban communities than in large cities. Thus, ensuring the presence of these buildings in the central city contributes to the vitality of the downtown. A study by the University of Wisconsin Extension examined comparable communities with county government seats to determine if the location of county buildings made a difference in the number of businesses located in the downtown. The study found that communities with "county seats had 8.4% more businesses in their downtowns in comparison to communities with few or no county offices downtown" (Grabow et al. 2005).

In Lawrence, MA, a city with a population of about 72,000 residents, the federal government's decision in 2008 to build a $15 million, 30,000-square-foot building to house the Citizenship and Immigration Services on 2 Mill St., spurred new business growth in the city's downtown. The opening of the immigration building had a multiplier effect on the economy of the downtown, with several businesses opening shortly afterwards. Conversely, the relocation of the Post Office in Hudson, OH, outside the central business district in 1997 had a significant debilitating effect on the city's downtown.

Perhaps no controversy relating to the location of a civic building in recent memory rivals that of the Ronald Reagan Federal Office Building and Courthouse in downtown Harrisburg, PA, and shows how a city squandered an opportunity to enhance the health of its downtown. In 2004, the U.S. General Services Administration (GSA) decided to replace the Ronald Reagan Federal Office Building and Courthouse in downtown Harrisburg because it did not meet post-9/11 security requirements. The search for a site to relocate the new courthouse initially yielded three sites. All three were eventually dropped because it would have required displacing low-income residents in the community. Consideration was then given to rebuilding the Courthouse at its current site in the 800 block of Market Street. A study paid for by the General Services Administration (GSA) concluded that, "the current site best serves the federal government and the community, maximizes investment in the City of Harrisburg and minimizes required local investment" (*Patriot News* 2008). The judges who worked in the courthouse equally favored a downtown location, as it would keep them downtown and near other civic amenities.

In 2006, the GSA conducted a new site search and narrowed the results to ten locations, three of which were located downtown. In June 2007, the GSA narrowed the potential sites down further by choosing two sites, both located in the downtown area. In 2007, U.S. Senator Arlen Specter and U.S. Rep. Tim Holden toured the proposed grounds with Harrisburg Mayor Stephen Reed. Shortly after, Specter drafted a letter to GSA Administrator Lurita Alexis Doan asking for clarification on why the agency chose the two locations. He also asked for appropriate consideration of sites supported by the City of Harrisburg, one of which was a vacant lot at the corner of 6th and Reily Streets. In the letter, Specter called attention to the objective of the federal government in the mid-1980s to locate projects in areas that best promote economic development. He also requested that the cost of the project be further analyzed, arguing that the downtown sites would require business relocation, costly demolition, and expensive high-rises, whereas the other sites, especially 6th and Reily, were expansive and shovel ready.

A coalition of neighborhood groups, local unions, realtors, and economic development groups banded together to form the Rite Site Harrisburg Coalition (RSHC), a group focused on advocating for the 6th and Reily location of the federal courthouse (Sheffield 2008). In 2008, the GSA released a statement that the 6th and Reily Street location was reviewed in comparison to the downtown site, and that the downtown option was still more cost effective because the 6th and Reily location would require the investment of $16 million for a parking garage and upgrades to 7th Street. In addition, $700,000 in subsidies would be needed to support commercial development for ten years, resulting in a loss of $36,000 annually on the tax rolls. Mayor Reed and other city officials countered these arguments by stating that the 6th and Reily location would save taxpayers $31 million. They also contended that the parking garage would have to be built anyway.

While the downtown location was more accessible and close to city amenities such as museums and restaurants, after six long years of debate over the location of the federal courthouse, the GSA was pressured to relocate the courthouse at 6th and Reily. The relocation cost $135 million and has had an effect on the downtown's health and economy (Thompson 2010).

Civic buildings create foot traffic in the downtown and help support local businesses such as restaurants where the downtown workers eat, businesses related to the legal profession such as attorney offices, title companies, and retail businesses such as coffee shops and bars. Ensuring the continuous presence of these buildings in small-city downtowns is critical to downtown renewal. Communities that capitalize on and promote such civic activity in the downtown will remain healthy. Those that neglect to capture the advantages that civic buildings bring to the downtown will see their downtown development efforts falter.

Resilient Downtowns

Fourteen small cities across the United States are selected as case studies for the resilience of their downtowns. The cities are selected to represent the five geographic regions of the United States and provide examples of successful downtown revitalization approaches that are appropriate for small-city downtowns. The selection of the cities in each region is based to a large extent on their reputation for accomplishing what many a small city is striving to achieve with their core areas. Most are recognized nationally and have received designations from professional organizations such as the American Planning Association and the National Main Street program, among others. Common to all cities in the sample is that their redevelopment approach went beyond the traditional Main Street four-point approach of commercial redevelopment. The strategies were comprehensive in nature and included housing, tourism, historic preservation, parking, and other neighborhood revitalization strategies. While most of the case study communities are not certified Main Street communities, they have demonstrated much success in revitalizing their downtowns.

As we will see in the chapters that follow, these communities have used a variety of approaches to bring their downtowns back to life. As a result, they have achieved positive outcomes in one or more of the following areas in their downtowns: they have i) grown their downtown residential population, ii) increased the assessed value of downtown properties, iii) augmented the number of housing units downtown, iv) attracted high-income residents to the downtown, v) increased the daytime population of their downtown, vi) preserved a significant number of their heritage resources, and have consistently done so for decades.

Another common denominator for the case study communities is that civic leaders in these cities recognized the importance of downtown to the overall health and image of the communities and therefore took action to reverse the trend. Here is how the City of Lafayette, IN, justified the need for redeveloping its downtown:

> There is a truism in the business of Downtown enhancement, which holds that "As the Downtown goes, so goes the town." This is true since an economically healthy and sustainable Downtown creates a vibrant image for the city in which it is located, which in turn enables that city to attract jobs, professionals (such as doctors and teachers), and additional residents—thereby enhancing the quality-of-life enjoyed by all residents of that city. And, the opposite is also true … An ailing Downtown casts a negative image; dragging down the entire city and the quality-of-life that city can offer its residents.
>
> (HyettPalma 2007, p. 8)

In the chapters that follow, the downtown redevelopment strategies of the selected cities will be discussed. Chapter 2 discusses the historical and regional context of the fourteen resilient downtowns. Chapters 3–6 examine expanded downtown revitalization strategies that go beyond retail development to include housing, residential, and tourism development. Chapter 7 shows how quality development of the physical environment through place making can have a lasting impact in creating residential and retail demand. Chapter 8 discusses how the resilient communities have weathered the recent economic recession and other downturns and remained healthy. The concluding chapter ties the book together and highlights the need for an expanded and "en-RICHED" approach that goes beyond the Main Street four-point strategy of downtown renewal.

 Please visit the companion website at http://routledge.com/cw/Burayidi for additional resources.

CHAPTER 2

Historical and Regional Context
of the Resilient Downtowns

Downtowns are the original sites where cities were first settled. In the United States, the favored sites have typically been those that facilitated the transportation of goods from one location to another. As a result, proximity to rivers and railroads were the preferred sites for early settlements. At the city core was a mix of uses, as residents operated businesses from their homes. Commercial, entertainment, as well as civic and cultural activities intermingled in the downtown. This was equally true in the cities with resilient downtowns. As shown in Table 2.1, most of the cities were planned during, or prior to, their settlement. Land was reserved at the town center for civic, retail, religious, and educational uses. Town squares and plazas were provided as communal and social meeting grounds at the town center. Government buildings, such as courthouses, were also provided. Residential development surrounded the town centers and built out from the core.

As industry proliferated in the city, the intermixing of land uses became a problem and people became more aware of health concerns. Those who could afford it left the downtown for better locations at the fringe where there was serenity in the countryside and less pollution. Spatial differentiation gradually took place with the downtown becoming the location of heavy industry and the abode for new immigrants who could not afford higher housing costs at the fringe. The advent of the railroad and the highway led to further spatial differentiation by making it possible for the nouveau riche to live farther away from the downtown. Suburban neighborhoods were built to cater to those who chose the Jeffersonian dream of living close to nature.

By the mid-twentieth century, there was a stark spatial demarcation between the downtown, the central city, and the suburbs. Increasingly, downtowns became identified with blight, poverty, and the social malice of urban life. The residential areas immediately surrounding the downtown had denser housing with a variety of architectural styles and niche retail businesses. Central city neighborhoods, especially in large cities, were also identifiable by their diversity of racial and ethnic groups, but were starting to suffer from archaic infrastructure. The suburbs became the bedrooms for the middle class; a place of "order" from the chaos of the central city. To prevent the problems of the central city from encroaching on the suburbs, Euclidean zoning was used to keep out all but single-family residential land uses. In comparison to the central city, suburbs were identifiable by their lack of housing and sometimes racial/ethnic diversity. To facilitate the easy commute of the middle class to the central city, wide residential and collector streets were designed to accommodate the automobile. At the same time, sidewalks were discouraged in the suburbs as these were anathema to the automobile and might invite the wrong crowd.

Table 2.1 Cities and their downtown uses at time of settlement

City	Layout of Original Settlement	Author of Original Settlement Plan	Major Land Uses at City Center
Middletown, CT	Unplanned	Settled in 1650 and incorporated in 1784	Church, Grist Mill, Schoolhouse, Meeting House, Tavern, Commerce.
Wilmington, DE	Planned	Thomas Willing 1731 (Founder)	Grid street pattern, Town Hall, Willington Square, Retail.
Greenville, SC	Planned	Lemuel Alston, 1797	11,023 acres Courthouse, Jail, Churches, Commercial Uses.
Hendersonville, NC	Planned	James Dyer Justice, 1841	79 acres Town Hall, Library, Hospital, Cemetery, Churches, Schools, Courthouse, Commerce.
Charlottesville, VA	Planned	Dr. Thomas Walker 1818	50 acres Grid streets, Town Hall, Courthouse, Residential, Jail, Institutional, Churches.
Mansfield, OH	Planned	Joseph Larwell, James Hedges, and Jacob Newman 1808	109 acres Public Square, Courthouse, Jail, Schoolhouse, Church, Commerce.
Ripon, WI	Unplanned	Settled in 1844	College, Residential.
Holland, MI	Unplanned	Van Raalte, 1847	Grid Streets, Market Square, Light industry, Residential.
Lafayette, IN	Planned	William Digby, 1824	84.23 acres Public square, Courthouse, Commerce, Offices.
Fort Collins, CO	Planned	Jack Dow and Norman Meldrum, 1866	935 acres. Post Office, Jail, Courthouse, College, Schools, County Building, Parks, Zoo, Cemetery.
Santa Barbara, CA	Planned	Salisbury Haley, 1851	Courthouse, Town Hall, Theater, Plaza.
Chico, CA	Planned	J.S. Henning, 1860	50 Blocks Grid streets, Town Center, Churches, Woodman's Academy, Salem Street School, Town Hall, Park, City Plaza.
Nacogdoches, TX	Planned	Don Antonio Gil Y'Barbo, 1779 Captain A.A. Nelson 1840	Old Stone House, Washington Square.
Santa Fe, NM	Planned	1608	Palace of the Governors, Plan based on Law of the Indies Town Planning Principles.

However, as a result of Euclidean zoning, suburban neighborhoods could not accommodate civic and cultural uses and the downtown remained the ideal place for such events as festivals and parades. More importantly, it became increasingly evident that there were significant ties that bound the suburbs to the central city and downtown. Like the heart of a living organism, the suburbs could not go on for too long without a healthy downtown. Thus, by the latter part of the twentieth century, civic leaders began to infuse a cocktail of drugs to resurrect the dying heart. Today, downtowns remain the core districts of most cities, although they may no longer be the major central business district (CBD).

The CBD is a community's civic, commercial, financial, and economic nerve center. It is here that one would find professional offices such as medical, accounting, engineering, and architectural, as well as retail and governmental offices. The CBD is usually in the older part of the city and may be coterminous with the downtown, although in many cities it is much larger than what the city may consider to be the downtown. With the relocation of most major chain stores to sites along highways, a community's primary central business district may no longer be in the downtown, but along one or more of its major arterial roads outside of the downtown. In others, there may be more than one central business district with the downtown having niche businesses, while the highway locations house the chain stores and other big-box retail stores.

Other terms used simultaneously by cities to refer to their downtown include the business improvement district (BID), and historic district. BIDs are formed by associations of downtown businesses and property owners to improve conditions for their members. Local governments grant taxing authority to these organizations so they can raise funds from members through property taxes to enhance their business environment. Such funds have been used by BID organizations for revolving loans that are given to their members for facade improvements, business expansion, building improvements, etc. In many cases, the BID has the same geographic boundaries as the CBD of the community, but that is not always the case, nor is it required. Some cities also create historic districts to recognize and protect housing, buildings, and structures in an area that encapsulates the history of the community's development. Not all structures in the district have to be historic, thus a distinction is made between contributing and non-contributing structures in the area. The contributing structures have historic merit and add to the heritage value of the district. Non-contributing structures may lie in the district, but add no historic value. As downtowns have the critical mass of the original buildings of settlements, they became the sites of most historic districts. It is not uncommon for the terms "BID," "historic district," "central business district," and "downtowns" to be used interchangeably.

This book uses the operational definition of downtown as defined and described by the cities themselves. Because downtown boundaries are amorphous, census tracts are used for delimiting the boundaries of the resilient downtowns. In some communities such as Greenville and Middletown, the CBD is smaller than the downtown's boundaries. Figure 2.1 shows the boundaries of downtown Greenville, as well as the city's CBD. In Middletown, the downtown business district (DBD) which lies between Union Street in the south and Washington Street in the north and from

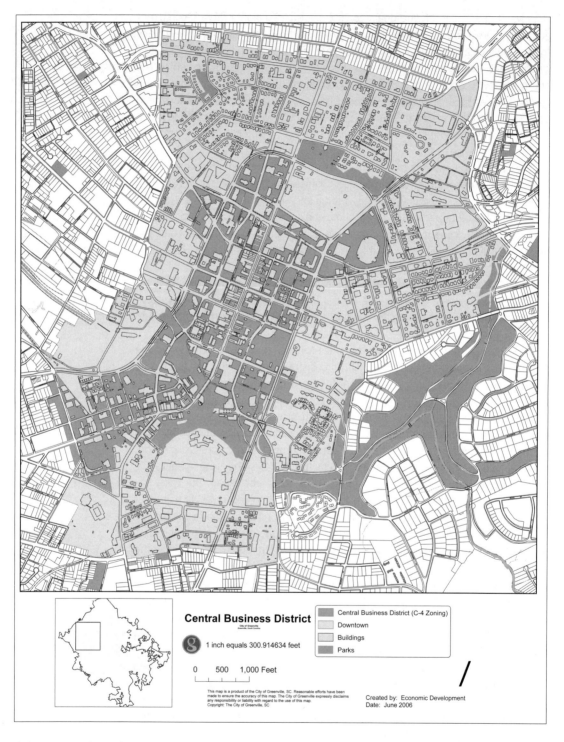

Figure 2.1 Boundaries of the CBD and downtown in Greenville, SC.

Credit: City of Greenville, SC.

General Plan Neighborhoods

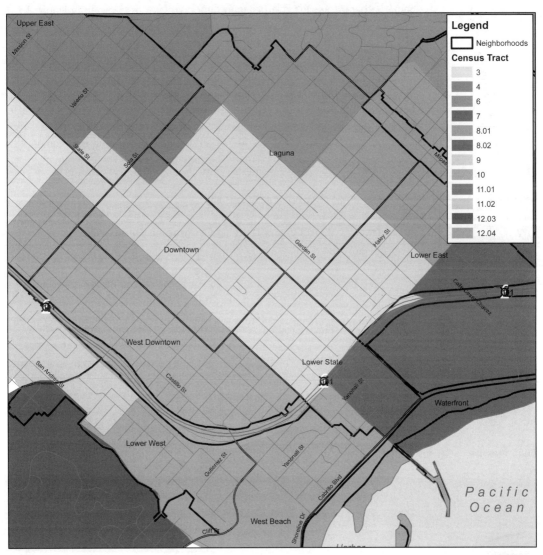

Figure 2.2 Santa Barbara downtown census tracts and neighborhoods.

Credit: City of Santa Barbara, CA.

Main Street in the east to Broad Street in the west is also a much smaller area than what is considered to be the city's downtown (see Table 2.2). In others such as Santa Barbara, the CBD is larger than the downtown as depicted in Figure 2.2. In this case, the downtown is part of Census Tract 9, but the CBD is much larger and includes all of Census Tracts 9 and 10. Since the Census Bureau no longer provides data on central cities, census tracts are a better way to tract socio-demographic data for downtowns. Table 2.2 shows the census tracts that are used to designate the downtown boundaries of the case study cities as well as the description of the geographic boundaries for each of the downtowns. It is the transformation taking place in these boundaries that is the basis of discussion in this book. While census-tract boundaries are not always coterminous with the geographic boundaries of the downtown, they provide a proximate statistical account for the downtowns.

Table 2.2 Cities and their corresponding downtown census tracts

City	2000 Census Tract	2010 Census Tract	Geographic Boundaries
Middletown, CT	Census Tract 5416	Census Tract 5416	Hartford Avenue in the north, to Union Street in the south, and the Connecticut River in the east to Broad Street in the west.
Wilmington, DE	Census Tract 1	Census Tract 28, Block Group 1	The riverfront to Washington Street, to 10th Street, and from Adam Street to 12th Street and Walnut Street.
Greenville, SC	Census Tract 2	Census Tract 2	Academy Street to the north to Academy Street in the west, and Pendleton Street in the west to Church Street in the east.
Hendersonville, NC	Census Tract 9912	Census Tract 9312	From 7th Avenue to the north, Church Street to the west, King Street to the east, and Kanuga Street to the south.
Charlottesville, VA	Census Tract 1 and 3.01	Census Tract 10	From Ridge Street in the West to Avon and 9th Street in the east and from High Street in the north to the Norfolk Southern Railroad in the south.
Mansfield, OH	Census Tract 1, 2, and 3	Census Tract 31	From Bowman Street to the west and Adams Street to the east, and from 5th Street to the north and 1st Street to the south.
Ripon, WI	Census Tract 416: Blocks 3000, 3017, 3018, 3019, and 3021. Census Tract 415: Blocks 2015, 2025, 2026, and 2027	Census Tract 416: Blocks 3000, 3017, 3018, 3019, and 3021. Census Tract 415: Blocks 2015, 2025, 2026, and 2027	Silver Creek/Jefferson Street in the north to Thorne Street in the south and from Ransom Street in the west, to Houston Street in the east.
Holland, MI	Census Tract 223 and Census Tract 224	Census Tract 249	From Van Raalte Ave in the west to Fairbanks Avenue in the east, and from 13th Street in the south to 3rd Street and Lake Macatawa in the north.

Lafayette, IN	Census Tract 6	Census Tract 6	From 4th Street in the west to 11th Street in the east and from Centennial Street in the north to South Street in the south.
Fort Collins, CO	Census Tract 1	Census Tract 1	Willow Street in the north to Olive Street in the south and from College Avenue in the west to Lincoln and Willow Street in the east.
Santa Barbara, CA	Census Tract 9	Census Tract 9	Micheltorena Street to the north, Castillo Street to the west, the waterfront to the south and Salsipuedes Street to the east.
Chico, CA	Census Tract 10	Census Tract 10	Normal Avenue to the west to Orient Street in the east and from Big Chico Creek to the north to Little Chico Creek to the south.
Nacogdoches, TX	Census Tract 9509 and 9510	Census Tract 9509 and 9510	North Street to the west, Mound Street to the east, Cox Street to the south and Mimms Street to the north.
Santa Fe, NM	Census Tract 4	Census Tract 4	The area surrounded by Paseo de Peralta Street.

Regional Context of the Resilient Downtowns

In Santa Fe, the downtown bustles with retail activity along San Francisco and the adjacent streets where merchants sell anything from brand name products to handmade goods. The streets are lined with healthy retail businesses, art galleries, restaurants, and specialty shops. In Wilmington, the downtown is on a rebound, experiencing population growth far in excess of that for the community as a whole. In Fort Collins, there is a healthy mix of retail, residential, art, and cultural activities that bring students from Colorado State University (CSU) and long-term residents to the downtown for entertainment and art walk. These are the symptoms of resilient downtowns, cities that have separated themselves head and shoulders above the crowd. Resilient downtowns are vibrant places with a mix of activity.

While resilient downtowns face similar difficulties as other downtowns in the country, they have managed to stay healthy by adopting successful and innovative revitalization approaches that have turned their downtowns around. Aristotle is said to have cautioned that, "If you would understand anything, observe its beginning and its development." In order to fully understand the resilient downtowns, we must first understand their origin and history. Figure 2.3 shows the fourteen communities selected from the five regions of the United States. They include: Middletown, CT, and Wilmington, DE, from the Northeast; Lafayette, IN, Holland, MI, Ripon, WI, and Mansfield, OH, from the Midwest; Charlottesville, VA, Greenville, SC, and Hendersonville, NC, from the Southeast; Fort Collins, CO, Chico, CA, and Santa Barbara, CA, from the West; and Santa Fe, NM, and Nacogdoches, TX, from the Southwest. They range in size from under 10,000 residents in Ripon, WI, to nearly 150,000 in Fort Collins, CO. In what follows, we look closely at these cities and their downtowns for a perspective of their development.

Figure 2.3 Regions of the U.S. showing case-study communities.

Figure 2.3 Regions of the U.S. showing case-study communities.

The Northeast Region

The Northeast Region comprises eleven states. These states were among the original thirteen colonies settled by European immigrants in the seventeenth century. They include: Connecticut, Delaware, Maine, Massachusetts, New Hampshire, New Jersey, New York, Pennsylvania, Rhode Island, Vermont, and Washington, DC. Close to sixty million residents live in this region. Early settlements occurred along rivers or waterways such as New York, NY, along the Hudson River, Providence on the north shore of the Severn River, and Wilmington, DE, along the Delaware River. Many of the colonial settlements in this region were planned. New Haven, CT, for example, is one of the first planned cities in the country, laid out in 1638. Other planned cities in the region include Annapolis, MD, Williamsburg, VA, Philadelphia, PA, and Washington, DC.

Cities in the Northeast Region developed with an economic base in one of the primary industries of the time, such as shipbuilding, fishing, iron work, and textiles. Later, steel became an important economic base for many major settlements, such as Pittsburgh, PA, and Newark, NJ. Following deindustrialization of economic activity in the 1970s, the region's economy diversified to include service, biotechnology, and information technology industries. The Northeast Region was perhaps the first to experience suburbanization. Levittown, NY, is credited as the first suburban development in the United States. Such development is often attributed to incentives provided to veterans from the federal government following World War II. Many of the new suburban developments catered to the needs of returning veterans. Levittown provided the template for suburban development around the country and the depopulation of the central city. The cities selected for their resilient downtowns in this region are Middletown, CT, and Wilmington, DE.

Middletown, CT

Established on the west bank of the Connecticut River in 1650, Middletown developed as an unplanned community. The Wangunks Native Americans who settled in the area called it "Mattabeseck" meaning "at a great river." The Native Americans gave land to the first English settlers of the area. It was renamed Middletown in 1653, perhaps because it is located midway between Windsor and Saybrook. The city was incorporated in 1784. The early settlers of the community were farmers and shipbuilders.

Agriculture provided the mainstay of the community in its early years, with wheat, rye, and oats as the main crops cultivated. The community's strategic location on the Connecticut River made it ideal for the growth of manufacturing industry. Steam from the river was used to generate power for the machinery of the mills to process grain and for the textile industry. Middletown's role as a port of entry for immigrants from Europe also contributed to the community's growth.

Land uses in the town included a church, a grist mill, a schoolhouse, a meeting house, a burial ground, a church, a tavern, a blacksmith shop, and a shoe business owned by Samuel Eggleston (Whittemore 1884). The first zoning ordinance was enacted by the City of Middletown in 1927. The city's 1955 plan sought to preserve the downtown as the commercial center stating, "The position of the downtown district as the shopping center for the City and surrounding area should be retained. Development of large-scale commercial centers in any other section should not be fostered. Small limited development of neighborhood shopping centers providing only convenience shopping should be provided for" (City of Middletown 1955, p. 4). However, construction of Route 9 in the 1950s and urban renewal in the 1960s greatly affected the downtown. The building of the Westfield-Meriden Mall along the highway attracted many of the national chain stores that were once located in the downtown such as Woolworth's Food Mart, LaBoca, and Kabachnicks. By the early 1970s, the vacancy rate for buildings in the downtown topped 60 percent. Also, the downtown lacked any connection to Wesleyan University and the river. In addition, the highway facilitated the development of new residential neighborhoods outside of the central city. As Warner (1990) observed, by the mid-twentieth century, the city was faced with similar issues that other small cities were facing. Middletown's downtown was in decline as many businesses and middle-class residents left the downtown for the suburbs.

In 1954, the city formed a redevelopment agency for the purpose of redeveloping blighted areas in the downtown. The first of the projects to be tackled by the agency was the Center Street project whose goal was to redevelop the two blocks east of Main Street and lying between Court Street and Williams Street (Dingwall Avenue). Other projects undertaken by the agency were the Metro south project, and the redevelopment of the Theater block. Urban renewal of the older neighborhoods resulted in the razing of blighted areas and the destruction of some of the city's most historic buildings. For example, the city's plan for the development of the Middletown Activities Center led to the demolition of 126 buildings, including the Governor Coughlin House, a 165-year historic building in the downtown.

In 1993, a Downtown Planning Committee was formed to help revitalize the central business district. This led to the development of the first downtown plan for the community, named *Downtown Visions: 2000 and Beyond*. The plan's goal was to create, "A thriving college town on the banks of the CT River." This plan, among others, resulted in a number of entities dedicated to the revitalization of downtown Middletown. The committee conducted a downtown market study and created a Design Review and Preservation Board. It also established a Main Street board of directors, who hired a downtown manager. A Downtown Business Improvement District was created in 2001 with the mission to, "Enhance the downtown through street beautification, public safety, marketing and business recruitment thus making it a desirable destination for residents and visitors seeking business, shopping, dining and entertainment opportunities" (City of Middleton n.d.). Several new developments occurred after the formation of the downtown redevelopment committee. Funds were raised to finance an artist cooperative that housed retail and gallery space for artists. A facade improvement program was also started to help spruce up buildings on Main Street, and a "Village District" was created between Wesleyan University and Main Street with strict guidelines for the neighborhood's development. In addition, Wesleyan University funded a Green Street Art Center downtown at a cost of $2 million.

In addition to the above investment, a $10 million police headquarters was completed on Main Street in 1999 that catered to a mix of uses, including retail on the ground floor. In the same year, a twelve-screen stadium-style theater opened in the downtown. In 2003, the historic National Guard Armory Building on Main Street was renovated into a hotel featuring 100 rooms.

Today, downtown Middletown is on a rebound with a mix of civic, cultural, retail, and residential uses. Some of these include a children's museum, Destinta Theater now called Metro Movies, and a community health center that provides retail space on the ground floor. Some three dozen eateries are located downtown, offering a wide choice of multicultural cuisines ranging from Italian to Chinese, Tibetan, Japanese, and Mexican to Middle Eastern.

Wilmington, DE

Wilmington was established by Swedish immigrants along the Delaware River in 1638. The town was platted for development by Thomas Willing in 1731 in a grid street pattern. Wilmington's downtown is located on the Cape Fear River. The city's central business district consists of approximately seventy blocks, situated between the Holmes and Memorial Bridges and extends irregularly east from the river to 4th and 5th Streets. In 1798, a town hall was built on the 500 block of Market Street and served as the locus of political and social gatherings for the elite in the community. A central square, Willington Square, was located on Market Street between 5th and 6th Streets. In addition, many of the city's commercial activities were located in this neighborhood. The city's development was influenced by its location and topography. Wilmington lies between the flat coastal plain and the hills to the east, a site that was favored by the city's elite. The Quaker Hill neighborhood was built in this area.

Wilmington's location also made it an ideal receiving center for commercial transportation of farm produce from the nearby communities of Cantell's Bridge, Duck Creek, Christiana, Newport, Stanton, and St. Georges. The produce was then shipped up the Delaware River to major cities such as Philadelphia. During the Civil War, gunpowder was transported by railroad cars and ships which passed through

Wilmington. Industrial development in the city took place along the Christina River. Heavy industries such as yacht building and shipbuilding also located along the Christina River and later the railroad tracks. An extensive park system was developed in the late nineteenth century, due to the generosity of William Bancroft, a successful businessman who donated land for the development of Rockford and Brandywine Parks.

In 1837, the Philadelphia, Wilmington, and Baltimore Railroad reached Wilmington. As with most other U.S. cities, railroads and highways increased decentralization of economic activity and made the middle-class suburban lifestyle possible. This led to a severe loss in population of the central city. The construction of I-95 led to the further destruction of several of Wilmington's most stable and historic neighborhoods. For example, land west of Quaker Hill was cleared to make way for the construction of I-95. Large tracts of land below 4th Street were also cleared for urban renewal.

In 1924, the city enacted a zoning ordinance to protect residential neighborhoods from encroachment from industry. In 1952, the city engaged the noted pioneer urban planner Harold M. Lewis as a consultant to prepare a comprehensive plan for the city. A Planning Commission was also formed in 1953 to deal with the "immediate problems of downtown parking and traffic; to find a site for relocation of the King Street Farmers Market; and to determine a route for the proposed limited access freeway that eventually became Interstate 95" (Wilmington Renaissance Corporation 2008, p. 5).

In 1993, the Wilmington Renaissance Corporation was created, "to develop and implement strategies that will increase the economic vitality of Downtown Wilmington, strengthen its role as a center for educational, cultural and social activity, and enhance its reputation as an exciting place to live and visit by marketing Wilmington's unique history and character" (Wilmington Renaissance Corporation 2012). In 1994, Downtown Visions, a non-profit organization, was formed with responsibility for keeping downtown clean, safe, and attractive.

In the last ten years, there has been over $2 billion in private investment in the city's CBD. A recent example of a redevelopment project in Wilmington is the Queen Theater on Market Street. Built in 1915 with a seating capacity of 2,000, the theater closed in 1959 and remained vacant until it reopened in 2011. A collaborative effort between Light Up the Queen Foundation, World Café Live and the Buccini/Pollin Group, a real-estate firm, restored the theater in 2011 at a cost of $25 million. The Buccini/Pollin Group alone has acquired or redeveloped close to $3 billion in real-estate assets in the downtown, including office, retail, hotel, and residential structures.

The revitalization of Wilmington's central business district is in full swing and is stimulating interest in the redevelopment of the area. There are over 300 businesses in downtown Wilmington including professional services, hotels, banks, restaurants, and retail businesses.

The Southeast Region

This region comprises twelve states: Alabama, Arkansas, Florida, Georgia, Kentucky, Louisiana, Mississippi, North Carolina, South Carolina, Tennessee, Virginia, and

West Virginia. It boasts the first permanent settlement in North America by the Spanish at St. Augustine, FL. Later, British colonists settled in the region in the seventeenth century and imported African slaves to work on cotton and tobacco plantations owned by European settlers. Colonies were also established by the French and Spanish in Florida and Louisiana. The Southeastern Region was mainly rural, with few urban settlements. Of the twenty largest cities listed in the census of 1890, New Orleans, LA, was the only city from the southeast included on the list.

The Southeast Region grew from the fertile lands that enabled settlers to grow and export agricultural produce such as cotton, sugarcane, and tobacco. While the economies of the original settlements in the region were based on agriculture, this region has now been transformed by the relocation of manufacturing firms, including the automobile, high-technology, service, and tourism industries. Consequently, this is now one of the fastest growing regions of the country. The southeast has also benefited from international migration from South America and from in-migrants from the northeastern and midwestern states of the United States. Greenville, SC, Hendersonville, NC, and Charlottesville, VA, are three of the resilient downtowns selected from this region.

Greenville, SC

The City of Greenville is located in the Appalachian Mountains, approximately halfway between Atlanta, GA, and Charlotte, NC, on Interstate 85. The city was built on land that originally belonged to the Cherokee Indians. The first European to settle in Greenville was Richard Pearis, who married a Cherokee woman and was given several tracts of land by the tribe. In 1797, Thomas Brandon purchased 11,023 acres of land and retained Lemuel Alston to plat the land for a village with a courthouse and a jail. The name of the original village was Pleasantburg, which later became known as "Greenville." The name was changed to Greenville in 1831, possibly in honor of Nathanael Greene, an American revolutionary general, or an early resident of the community, Isaac Green. The charter was amended in 1869 to give the settlement the title of a city (City of Greenville 2012).

In 1815, Alston sold his holdings and home at Prospect Hill to Vardry McBee of Lincolnton, NC. McBee brought in new businesses, tradesmen, and homebuilders to the village and provided land to each religious denomination to build a church. In time, the settlement attracted residents that sought escape from malaria and other diseases in the coastal region. Many of the original houses built in the 1850s have been preserved in the downtown district. These include Governor Middleton's House, the Fountain Fox Beattie House, the Elias Earle Town House, and the Josiah Kilgore House (City of Greenville 2012).

Downtown Greenville is also where the city's first settler, Richard Pearis, established his plantation in 1770 at the intersection of present-day East Court Street and South Main Street. It was here that Pearis built his house, established a trading post, dairy, blacksmith shop, grist mill, sawmill, and slave quarters (Huff 1995).

During the 1850s, the Greenville and Columbia Railroad reached Greenville, with a terminal constructed in the West End area. In 1869, the Southern Railroad started operations through Greenville. In addition to the expansion of the railroads, an oil mill was built on Augusta Street and the first real bridge was constructed across the Reedy River. A horse-drawn street railway began operations throughout the city at this time. By 1890, a city hospital and a second city hall were built. By the mid-nineteenth century, Greenville became known as the "Textile Center of the South" and an Exposition Hall was built for the display of textile products.

The streetcar and new wealth from the textile industry enabled Greenville's elite to build new residential neighborhoods outside the original downtown core. Among these were the Hampton-Pinckney neighborhood, Pettigru Street neighborhood, Pendleton Street neighborhood, the James and Earle Street neighborhoods, and the Overbrook neighborhood. As commercial development increased in the suburbs, downtown Greenville declined in population and economic health.

Revitalization efforts began in the 1970s in response to the decline in the city's downtown. This ambitious revitalization effort was led by Mayor Max Heller. The first major redevelopment project was the streetscape plan. Main Street was narrowed from four to two lanes, angled parking and decorative lighting were integrated, and trees were planted along the street. Falls Park was restored with the removal of the Camperdown Bridge across the river. In its place, the city undertook a $70 million renovation of Falls Park on the Reedy River and built a unique pedestrian suspension bridge over the river in 2004.

In the last decade there has been a significant increase in downtown living with the development of luxury condos, apartments, and lofts. A mix of retail, entertainment, the performing arts, and pedestrian-scale development have enlivened the downtown and brought attention to the city from both near and far. Greenville has received national recognition for its innovative use of public–private partnerships which bring both sectors together on projects using carefully crafted development agreements to revitalize the city's downtown.

Hendersonville, NC

Hendersonville, NC, the county seat of Henderson County, is located between Greenville and Asheville. It was laid out near Mud Creek in 1841 on 79 acres of land donated by the area's largest landowner at the time, Judge Mitchell King. The plan for the city was prepared by Justice James Dyer and consisted of forty lots. This original layout was bounded by King and Washington Streets to the east and west, respectively, to the south by Caswell Street, and to the north by 7th Avenue. A square on Main Street was set aside for a courthouse, built in 1844. Zoning law in Hendersonville required Main Street to be 100 feet wide so that "a carriage and four horses could turn around without backing" (Bailey & Barber 1988, p 55). Early industry in Hendersonville was agriculture (particularly fruits), furniture, and brick making.

Hendersonville grew rapidly in the mid-1800s due to its accessibility to the Buncombe Turnpike. Completed in 1827, the turnpike stretches from Asheville to Greenville. The completion of this highway made Hendersonville accessible to the Blue Ridge Mountains and facilitated the transportation of surplus farm produce to large market centers. The Spartanburg and Asheville Railroad, which was later absorbed by the Southern Railway in 1902, reached Hendersonville in 1879. The railroad helped establish the city as a tourism destination for travelers from Florida and Georgia to the Blue Ridge Mountains for recreational pastimes. The railroad also extended the physical growth of the city from its original plat to a one mile radius.

Hendersonville's civic and cultural buildings were located in the downtown. These included the town hall, cemetery, the People's National Bank (built in 1910), the Greenville County Courthouse (1844), Rosa Edwards School (1912), 6th Avenue School (1916), as well as the Public Library (1914) and hospital. Several churches were also located in this neighborhood including the Western Baptist Church (built in 1858), the St. James Episcopal Church (1843), the Baptist Church (1848), the Methodist Church (1852), and the Presbyterian Church (1852).

Tourism contributed to the growth of the city in the late nineteenth century and several hotels were built to accommodate tourist activity. The majority of these hotels were built in the downtown. Wheeler Hotel, with one hundred rooms and a dance hall, was built in 1895. Wayside Inn, the Chewning House, Cedars, the Aloha Hotel, the Kentucky Home, and the Smith-Williams-Durham Boarding House were built shortly thereafter.

Residential development also grew rapidly by the late nineteenth century, particularly west of Main Street. Residential segregation occurred along socio-economic class lines. The working class lived in neighborhoods near the railroad lines, while the wealthier residents in the community resided west of Main Street along 4th and 5th Avenue. The dominant architecture of the time was Greek revival, the I-house style, Queen Anne, the Classical Revival, and the Colonial Revival styles. After World War II, the advent of the automobile led to the decentralization of commerce and residential development away from the city's core area. This accelerated after the completion of Interstate 26 and 40, which made the outlying areas more accessible, resulting in the development of new residential suburbs such as Osceola Lake, Mountain Home, and Druid Hills.

In the urban renewal era, several buildings in the CBD were demolished, leading to the destruction of some valued historic property, including the Marlborough Hotel, located at the corner of Church Street and Fifth Avenue West. Downtown Hendersonville faced its first competition with the opening of Rose's store in 1967 in a shopping center to the south of the city. Hendersonville's downtown started to suffer from blight, high vacancy rates, and declining property values. In 1974, a county-wide valuation of property found that downtown property values had dropped by 20 percent, while property values in other areas of the city had increased 40 percent or more (Edney 1997). The property value study provided clear evidence that the downtown was struggling and that something needed to be done about it.

In 1972, a group of downtown business owners formed the downtown Hendersonville Merchants Association (HMA) to try to save the downtown. However, the effort to revitalize the downtown was a community-wide endeavor. Of the thirteen members of the downtown merchants association, seven had no businesses in the downtown. Jim Taylor, the manager of Rose's store, a major competitor to downtown businesses, was a member of the HMA.

Following the formation of the HMA, twelve members from the city went to Grand Junction, CO, to study the revitalization programs of the city's downtown. Upon their return, they proposed the creation of a "special tax district" to raise revenue for downtown's development. They aimed to persuade business owners in the county to approve a three mill tax on themselves to help retire a loan for the redevelopment of the downtown. The HMA Board convinced 250 business owners in the county, many of them not affiliated with the downtown, to sign a commitment to each pay $1,000 to retire a loan incurred by the downtown organization if the mill rate was not sufficient to repay the loan. The financial commitment from business owners provided the necessary funding to begin the revitalization of downtown Hendersonville.

Between 1974 and 1977, the HMA focused on the redesign of Main Street to make it pedestrian friendly. The street was narrowed from four lanes to a two-lane serpentine street with wide sidewalks, angular parking, and landscaping. A downtown development organization, Downtown Hendersonville, Inc., was formed in 1986 for the purpose of bringing the downtown back to health.

Today, downtown Hendersonville is on an upswing. Storefronts are fully occupied. Retail business is thriving, and upper-floor apartments and condominiums are catering to the needs of many city residents who choose to live downtown.

Charlottesville, VA

Charlottesville is located on the Rivanna River and the Three Notch'd Road (now US Route 250). It was established in 1761 as the county seat of Albemarle County. Charlottesville's name is derived from Queen Charlotte Sophia of Mecklenberg, the wife of King George III. Land for the establishment of the town was purchased from Colonel Richard Randolph. The town was laid out on fifty acres of twenty-eight block grids. Two acres of land were set aside for a courthouse on the northern edge of the town. The plan designated the east/west streets to have a width of 66 feet and the north/south streets to be 33 feet wide.

The town grew slowly due in part to its location on a non-navigable creek, at a time when most forms of transportation depended on waterways. By 1765, only twenty lots of the platted land had been developed. In 1835, the Courthouse Square area had two hundred, mostly brick houses, four churches, three hotels, and a number of businesses. In addition to the courthouse, other civic buildings in the downtown included a jail and some educational institutions. These included Jefferson Central College (1816), the University of Virginia (1825), and McGuffey Primary School (1916) built on 2nd Street.

Religious institutions were centrally located in the city's downtown. In 1825, Christ Episcopal Church, designed by Thomas Jefferson, was built at 116 West High Street. Other churches with a downtown location were First Christian Church (1897) at East Market and 1st Street, the Roman Revival Holy Comforter Church at East Jefferson Street (1925), the Colonial Revival First Methodist Church (1924) at 101 East Jefferson Street, and First Presbyterian Church (1955) at 500 Park Street.

When Marquis de Lafayette visited the city in 1824, there were only six hundred residents. In 1836, the population had increased to 957. At that time, Charlottesville had four churches, three hotels, one tavern, two bookstores, two drug stores, twenty retail outlets, two schools, a library, a printing office, and a volunteer fire department. By 1853, the city's population had grown to 2,600 and there were four churches, two banks, and four newspapers. Around the same time, a town hall was constructed downtown and used for public events and theatrical productions (Dabney 1951).

The railway played a role in the early growth of Charlottesville. In 1850, Virginia Central Railroad reached Charlottesville and linked the city to the eastern and western regions of the state. In 1852, the Orange and Alexandria Railroad linked the city to the south and north. Thus, Charlottesville became the transportation hub for agricultural and manufactured products, due to the easy access that the railroads provided for transportation of goods to and from the city. Industry grew and prospered in the town in the 1870s. Major industries in the city at that time were the Charlottesville Woolen Mills, R.F. Harris & Sons, a business that supplied farm equipment, and Charlottesville Milling and Manufacturing Co., a wagon and carriage manufacturer.

The railroad lines also impacted on the city's development in another way. The intersection of the two railroad lines divided the city into four quadrants, with the favored neighborhoods located west of 1st Street. Other choice neighborhoods were located at University Circle, Oakhurst Circle, and Altamont Circle. Queen Anne and Colonial Revival were the preferred architectural styles of the period.

Suburbanization began in Charlottesville toward the end of the nineteenth century, the result of the railway lines that connected the city to the outlying undeveloped areas. Thus, after a century of prosperity, downtown Charlottesville witnessed a decline in business. This was attributed to the development of new suburban centers on the perimeter of the city. Downtown neighborhoods along High and Park Streets were converted to offices. Vinegar Hill, a predominantly African-American business and residential area, was razed in 1964 for urban renewal.

Today, downtown Charlottesville is prospering. This upswing started in the early 1970s when Lawrence Halprin & Associates were hired to prepare a master plan for the city. Restoration of residential structures on North 1st Street marked the beginning of renewed interest in Downtown and the Courthouse neighborhood (Johnson 1988).

The Midwest Region

The Midwest comprises twelve states. These include Illinois, Indiana, Iowa, Kansas, Michigan, Minnesota, Missouri, Nebraska, North Dakota, Ohio, South Dakota, and Wisconsin. According to the U.S. Census Bureau, close to seventy million people live in this region. The Midwest is also referred to as the "heartland of the United States." The attribute of this region as "middle America" was made famous in a study of Muncie, IN, by Robert Staughton Lynd and his wife, Helen Merrell Lynd. The studies were subsequently published as the Middletown Studies in two books: *Middletown: A Study in Modern American Culture* (1920) and *Middletown in Transition: A Study in Cultural Conflicts* (1937). The books provided a snapshot of what is regarded as life in a typical American city. Thus, midwestern cities are regarded as characteristic of American cities and culture. The topography of the land and the fertile soils in the region support the cultivation of diverse crops, including wheat, oats, and corn, hence also giving the region the name "breadbasket" of the United States.

Early settlement occurred in the 1800s when the French established fur trading posts in the region. Several military forts such as Fort Wayne, Fort Crawford, Fort Snelling, and Fort Atkinson were built in the region to protect settlers from Native American attacks. Many of these forts, such as Fort Wayne, remain today as fully fledged settlements. In the nineteenth century, access to navigable waters like the Ohio and Mississippi Rivers attracted manufacturing plants to the region. The waterways presented opportunities for businesses to ship finished goods to major urban centers.

Industrial development in the nineteenth century led to the expansion of large urban centers in the region, as rural farm workers migrated to cities for jobs in manufacturing plants and a better quality of life. Cities such as Chicago, Detroit, and Milwaukee saw their populations triple in this period of industrialization. Because cities in this region depended so heavily on manufacturing, they also bore a greater burden of deindustrialization in the 1970s. As manufacturing plants closed and moved to lower wage locations in other regions and abroad, the region witnessed high levels of unemployment and abandoned buildings. This gained the region the infamous nickname "the rustbelt" region. The four communities selected in this region provide exemplary approaches to downtown revitalization. They are Holland, MI, Lafayette, IN, Mansfield, OH, and Ripon, WI.

Lafayette, IN

Lafayette, IN, is located in Tippecanoe County. The city was founded by William Digby, who purchased 84.23 acres of land in 1824 on the Wabash River for the establishment of the town. In May 1825, he platted 140 lots and named the community Lafayette after the Marquis de Lafayette, the French hero of the Revolutionary War. Across from the Wabash River is West Lafayette, home of Purdue University. These two communities make up the metropolitan area of Lafayette and are economically and socially integrated with each other (Martin & Woods 1994).

Like many of the early settlements, downtown Lafayette was the hub of commercial and civic activity. It was where the courthouse, a public square, retail and wholesale businesses, banks and professional offices were located. Lafayette's growth is attributable to its strategic location as a transportation center, first by water and later by rail. The city's location on the Wabash River facilitated the transportation of farm produce to other urban centers in the region. This role was further strengthened when the Wabash and Erie Canal were completed in 1843. Until its close in the 1870s, the canals were the major means of transporting goods from the region to cities such as Chicago and Detroit. The Monon Railroad reached Lafayette in the 1840s and carried passengers and cargo directly to Chicago, St. Louis, Louisville, Indianapolis, and Toledo. Factories located near the railroad and along the river for easy access to transportation. Among them were ALCOA and Rostone Corporation.

The location of Purdue University in 1869 across the Wabash River in West Lafayette provided further impetus to the development of Lafayette. The presence of a university helped so much that the city's population grew from 2,000 residents in 1840 to 13,506 in 1870. After Lafayette suffered a devastating flood in 1913, the city hired Lawrence Sheridan to prepare a redevelopment plan to guide the future growth of the city. Among the proposals made in the plan was the relocation of the railroad from the downtown to ease traffic congestion. He also made proposals for zoning and thoroughfare improvements.

The factors that contributed to the growth of Lafayette are summed up by a report of the U.S. Department of Interior (1976, p. 3):

> Lafayette's expansion in the last quarter of the 19th century and the beginning of the 20th was influenced by the developments in technology, by the new movements in urban planning, and by local developments, such as Purdue University. The building of the Street Railway and the Belt Railway allowed housing and industry to expand to the East, away from the Wabash River, and the building of Purdue University among others brought about expansion west of the Wabash River.

This eastward expansion away from the central city affected the health of the downtown. By the 1960s, downtown Lafayette began to suffer population decline and blight. After U.S. highway 52 was constructed, it became the preferred location for industry and businesses, thus pulling new development toward this corridor.

After years of decline, downtown Lafayette is now experiencing a period of reinvestment. Perhaps the catalyst for growth was the relocation of the railroad tracks from the downtown at a cost of $185 million. Downtown Lafayette is now a mixed-use neighborhood with entertainment, retail, housing, professional offices, and civic and cultural amenities. Many of the new projects completed in downtown Lafayette include a public library, a main street pedestrian bridge, Courthouse Square, and Riehle Plaza.

Holland, MI

In 1847, Reverend Van Raalte led Dutch Calvinists to the banks of Lake Macatawa, where they founded the Town of Holland. The grid street pattern was used to plat the city, with settlement occurring around a market square that is today the site of Centennial Park. The original grid system remains today in the downtown.

Tourism flourished in Holland following the completion of a channel that linked the settlement to Lake Michigan and opened it to shipping lanes from Chicago. Hotels such as Hotel Ottawa and Hotel Macatawa were built along the lake to cater to vacationers. By 1890, the town's population had grown close to 4,000 residents. Another reason for the growth of the community was the establishment of Holland Academy in 1850 on land provided by Van Raalte, an institution which later became known as Hope College (Van Reken 1977).

Like many midwestern cities, Holland's growth is attributable to industry, specifically furniture and lumber-related businesses. Companies originally based in Holland included Bay View Furniture, West Michigan Furniture, Ottawa Furniture, and the Holland Furniture companies. Additionally, factories such as Cappon-Bertsch Leather Company, Heinz Pickling Works, and Bush and Lane Piano Company thrived in the early days of the community.

Following Dutch tradition, tulip bulbs were imported from the Netherlands to beautify the city. These were planted along the streets and in city parks. This spawned the Tulip Time Festival, which was first held in 1930 and now attracts thousands of tourists to the annual downtown event (Vande Water 2002). Opportunities for farm work attracted Hispanics who began settling in the city in the 1940s, transforming a predominantly Dutch city into a multicultural settlement.

Holland endured a major fire in 1871 that decimated the entire community, including the downtown. However, the city was rebuilt and today Holland's downtown still reflects the city's Dutch heritage. More obstacles arose from the completion of the U.S. 31 Highway, which drained many shops from the downtown to locations along the highway. The downtown further suffered after the completion of the I-196 expressway in the 1970s. Anchor stores such as JCPenney, Woolworth, and Steketee's relocated to the mall at the fringe of the city. By making land outside the central city more accessible, the highway pulled residents and businesses to the outskirts and made the development of new suburbs such as the Townships of Park, Laketown, and Holland feasible.

To stem the tide of downtown decline, the City of Holland prepared a master plan in 1953 to guide the city's development and in 1979 a Downtown Development Steering Committee was formed to provide guidance for the redevelopment of the downtown. These efforts culminated in the formation of a Downtown Development Authority (DDA) in 1995 to address the issue of downtown business retrenchment. The DDA also prepared a downtown strategic plan to jumpstart revitalization efforts.

Several downtown projects were completed in the 1990s as well: the Amtrak Railroad Station was restored; the old Post Office was converted into the Holland Museum; Freedom Village was built; and Hope College's Haworth Inn and Conference Center was completed. A snowmelt system was installed on downtown streets and sidewalks, making navigation of the downtown comfortable for tourists and residents alike. All of these developments helped to reset the downtown. A renewed downtown is anchored by local retailers such as Outpost and national retailers such as Talbots, Chico's, and Joseph A. Banks. The city has won many accolades for its downtown, including "Great American Main Street" by the National Trust for Historic Preservation.

Ripon, WI

Ripon's history dates back to 1844 when a group of twenty Phalanx moved north from the Kenosha region to form a utopian community. The city was named after the ancestral home of David Mapes, one of the city's first settlers who originated from the City of Ripon in Yorkshire. The settlement was incorporated in 1858. In line with their utopian ideals, the group built communal facilities such as the "long house" near present-day Ceresco Park and Ripon College, a private liberal arts college that to this day is a mainstay of the community. Ripon grew in population, largely due to the efforts of Mapes who donated land for new settlers and for the establishment of the college. Mapes secured railroad tracks through the city to Milwaukee and convinced the federal government to build a post office in the community (Miller & Pedrick 1964).

Ripon's downtown stretches from Fond du Lac Street on the south to Jackson Street in the north along the Watson Street corridor. It is bordered in the east by the Mill Pond neighborhoods and to the west by Ripon College. Ripon's downtown consists of historically significant brick architectural buildings, including the Marcus Theater, the Maples House, and the First National Bank building.

Ripon Main Street, Inc., was established in 1989 as a non-profit organization to oversee redevelopment of the Business Improvement District. The organization is made up of 100 property owners and 125 member businesses. Ripon Main Street works to improve the quality of the downtown, to create an identity for the CBD, and to ensure its economic prosperity.

The downtown is experiencing significant reinvestment, with the infusion of money from both the public and private sectors to the tune of $14 million. Among these is the Watson Street renovation, the refurbishing of Pratt's Block, and the Scott Street building. These buildings have become choice places of residence for college students, professors, artists, and young professionals. Since the formation of Ripon Main Street, Inc., vacancy rates in the CBD have dropped from 26 percent to less than 7 percent, and assessed values have increased over 74 percent. These improvements have gained the city national prominence. In the last decade, the city has been semi-finalist three times for the Great American Main Street Award. In 2011, *Budget Travel Magazine* named Ripon one of the "Coolest Small Towns in America."

Mansfield, OH

The first permanent European settler in Richland County was Jacob Newman, who constructed a cabin on the bank of the Rocky Fork River in 1807, three miles southeast of present-day Mansfield. The site was chosen for its proximity to the "Big Spring" which provided settlers with a source of fresh water. Mansfield was platted for development by Jacob Newman and Joseph Larwell in 1808. The original plat consisted of 276 lots bound by Adams, 4th, Mulberry, and 1st streets, with a centrally located public square. In 1812, two blockhouses were constructed on the public square to provide a safe haven for settlers in the event of an Indian attack. The blockhouses were also used as a courthouse, jail, schoolhouse, a makeshift church, and later, as the town's first post office.

Economic activity in Mansfield centered on the public square. A farmer's hay market and the first store, which also doubled as an emporium and saloon, were built at the corner of North Park Street and Main Street. In 1831, a stagecoach line linked Mansfield to Sandusky, Norwalk, Mount Vernon, and New Haven. Mansfield became a trading and manufacturing town, due in part to its location at the intersection of four railroad lines. By 1820, the city had thirty houses and several retail businesses. Mansfield was incorporated as a village in 1828 and by 1845 the population had reached 3,000 people. Mansfield incorporated as a city in 1857 with a population of 5,121.

In 1849, the Pittsburgh, Fort Wayne, and Chicago Railway (later Pennsylvania Railroad mainline) reached Mansfield. Then the Atlantic and Great Western Railroad (later Erie Railroad mainline) reached Mansfield in 1863. Rail transportation transformed the town from agricultural to an industrial and commercial center. Railroad tracks were located north of the city in what was known as the "flats." Most industries located in this area to take advantage of easy access to transportation for their products. One of the first industries in the city was Hall & Allen foundry, a manufacturer of steam engines and mill equipment. Mansfield Machine Works, another major employer in the city, manufactured steam engines, saws, mill machinery, and pumps. Other manufactured products in the city included doors, brass objects, linseed oil, and paper boxes. In the 1920s, the town's growth was aided by the stove industry, namely Westinghouse and Tappan Stove Company.

The city's growth was also influenced by the highway system. The east–west highway corridor, the "Ohio Market Route 3," ran through Mansfield. In 1913, this route was chosen to be part of the Lincoln Highway that connected New York to San Francisco. Housing for the working class developed near the industrial area. Planned suburban neighborhoods such as Woodland Farms, built by developer James M. Dickson in 1920, were developed away from this area.

The deindustrialization of economic activity greatly affected Mansfield, especially after the steel recession of the 1970s. The relocation and closure of manufacturing plants had ripple effects on other businesses in the community, especially those located in the downtown along Park Avenue West and Lexington Avenue. These businesses fled the downtown to the neighboring city of Ontario. Thus, Mansfield lost its advantage as a retail hub for Richland County and north-central Ohio.

Downtown Mansfield began to deteriorate, as retail business relocated to the Miracle Mile along Park Avenue West outside the downtown. The construction of a regional shopping mall in nearby Ontario further added to the decline of downtown. The 4th and Main neighborhood was especially affected by this turn of events and became the brunt of jokes by Bill Cosby when he visited the city in 1984. Shortly thereafter, Mayor Ed Meehan embarked on the redevelopment of the North Main Street neighborhood. The city pledged $300,000 and private contributions of $600,000 were raised to build a hand-carved carousel. The launching of the carousel in 1991 had multiplier impacts on the rest of the downtown. Downtown Mansfield is now thriving.

The Southwest Region

The Southwest Region of the United States stretches from the coast of Texas to the Colorado River in the west and is bordered to the south by Mexico. Four states make up this region. They are Arizona, New Mexico, Oklahoma, and Texas. The common characteristic of this region is its aridness. Because of its desert climate, settlement and agricultural development is dependent on availability of water, which is provided to settlements in the region from the Rio Grande and the Colorado Rivers. The Theodore Roosevelt Dam (1911) and the Hoover Dam (1936) supported the development of settlements in this region.

The discovery of oil in the twentieth century provided a boost to the Southwest's economy, especially in Oklahoma and Texas. Houston and other port cities have also benefited from export of goods, particularly in petrochemicals. The region has seen growth in industry in the last two decades, following the relocation of aeronautics, automobile, and aluminum industries. The Southwest also benefited as a destination of choice for retirees and for heritage tourists interested in learning about Indian and Spanish-American cultures. We examine the downtown redevelopment efforts of Nacogdoches, TX, and Santa Fe, NM, for insight.

Nacogdoches, TX

Located on hilly terrain, Nacogdoches is described as the "Oldest Town in Texas." Settlement of the community dates back to 10,000 BC when Native Americans built lodges on two creeks: Lanana Creek on the east and Bonita Creek on the west (Ericson 2003). The city center is located at the fork of these two creeks. Nacogdoches is also located along the Old King's Highway, which was the first important road built through Texas. Thus, Nacogdoches became a market center for travelers along the King's Highway. Even in its early days, Nacogdoches was a gateway for trade from Natchitoches and New Orleans. The city's location made it a significant player in politics and the military escapades between Mexico, Spain, and later the United States.

The town owes its growth to agriculture and trade. Nacogdoches was first laid out by Don Antonio Gil Y'Barbo in 1779. He is also credited with building the city's Old Stone House, erected on the northeast corner of Town Square, and for writing the city's development code. Later in 1840, Captain A.A. Nelson surveyed the city streets and gave each a name.

Civic and cultural activities took place in the downtown. The center of the city was devoted to a mix of uses including retail, civic, and cultural buildings. In the early 1800s, the city's economy was based primarily on agriculture. Cotton, tobacco, and timber were produced in the city. In 1845, Haden Edwards, Charles S. Taylor, and J. R. Arnold donated 21.5 acres of land for a city square, now known as Washington Square. The square is bounded by Hughes, Mound, Edwards, and Fredonia Streets. The Old Stone Fort was constructed in the town center by Antonio Ibarvo, one of the early settlers of the area. It became the civic center for the community where business and public meetings took place. Residential neighborhoods sprang up on the south side of the community along east Pilar Street, with Henderson Road as the preferred residential area for the city's elite. The prominent Judge William Hart and Thomas J. Rush resided in this neighborhood.

The city's growth faltered in the mid-1800s as the old San Antonio Road that linked the city east and west became impassable. At the same time, the existing railroads, ships, and steamboats in the region routed people around Nacogdoches. However, oil was discovered in the area and the first well was drilled in 1861. Together with the arrival of the Houston, in addition to the East and West Texas Railroad in 1883, the city was transformed into a thriving commercial center. The railroad, like highways 59 and 259, changed the flow of commerce from east/west to north/south. The highways also led to the spatial restructuring of retail activity from the downtown to areas along North Street.

Nacogdoches is the headquarters for Texas Farm Products, a state leader in the manufacturing of fertilizer, animal feed, and animal health products. The city is also a state leader in the broiler industry, with several poultry hatcheries, feeders, and processing plants located in the city. Newer industries include banking, recreation, and medical services. Another important asset to the community is the Stephen F. Austin State Teachers College (now Stephen F. Austin State University), which was established in Nacogdoches in 1923. Nacogdoches has used historic preservation to restore many of its historic downtown buildings and is a leader in downtown revitalization.

Santa Fe, NM

Santa Fe was a minor settlement of Pueblo Indians before the Spanish conquest and settlement in 1598. It was founded in 1608 and was made the official Capital of Nuevo Mexico (a province of New Spain) in 1610. It is the second oldest city founded by European colonists in the United States. Only St. Augustine, FL, founded in 1565, is older. There is a claim that the Palace of the Governors, an adobe structure built in the city around 1200, is the oldest building in the United States.

Santa Fe was laid out in accordance with the Laws of the Indies town planning principles; a set of 148 rules adopted by the Spanish crown at the time to guide Spanish colonists in locating, building, and populating settlements. These principles were signed into law in 1573 and represent perhaps the first comprehensive guidelines for city planning and development. Among these is the requirement for a central commons where people can gather to socialize, in addition to a stipulation that buildings should be of similar styles to ensure good aesthetics for the community.

The Palace of the Governors forms the north edge of the central plaza. To the east is the Cathedral of Saint Francis of Assisi. A grid street pattern radiates out from the central plaza. The city's downtown is nearly 300 acres and includes properties within and adjacent to the Paseo de Peralta loop and Guadalupe Street.

Santa Fe's growth has been influenced by its topography and availability of water. Hills to the north and northeast of the city constrained residential development. Almost all civic and cultural institutions were located in and near the central core. Some residential development took place along the banks of the Santa Fe River and the Acequia Madre, the primary irrigation ditch. Santa Fe grew in a compact form. In the early years of the city's settlement, the population was confined within a half-mile radius of the central core. The population and economy grew rapidly in the 1880s, with the development of the railroad (Noble 2008).

A mix of uses including schools, retail and other businesses were all within walking distance of most residents. In 1958, the city adopted an ordinance requiring all buildings in the city to be of the Spanish-Pueblo style. This was meant to reflect the adobe architectural history of the city's past. As it grew, residential uses and retail serving the local population moved out of the central core to the surrounding area. This resulted in a decline in residential population in the downtown.

Santa Fe's nickname, "The City Different," exemplifies the uniqueness of culture and architecture in the city. A "City Different" plan was prepared for Santa Fe in 1912. Currently, Santa Fe's downtown revitalization efforts center on historic preservation and tourism to capitalize on the city's cultural and architectural assets. The downtown vision plan, prepared in 2007, outlines the city's strategy to "preserve the essential elements that make downtown special, while proactively establishing a template for measured growth that benefits the community at-large."

The Western Region

The Western Region was the last portion of the United States to be settled. Although Native Americans already inhabited the area, it was not until the mid-1800s that European pioneers ventured into this region of the country. The West is geographically diverse, with plains, mountains, and deserts. The region comprises eleven states: Arizona, California, Colorado, Hawaii, Idaho, Montana, Nevada, Oregon, Utah, Washington, and Wyoming. Most of the land in these states was formally owned by France and was sold to the United States in the Louisiana Purchase of 1803. In 1848, Mexico ceded all land north of its current borders to the United States. The quest for land west of the Mississippi and the gold rush led to the settlement of the western region.

The Federal Land Ordinance of 1785 governed the survey, distribution, and sale of land in the West. Land was surveyed and divided into square townships of six miles on each side. It was then subdivided into a square of one mile on each side and then into 160 acre lots. These lands were sold to bidders at a public auction for $1.25 per acre.

The transcontinental railroads, completed in 1869, also contributed to the commercial viability of the region and to population growth, and commerce. Unlike cities in the Midwest that were dependent on manufacturing, cities in the West developed from extractive industry such as mining, fishing, and logging for their economic growth. Communities in the West were impacted by deindustrialization, as other regions of the country. Chico, CA, Fort Collins, CO, and Santa Barbara, CA, are the three exemplary downtowns selected from this region.

Fort Collins, CO

The City of Fort Collins was settled on the Cache la Poudre River as a military post in 1864 and is named after Colonel William O. Collins. The fort was abandoned in 1867 by federal order, but a handful of civilians received permission to remain on the site. Later, a site now known as Old Town was platted for settlement by Jack Dow and Norman Meldrum. This site extended from the Cache la Poudre River to Mountain Avenue and from Riverside Avenue to College Avenue. Land was allocated for the construction of several civic buildings including a college, schools, churches, a hotel, county buildings, parks, a zoo, and a cemetery. The Homestead Act of 1862 offered land to Union army veterans, citizens, and immigrants who planned to become citizens. Homesteaders could acquire up to 160 acres of land at a small cost after living on and improving it. After the cessation of hostilities between Native Americans and settlers, many soldiers from the fort either purchased or claimed land in the area. Some brought their families to the area to settle as squatters. Among the early settlers were Norman H. Meldrum, John H. Mandeville, and Fred Wallace.

In 1886, the commercial area of the town covered approximately 43 acres and stretched from Jefferson Avenue on the northeast, to the intersection of College and Mountain Avenue in the southwest. Most of the buildings in the commercial core were one to two stories in height, with the exception of the Tedmon House, Collins House, the Opera House, and Poudre Valley Bank/Linden Hotel that were three stories each. The downtown also had a number of residential units, especially on the upper floors of downtown businesses. Public facilities included the town offices on Walnut Street between Pine and Linden, the post office at the corner of Linden and Mountain, and a frame office and stone jail located on Courthouse Square at Mason Street and Mountain Avenue.

The earliest businesses established in Old Town were mercantile stores supplying foodstuff and basic manufactured goods, drug stores, and mills for the processing of wheat and corn. Civic business was conducted downtown in Old Grout, a building that was also used for church services, court hearings, and theatrical entertainment. The relocation of the county seat from Laporte to Fort Collins in 1868 boosted the community's development. By 1880, the census showed Fort Collins had 1,356 inhabitants and was the twelfth most populous municipality in the state.

The Fort Collins town plat of 1873 was roughly 935 acres in size. As population increased, more residential additions were platted. The first residential subdivisions were platted in 1881 following the platting of the original town. Earliest development activity included the Harrison addition (1881) and the Lake Park addition (1881). Other major subdivisions platted before 1900 included the Doty and Rhodes Subdivision (1883), the A.L. Emigh Subdivision (1886), the Loomis addition (1887), and the West Side addition (1887). By the end of the nineteenth century, Fort Collins had grown to approximately 1,100 acres in size (City of Fort Collins 1991).

The Union Pacific railroad reached Fort Collins in 1877, followed by the Greeley, Salt Lake, and Pacific (GSL&P) railroad in 1882. In clearing the right of way for the Union Pacific railroads in 1910, a sizable number of the city's most historic structures along Jefferson Avenue, including many historic residences, were destroyed. By the mid-1890s, residential areas within the city had expanded, with affluent residential neighborhoods located to the south and west of downtown and the less preferred residential areas to the northwest between Jefferson Street and the river. By 1925, the central business district covered approximately 76 acres extending from Willow Street on the northeast, west to Howes Street, and south to Mountain Avenue and Olive Street. By 1925, very few residential uses remained in the CBD, as the area was taken over by retail, commercial, service, and financial businesses.

Fort Collins has taken a proactive approach to downtown revitalization. The city established the Downtown Business Association (DBA) in 1982 to promote downtown business. This organization is self-funding and has generated over $1.5 million in income over the last decade that is reinvested in the downtown. It also organizes free events that draw thousands of residents to the downtown. The DBA has over 225 members representing businesses in the arts, entertainment, retail, restaurants, professional, and service sectors. The Downtown Development Authority (DDA) was also created by the city in 1981 to leverage private development in the CBD using tax increment financing (TIF). Fort Collins' downtown is a lively and aesthetically pleasant district that has been redeveloped with a mix of uses. Few downtowns in the country compare to this one-of-a-kind place.

Santa Barbara, CA

Like Fort Collins, Santa Barbara began as a Spanish presidio, a military fortress for Spain. In 1782, soldiers who came to build the presidio brought along their families and settled in the community once their service was completed. The city got its name from Saint Barbara, a name that was given by Sebastian Vizcaino in gratitude for surviving a violent storm on the Channel in 1602 on the eve of the feast day of the saint. The City of Santa Barbara was laid out as Central City in 1875. It grew during the era of the California Gold Rush with the discovery of gold at Sutter's Mill in the Sierra foothills and as an oil boom town in the 1800s. In World War II, Santa Barbara served as both a military base and as a site for the treatment of wounded servicemen. A cluster of adobe residences around the presidio formed the heart of what is now the downtown.

Santa Barbara incorporated as a city in 1850. As immigrants from the east came to settle in the city, the haphazard collection of adobe buildings gradually gave way to a planned city grid. In 1851, Salisbury Haley was hired to survey and layout the city in square blocks of 450 feet on each side. Unfortunately, Haley used a defective chain that was held together in some places with oxhide, a material that contracted and expanded depending on the time of day. Thus, his measurements were off in several places, resulting in city square blocks that vary in size from 457 to 464 feet on the side. This irregularity in blocks and street layout persists in the city to this day (City of Santa Barbara 2000).

Santa Barbara grew as a tourist resort in the latter 1800s, propelled by railroad lines that linked the city to San Francisco and Los Angeles. One notable development was a movement in the early twentieth century to beautify the city. This movement was led by Bernard Hoffman and Pearl Chase. The objective was to develop an urban design and architectural theme around the Spanish Colonial style and harmonize this with the pueblo buildings in the city. This goal came to fruition ironically when the city suffered an earthquake in 1925. The earthquake destroyed several buildings and prompted the incorporation of the architectural enrichment and city beautification principles that were advocated by Hoffman and Chase. Notable buildings that used these design principles were the County Courthouse and Lobero Theater on Canon Perdido Street that are built in the Spanish-Moorish style.

Suburbanization took hold in Santa Barbara with the development of new neighborhoods west of the downtown including San Roque, Hope Ranch Annex, and Goleta Valley. Shopping centers also developed to serve the suburban population away from the downtown in Loreto Plaza, Five Points, and La Cumbre Plaza. However, in 1975, the city council passed a resolution limiting expansion of the city. This had the effect of making housing less affordable in the city, but has provided an impetus for the redevelopment of the downtown.

The Santa Barbara Downtown Organization (SBDO) was formed in 1967 by then Mayor Don MacGillivray. The goal for the formation of the organization was to help the downtown compete with the newly built La Cumbre Plaza, a suburban mall north of Santa Barbara. The SBDO was charged with three main objectives: to prepare a plan for the improvement of public and private property in the downtown; to work toward attracting a department store to the downtown; and provide free parking to patrons of the downtown.

A beautification committee was also formed to bring about aesthetic improvements to State Street. A plaza was designed by architect Robert Ingle Hoyt in 1967, which helped attract some chain stores to the downtown. Parking was made free through contributions by downtown merchants to a parking improvement program. Downtown Santa Barbara offers world-class dining, entertainment, culture, and architecture. It is a vital part of the community.

Chico, CA

Chico is located in the northern Sacramento Valley. It was founded in 1860 by John Bidwell and incorporated as a city in 1872. Bidwell purchased Rancho Arroyo Chico from William Dickey in 1849 and commissioned J.S. Henning in 1860 to plat a town of fifty city blocks on land lying between Little Chico Creek and Big Chico Creek for development. The city was subsequently laid out in a grid street pattern. Henning designated land along the Shasta-Tehama Road for the town center. This still remains the core commercial and cultural center of Chico. Downtown Chico is about ten blocks long and five blocks wide. It is bounded by residential neighborhoods west of Normal Avenue and east of Plume Street. Little Chico Creek lies south of the downtown. To the north are Big Chico Creek and the CSU Chico campus.

Chico's development is in part a reflection of Bidwell's vision. The city's wide, tree-lined streets were designed to give the impression of spaciousness. Each religious denomination was given a block on which to build a church. By 1970, there were seven churches in downtown Chico. Bidwell also donated land to build schools including Woodman's Academy, built in 1862 on Block 81, and the Salem Street School, built in 1866. A Town Hall was built following incorporation of the city in 1872. In 1905, Annie Bidwell donated 2,250 acres of land for the development of Bidwell Park, near Big Chico Creek (Moon 2003).

The first grist mill in Northern California was built by Bidwell in 1853. The mill helped transform the City of Chico from a cattle ranching economy to a grain production economy. Chico also became a major economic and transportation hub for agricultural products such as wheat and lumber. The California and Oregon Railroad reached Chico in 1870 and linked the city to the rest of the region. It also facilitated the development of new suburbs. Two new subdivisions were added to the city just south of Little Chico Creek in the 1870s: the Chapman addition and the Oakdale subdivision. In 1889, a new 200-block suburb was also platted for development by Bidwell between Rancheria Lane (Sacramento Avenue) and Lindo Channel. Later, the company town of Barber was built around the Diamond Match Company plant located south of Little Chico Creek.

While the development of Chico was fueled by the lumber industry, the city also benefited from the establishment of the State Normal School of California in 1889 that is now the California State University, Chico. The campus was built on the south banks of Big Chico Creek and 1st Street. The expansion of the university southwards has, however, had a negative impact on the older residential neighborhoods in this area. This has resulted in the demolition of some of the older houses for the provision of student rentals. The first Chico General Plan was adopted in 1961 and was updated in 1976, 1994, and 2011. Each update included sub-area plans for the revitalization of the downtown. In 1975, the non-profit, member-financed organization the Downtown Chico Business Association (DCBA) was formed. The DCBA promotes events and seeks to maintain downtown as the community's civic, cultural, and business center.

In recent years, the City of Chico has made significant public investment in restoring many of its downtown buildings as a redevelopment strategy. In 2009, the city's 1910 municipal building was completely restored. The city's 138-year-old public square, Chico City Plaza, was also redesigned and reconstructed. The downtown has gained the attention of other cities and professional organizations and is regarded as one of the best downtowns in the state of California.

Reprise

All of the cities, regardless of region, experienced a period of economic growth fueled by natural resources, industry, mining or trade followed by a period of decline and revitalization. We also saw that civic, cultural, commercial, and religious buildings were centrally located in the cities. The railroads and highways also had an influence in the decentralization of residents and businesses to the fringe. It took civic leadership to intervene and jumpstart the revitalization of the downtowns. Often, this involved a public–private partnership. The rest of this book will focus on the steps taken by these communities to revitalize their downtowns.

 Please visit the companion website at http://routledge.com/cw/Burayidi for additional resources.

CHAPTER 3

Cultivating Downtown Living

Resilient downtowns are healthy downtowns. They are vibrant places where people work, eat, play, and live. In these downtowns, the residential population is growing, businesses are thriving, and public spaces are inviting and well patronized. Cities with resilient downtowns cultivate downtown living because housing has ripple effects on the rest of the downtown economy. As Sasaki Associates observed with respect to Greenville, "Resident households create 24-hour vibrancy downtown. Households demand goods and services and, as such, support downtown retail and service establishments … A strong downtown residential base enlivens the streets, supports retail, and attracts office uses" (Sasaki Associates 2008, p. 68).

Cities with resilient downtowns often start by conducting a housing assessment to gauge the level of demand for housing and to identify strategies for meeting these housing needs in the downtown. In 2006, the Wilmington Renaissance Corporation (WRC) retained the services of The Vincent Group to assess demand for downtown housing. The firm conducted a web-based survey that received responses from 772 residents and held three focus group meetings. The study found that of those that are likely to move within a year, 30 percent would consider living downtown. Furthermore, the demographic group that is most likely to consider living downtown is young, has no children, and works in professional and management jobs. The study also found that "downtown residential demand will be generated by empty-nesters, students, and people relocating to the area" and that "downtown development can attract people working downtown who share lifestyle characteristics consistent with an urban lifestyle" (The Vincent Group 2006, p. 6).

Downtown Mansfield, Inc., the City of Mansfield's downtown development organization, also sees housing as central to the development of the city's downtown:

> For the past few years, issues related to housing in various areas close to and within DMI's program area have become a greater concern. We understand the relationship between housing and business and the importance of each entity's role to the sustainability of the other. We feel that in order to effectively restore downtown Mansfield, we must also address the issues regarding housing.
>
> (Downtown Mansfield, Inc. 2010)

To assess housing need in the downtown, the City of Mansfield hired Danter Company in 2011 to study the potential for downtown housing. Following field studies, telephone interviews, and case studies, the firm found that downtown

Mansfield could support as many as fifty new market rate and subsidized housing units per year. Additionally, the company found that one-third of those surveyed would consider living downtown if the appropriate housing were provided.

As stated by Mansfield Alliance (2003, p. 107), "Analysis of the demographic and psychographic characteristics of Mansfield residents identified a number of characteristics that would seem to support a higher potential demand for downtown housing, including a significant increase in non-traditional households and households without children."

Similarly, the City of Santa Barbara retained the services of Peikert Group Architects, LLP, to assess the feasibility of developing downtown surface parking lots into parking structures, with upper-floor residential housing. The firm identified the Louise Lowry and Cota Commuter lots as the most feasible for such a conversion to residential development noting that, "the City could generate between $2.1 and $2.2 million from a market rate ownership project on the Louise Lowry lot, and approximately $4.4 million for the same type of project on the Cota lot" (Peikert Group Architects, LLP 2003, p. 12).

In 2007, the City of Greenville began a downtown planning process to involve stakeholders in the development of strategies to guide downtown development for the next three decades. The process was led by Sasaki Associates, Inc., and also included W-ZHA, a firm that was retained to provide real estate and market analysis, and Craig Gaulden Davis for guidance on architecture. The downtown strategic plan noted that the city's downtown captured only 10 percent of the potential housing market, and that young professionals, non-traditional families, empty nesters and the elderly should be a target for downtown housing:

> Downtown Greenville has recently experienced considerable downtown residential development. A majority of this development, however, is high income households of one and two people. Housing opportunities for younger households, family households, and middle income households are limited to downtown's surrounding older neighborhoods.
>
> (Sasaki Associates 2008, p. 68)

According to a study by Randolph McKetty & Associates, almost half of the families in the City of Greenville were non-traditional families. The elderly aged 65 years and older owned 33 percent of all owner-occupied housing units in the city, but comprised 12.9 percent of the population, while 34.2 percent of the population were young professionals (20–39) (Randolph McKetty & Associates 2005, p. 15).

Similarly, a downtown housing market study was conducted for the City of Middletown by RKG Associates in 2010. The study found that the downtown population grew by 1.3 percent, but the number of households increased by 3.5 percent between 2000 and 2010, an indication of decreasing household size. The report projected an increased demand for condominiums in the downtown and that the groups that were likely to be purchasing these were young professionals (25–34 years) and the elderly: "The Downtown has a small concentration of condominiums, and there is a forecasted demand for approximately 20 condominiums in the downtown annually, with much if not most of this demand captured by ownership turnover in existing condominium units" (Milone & MacBroom, Inc. 2011, p. 6).

As these studies reveal, not all population groups embrace urban living. The demographic group that is most amenable to living downtown is empty nesters who are post-child-raising and may either be retired or be in the pre-retirement age. Young professionals also prefer urban lifestyles because of the close proximity to city amenities, entertainment, shops, and culture. Cities with resilient downtowns provide housing that target both of these demographic groups.

The Evidence

Table 3.1 shows that eight of the fourteen cities had a growth in their downtown resident population between 2000 and 2010. Furthermore, although the overall city population for Wilmington and Santa Barbara declined from 2000 to 2010, these cities saw a growth of their downtown population.

Tables 3.2 and 3.3 provide data on housing unit and median income change for the cities and their downtowns, respectively. In Table 3.2, we see that there was a growth in downtown housing units from 2000 to 2010 in all but five of the cities (Mansfield, Ripon, Holland, Chico, and Santa Fe). The number of housing units in downtown Wilmington increased from 363 units in 2000 to 1,057 in 2010, a growth of 191 percent. Similarly, the number of housing units in Santa Barbara increased by 24 percent, from 1,408 to 1,746 housing units in the decade. By contrast, the number of housing units in downtown Holland decreased from 2,356 in 2000 to 2,054 in 2010. The table also shows that seven downtowns had a faster growth in housing units than for their cities in the same period.

Table 3.1 City and downtown population change, 2000–2010

City	City Population			Downtown Population		
	2000	2010	Percentage Change	2000	2010	Percentage Change
Middletown, CT	43,167	47,648	10.4%	1,304	1,540	18.1%
Wilmington, DE	72,664	70,851	−2.5%	730	1,365	87.0%
Greenville, SC	56,002	58,409	4.3%	539	954	77.0%
Hendersonville, NC	10,420	13,137	26.1%	2,336	2,240	−4.1%
Charlottesville, VA	40,099	43,475	8.4%	2,440	2,783	14.1%
Mansfield, OH	43,167	47,648	10.4%	5,327	2,428	−54.4%
Ripon, WI	6,828	7,733	13.3%	309	272	−12.0%
Holland, MI	35,048	33,051	−5.7%	8,536	6,958	−18.5%
Lafayette, IN	56,397	67,140	19.1%	561	806	43.7%
Fort Collins, CO	118,652	143,986	21.4%	2,485	2,487	0.1%
Santa Barbara, CA	92,325	88,410	−4.2%	3,219	3,266	1.5%
Chico, CA	59,954	86,187	43.8%	4,970	4,801	−3.4%
Nacogdoches, TX	29,914	32,996	10.3%	6493	7352	13.2%
Santa Fe, NM	62,203	67,947	9.2%	556	336	−39.6%

Source: U.S. Census: Profile of General Population and Housing Characteristics, 2010 Demographic Profile Data. American FactFinder. United States Census Bureau.

Table 3.2 Housing unit change for cities and downtowns, 2000–2010

City	City Housing Units			Downtown Housing Units		
	2000	2010	Percentage Change	2000	2010	Percentage Change
Middletown, CT	19,697	21,223	7.7%	808	872	7.9%
Wilmington, DE	32,138	32,820	2.1%	363	1,057	191.0%
Greenville, SC	27,295	29,418	7.8%	467	840	79.9%
Hendersonville, NC	5,181	7,744	49.5%	1,147	1,232	7.4%
Charlottesville, VA	17,591	19,189	9.1%	1,413	1,623	14.9%
Mansfield, OH	22,267	22,022	−1.1%	1,464	1,285	−12.2%
Ripon, WI	3,118	3,306	6.0%	225	220	−2.2%
Holland, MI	12,533	13,212	5.4%	2,356	2,054	−12.8%
Lafayette, IN	25,602	31,260	22.1%	423	542	28.1%
Fort Collins, CO	47,755	60,503	26.7%	1,417	1,550	9.4%
Santa Barbara, CA	37,076	37,820	2.0%	1,408	1,746	24.0%
Chico, CA	24,386	37,050	51.9%	2,209	2,190	−0.9%
Nacogdoches, TX	12,329	13,635	10.6%	3103	3796	22.3%
Santa Fe, NM	30,533	37,200	21.8%	368	339	−7.9%

Source: U.S. Census: General Housing Characteristics, 2010 Census Summary File 1, 2000 and 2010 Demographic Profile Data. American FactFinder. United States Census Bureau.

Table 3.3 compares downtown median income to city median income for 2000 and 2010. The table shows that the median income for downtown households grew in every city except Holland, where median incomes dropped by 2.9 percent. Downtown median incomes also grew faster than city median income in eleven of the fourteen cities—the exception being Hendersonville, Holland, and Nacogdoches. Between 2000 and 2010, downtown median income grew by almost 42 percent in Charlottesville, while the city's median income grew by 36 percent. Table 3.3 also shows that the median household income of downtown residents grew as a percentage of overall median household income in the city. The exceptions are Holland, Santa Barbara, and Fort Collins. For example, between 2000 and 2010 the median household income for the City of Nacogdoches grew by 13 percent, but the downtown median household income grew faster, by 28 percent.

Between 2000 and 2010, eight of the cities had a growth in three of the indicators that are used to gauge the health of the downtowns: a growth in downtown population, a growth in downtown housing units, and a growth in downtown household median incomes. These cities are Middletown, Wilmington, Greenville, Charlottesville, Lafayette, Fort Collins, Santa Barbara, and Nacogdoches. The resilient downtowns capitalized on national demographic shifts that favor downtown living to grow their downtown population. These shifts have included a growth in non-traditional families and lifestyle changes favoring more compact and walkable neighborhoods. These population cohorts have a higher preference for downtown living than other demographic groups. Table 3.4 shows data for non-family households and one-person households in the fourteen cities. Table 3.5 shows similar data for the downtowns of the cities. In Table 3.4 we see that there

Table 3.3 City and downtown household median income, 2000–2010

City	City Median Income 2000	City Median Income 2010	City Percentage Change	Downtown Median Income 2000	Downtown Median Income 2010	Downtown Percentage Change	Downtown Income as a Percentage of City Income 2000	Downtown Income as a Percentage of City Income 2010
Middletown, CT	$47,162	$57,655	22.2%	$13,699	$19,329	41.1%	29.0%	33.5%
Wilmington, DE*	$35,116	$38,386	9.3%	$32,969	$59,464 *	80.4%	93.9%	155.0%
Greenville, SC	$33,144	$40,291	21.6%	$13,750	$37,250	170.9%	41.5%	92.5%
Hendersonville, NC	$30,357	$37,079	22.1%	$21,667	$23,688	9.3%	71.4%	63.9%
Charlottesville, VA	$31,007	$42,240	36.2%	$37,949	$53,732	41.6%	122.4%	127.2%
Mansfield, OH	$30,176	$32,797	8.7%	$19,105	$22,277	16.6%	63.3%	67.9%
Ripon, WI	$37,399	$40,740	8.9%	$39,868	$43,512	9.1%	106.7%	106.8%
Holland, MI**	$42,291	$42,987	1.6%	$37,563	$36,462	-2.9%	88.8%	84.8%
Lafayette, IN***	$35,859	$37,605	4.9%	$16,750	$28,239	68.6%	46.7%	75.1%
Fort Collins, CO	$44,459	$49,589	11.5%	$21,313	$27,500	29.0%	47.9%	55.5%
Santa Barbara, CA	$47,498	$61,665	29.8%	$27,108	$27,281	0.6%	57.1%	44.2%
Chico, CA	$29,359	$41,835	42.5%	$18,140	$30,136	66.1%	61.8%	72.0%
Nacogdoches, TX	$22,700	$25,726	13.3%	$16,192	$20,646	27.5%	71.3%	80.3%
Santa Fe, NM	$40,392	$49,947	23.7%	$33,688	$61,757	83.3%	83.4%	123.6%

Notes
* For 2010, the median income for Census Tract 28 was used for the downtown since the Census Bureau did not report median incomes for Block Group 1 of Census Tact 28.
** Median income for Census Tract 223 was $33,676 and for Census Tract 224, it was $41,450. The average of the two tracts was used for the downtown median income in 2000.
*** The 2010 data for Census Tract 6 is taken from the 2009 ACS five-year estimates as this tract was merged with Census Tract 111 in the 2010 census.

Source: U.S. Census: Profile of Selected Economic Characteristics: 2000 Census, Summary File 3 (SF 3)—Sample Data; and Selected Economic Characteristics: 2006–2010 American Community Survey, 5-Year Estimates. American FactFinder. United States Census Bureau.

Table 3.4 Non-family households in cities, 2000–2010

City	One-Person Households			Non-Family Households		
	2000	2010	Percentage Change	2000	2010	Percentage Change
Middletown, CT	6,491	7,100	9.4%	8,161	8,907	9.1%
Wilmington, DE	10,615	10,892	2.7%	12,736	13,217	3.8%
Greenville, SC	9,957	10,686	7.3%	11,809	12,772	8.2%
Hendersonville, NC	1,836	2,976	62.1%	2,022	3,341	65.2%
Charlottesville, VA	5,888	6,063	3.0%	9,225	10,260	11.2%
Mansfield, OH	7,018	6,941	−1.1%	8,147	8,041	−1.3%
Ripon, WI	993	1,115	12.3%	1,163	1,284	10.4%
Holland, MI	3,214	3,577	11.3%	4,043	4,428	9.5%
Lafayette, IN	7,990	9,948	24.5%	10,390	12,682	22.1%
Fort Collins, CO	11,944	16,399	37.3%	20,102	26,681	32.7%
Santa Barbara, CA	11,706	11,937	2.0%	16,651	17,216	3.4%
Chico, CA	6,874	10,419	51.6%	11,835	17,356	46.7%
Nacogdoches, TX	3,762	4,274	13.6%	5,288	5,816	10.0%
Santa Fe, NM	10,029	12,934	29.0%	12,587	15,768	25.3%

Note
One-person households are a subset of non-family households.

Source: U.S. Census: Households and Families: Census 2000 Summary File 1 (SF 1) 100-Percent Data; and Households and Families: 2010 Census Summary File 1. American FactFinder. United States Census Bureau.

Table 3.5 Non-family households in downtown, 2000–2010

City	One-Person Households			Non-Family Households		
	2000	2010	Percentage Change	2000	2010	Percentage Change
Middletown, CT	410	409	0.0%	494	499	1.0%
Wilmington, DE	136	512	276.5%	183	614	236.0%
Greenville, SC	319	410	28.5%	340	477	40.3%
Hendersonville, NC	457	443	−3.1%	508	517	1.8%
Charlottesville, VA	715	754	5.5%	839	934	11.3%
Mansfield, OH	465	424	−8.8%	525	482	−8.2%
Ripon, WI	119	89	−25.2%	138	102	−26.1%
Holland, MI	682	671	−1.6%	986	927	−6.0%
Lafayette, IN	307	256	−16.6%	314	390	24.2%
Fort Collins, CO	733	806	10.0%	1,082	1,160	7.2%
Santa Barbara, CA	634	875	38.0%	821	1,078	31.3%
Chico, CA	786	737	−6.2%	1,521	1,533	0.8%
Nacogdoches, TX	976	1171	20.0%	1362	1,696	24.5%
Santa Fe, NM	228	156	−31.6%	251	171	−31.9%

Note
One-person households are a subset of non-family households.

Source: U.S. Census: Households and Families: Census 2000 Summary File 1 (SF 1) 100-Percent Data; and Households and Families: 2010 Census Summary File 1. American FactFinder. United States Census Bureau.

has been a growth in non-family households in every city, with the exception of Mansfield, where this demographic group dropped by 1.3% between 2000 and 2010. We also see in Table 3.4 that the one-person household, a segment of non-family households, grew in all cities in the decade except for Mansfield. For example, this population cohort grew by about 52 percent in Chico between 2000 and 2010 and by 37 percent in Fort Collins in the same period.

Table 3.5 displays data for non-family households in the downtowns of these cities. The table shows that non-family households grew in nearly every downtown between 2000 and 2010, with the exception of downtown Mansfield, Holland, Ripon, and Santa Fe. In Mansfield, the non-family households in the city's downtown dropped by 8.2 percent. In downtown Santa Fe, it declined by almost 32 percent. Six downtowns saw double-digit growth in their non-family household population. These include Wilmington, Greenville, Charlottesville, Lafayette, Santa Barbara, and Nacogdoches. Greenville had a growth of 40 percent in this population cohort; Nacogdoches had a growth of 25 percent; and Santa Barbara grew by 31 percent. Wilmington's non-family households quadrupled. There was also a growth of single-person households in the downtowns of six cities.

Attracting Empty Nesters to Downtowns

A study for the American Association of Retired Persons (AARP) found that, on average, men and women outlive their ability to drive by six and ten years, respectively (Nathans 2011). Thus, the elderly prefer to live close to city amenities so they do not have to rely on motorized transportation for activities of daily living. This in part explains why retirees, baby boomers, and empty nesters are showing a greater preference for downtown living.

Gail and Gene Zannon of Santa Barbara are typical of empty-nester households that are attracted to downtown living. The Zannons have owned a commercial property in downtown Santa Barbara at 407 State Street since 1981. Built in 1914, the property sits on a downtown lot measuring 25 ft. on the street frontage by 125ft. The building is sandwiched between two properties on both sides of State Street. Behind the building, the undeveloped land was previously used as a parking lot (see Figures 3.1 and 3.2). They rented out the lower floor of the building for commercial uses and run their marketing, direct mail, and magazine publishing business on the upper floor.

The Zannons lived in the suburbs until their children grew up and left home. In 2002, they decided to add a residential unit to their commercial property and move downtown themselves. After speaking with several architects, they hired Jeff Shelton, an award-winning architect in Santa Barbara, to design the house to meet their needs. In particular, they wanted the house to have enough lighting on the second floor to accommodate their passion for gardening. In 2003, the Zannon's building won the George Washington Smith Award for exemplary design in architecture. The city now uses their house to showcase appropriate infill housing development. The Zannons have provided tours of their house to representatives from other municipalities that want to emulate their example. I met with Gene and Gail on the upper floor of their property to learn of their transition from suburban

Figure 3.1 Front view of the Zannons' house in white wash at 407 State Street, Santa Barbara, CA.

to downtown living. I was curious to know why they chose to live downtown and what it is that cities could do to entice other baby boomers to live downtown.

The Zannons' residence is surprisingly opulent. It has three floors, three bedrooms, two living rooms, a two-car garage, and an airy second-floor balcony that connects the residential unit to the two-story building that fronts State Street. I learned that the couple chose to move downtown because it was convenient for their needs. They do not have to drive in order to get to work or to access city amenities, because these are within walking distance. At the time they made the move, their children did not think they would last downtown and gave their parents six months before they would move back to the suburbs. Gail quipped that they have outlived their children's expectations and even their kids now see the benefits of downtown living. The Zannons also noted that they are not the only baby boomers living in the block: three or four other similar families live nearby.

During the time that the Zannons moved downtown, the City of Santa Barbara was encouraging downtown living, but provided no incentives for doing so. Furthermore, the process of adding on the residential unit to their downtown property took a lot of time and effort, as they had to fight the city's stringent development regulations every step of the way. The couple retained a consultant and spent $10,000 to dispute city regulations that made it difficult to add a residential unit to their property. For example, the city's regulations required that they provide two parking spaces for their add-on residential unit though they had tandem parking that accommodated two vehicles. The city also required the couple

Figure 3.2 Rear view of the Zannons' house showing the addition of the residential unit, Santa Barbara, CA.

to do a noise assessment and enclose their second-floor patio. Because of these requirements, the couple had to pay a consultant to take them through the hoops of the city's permitting process.

While the Zannons have no regrets about moving downtown, they are disturbed by the noise and other nuisance activities of their neighbors. They have filed a number of citizen reports to address these issues. Gail now serves on the downtown board because she wants to be part of the solution. Given the experience of the Zannons, I wanted their opinion on what cities can do to entice more baby boomers to choose downtown living over the suburbs. Gail took this question and made a rather poignant observation:

> It will be tough for a while because most cities don't have adequate staff to dedicate time to considering thinking outside the box. It used to be that cities will consider new ideas and work with property owners to accommodate their needs, but now unfortunately if an idea doesn't fit in the square box, it isn't allowed.

The morning after my visit with the Zannons, I met with Paul Casey, the Assistant City Administrator of Santa Barbara at City Hall. I told him of Gail's comments regarding the difficulties they had with adding to their building and moving downtown. Casey thought Gail's comments were a little exaggerated, but he was not surprised. He explained that there is tension in the community on growth and development issues. He cited the city's strategy for increasing affordable, market-rate housing downtown through increased densities, which he said pitted "slow-growthers" against "smart-growthers" and stated that this has been the case in Santa Barbara for the last ten years. He also said that some people think the community is moving too fast in approving building and housing permits and, as a result, the character of the downtown is changing. However, others think the city is putting too many impediments in the way of developers. In Casey's assessment, the city is doing a good job in mediating between these two opposing camps. He pointed to the quality of the downtown as evidence, one he attributes to the attention the city pays to detail in the development review process.

Before leaving the residence of the Zannons, I asked what advice they would give to cities that want to attract baby boomers to live downtown. One factor is crucial to making this work, Gail and Gene both agreed: "Cities have to encourage architects to get on board with innovative designs that meet the needs of baby boomers. Because there is no land available downtown for ground-floor gardens, downtown housing units must be designed to allow enough lighting for those who want to engage in gardening on upper floors." This may be a reflection of their passion for gardening, but the same observation was made by Greg Holcombe, a Harvard-trained urban planner who works for Riverview Group in Holland. Greg has lived in downtown Holland for over twenty years and likes the convenience that the downtown offers to city amenities and his place of work. He is excited to be in the mix of the different downtown activities. The one aspect he would change about living downtown is to add a roof-top garden to his condominium so he can engage in gardening in his spare time.

In examining Table 3.6, there is evidence that resilient downtowns are not capturing this demographic group, at least not yet. Except for the City of Lafayette which saw an 87 percent growth in the size of the elderly population between 2000 and 2010, all the other cities had a decrease in the elderly population in their downtown.

Attracting Young Professionals to Downtowns

The other demographic group that is attracted to downtown living is young professionals. This demographic group values the variety and diversity of urban life. Young professionals also like to live in close proximity to each other, so they can socialize and trade ideas. Because this group is just starting out in life, they have no children to worry about and do not need large backyards. We saw this trend manifested in Table 3.5 where most downtowns had positive growth in their one-person and non-family households. Contributing to this growth of young professionals in downtown Chico is Marci Goulart. Marci owns an interior design company and also works as a Senior Designer for Nantucket, a high-end furniture store at the corner of Broadway and 6th Street in downtown Chico. Her husband, Richard Wodrich, graduated from Ball State University in Indiana with a major in English and works in the radio business. I met with Marci on a pleasant afternoon at the downtown Nantucket store to get her views on downtown living for young professionals like herself.

Table 3.6 Elderly population (65+) change, 2000–2010

City	Elderly Population in City			Elderly Population in Downtown		
	2000	2010	Percentage Change	2000	2010	Percentage Change
Middletown, CT	5,786	6,285	8.6%	172	150	−12.8%
Wilmington, DE	9,123	8,185	−10.3%	36	6	−83.3%
Greenville, SC	8,081	7,468	−7.6%	175	154	−12.0%
Hendersonville, NC	3,248	3,963	22.0%	464	374	−19.4%
Charlottesville, VA	4,548	4,017	−11.7%	502	461	−8.2%
Mansfield, OH	7,633	7,504	−1.7%	360	266	−26.1%
Ripon, WI	1,304	1,316	10.9%	60	44	−26.7%
Holland, MI	4,740	4,538	−4.3%	885	794	−10.3%
Lafayette, IN	6,775	7,593	12.1%	67	125	86.6%
Fort Collins, CO	9,330	12,640	35.5%	323	298	−7.7%
Santa Barbara, CA	12,727	12,573	−1.2%	586	559	−4.6%
Chico, CA	5,932	9,178	54.7%	229	189	−17.5%
Nacogdoches, TX	3,312	3,347	1.1%	765	749	−2.1%
Santa Fe, NM	8,648	11,948	38.2%	314	210	−33.1%

Source: U.S. Census. Households and Families: Census 2000 Summary File 1 (SF 1) 100-Percent Data; and Households and Families: 2010 Census Summary File 1. American FactFinder. United States Census Bureau.

Marci was born and raised in Chico and grew up in the suburbs on a cul-de-sac. She enjoyed the many things that suburban life offered a child, like the large backyards and other children in the neighborhood with whom she played. However, after graduating from college, she no longer enjoyed the uniformity of the suburbs. When the couple could afford it, she and her husband bought two houses in the downtown: one that they live in and the other as a rental. She explained that she likes the energy of the downtown, with a variety of people and things to do. Her home is within walking distance of restaurants, the City Plaza, and Bidwell Park. In her neighborhood, there is a mix of housing types, all of which have their unique character so no house looks the same. Marci feels this makes the downtown neighborhoods more interesting than the suburbs. While the home Marci and Richard own has maintained its value, many homes in suburban Chico have decreased in value in the last ten years.

If there is a downside to downtown living, Marci noted, it is crime. Her house has been vandalized twice. She is also able to tell when the bars close at night, because of the noise from young college students returning to the campus. Despite these concerns, she has no regrets for choosing to live downtown. She likes the vibrancy of downtown life that is absent in the suburbs. Marci is on the city's Design Review Board and is keenly aware of some of the difficulties of increasing the downtown housing stock, because of the expense it takes to provide upper-floor housing in remodeled buildings. She sees the need for cities to provide more incentives to developers to offset the high cost of providing upper-floor apartments and lofts in downtown buildings. Another concern she has is with absentee landlords that buy single-family housing for the sole purpose of renting them out. She has seen first-hand how this has led to the lack of maintenance and eventual blight, thus turning once healthy owner-occupied housing neighborhoods into all rental-occupied neighborhoods. Her recommendation for the City of Chico and others is to enforce stricter building codes that will prevent such speculative housing from ruining entire downtown neighborhoods.

Enhancing Downtown Living

The experiences of the Zannons and Marci Goulart provide the backdrop for a discussion of the strategies that resilient downtowns are using to promote downtown living. Four main approaches are in wide use by these cities: i) changing the image of downtown to potential residents; ii) improving safety; iii) relaxing strict zoning and other regulations that are detrimental to development; and iv) providing incentives for redeveloping downtown properties into residential housing.

Changing Downtown's Image

Cities with resilient downtowns recognize that the first step to enhancing downtown living is to change the image of the downtown. Over the years as the middle class moved out to the suburbs, people have come to associate downtowns with crime, blight, and a place inhabited primarily by those "left behind." Changing residents' opinions about downtowns often requires a rebranding campaign. As the Wilmington Renaissance Corporation (WRC) in Delaware has rightly observed:

> In communities across the nation similar to Wilmington, more and more young professionals and empty nesters are choosing an urban lifestyle and returning to city living. Wilmington continues to see growth in residential opportunities in the Downtown and along the Riverfront. As these new residential neighborhoods continue to develop and grow it is essential that Wilmington presents a consistent message and image in regard to city living. Doing so will not only help fill the residential units already in existence but will create further demand for new units.
>
> (Wilmington Renaissance Corporation 2008, p. 11)

The WRC advocates for an increased police presence downtown to:

> Help dispel false negative perceptions that downtown is unsafe, to work with other partners such as the Department of Public Works and Amtrak to improve lighting in key areas of the downtown, to advocate for stricter enforcement of quality of life crimes, to increase positive media coverage of the downtown and use an image campaign to drum up downtown living.
>
> (Wilmington Renaissance Corporation 2008, p. 8)

A similar approach is taking place in Santa Barbara to change citizens' view of downtown. Here, it is the presence of the homeless population that is making people feel unsafe in the city's downtown. Others see Santa Barbara's downtown as different from how it used to be: a "mom and pop" business district that has been taken over by chain department stores. To address this, the Santa Barbara Downtown Organization, the Redevelopment Authority, the Visitors and Convention Bureau, and the city government have worked diligently to try to change the public's image of the downtown.

Recently, city government passed a strict anti-panhandling ordinance to control aggressive panhandling in the downtown. The ordinance makes it illegal to panhandle near bus stops, city parking lots or structures, and restaurants. The law bars the homeless from soliciting donations from people within 25 feet of an ATM machine or where there is a queue of more than five people waiting to enter a business or event. Most importantly, the ordinance makes it illegal to panhandle along State Street (the main downtown arterial) between the 400 Block to the 1200 Block, the 300 block north of Milpas Street to the 300 block south of Milpas Street, and on Cabrillo Boulevard between Calle Cesar Chavez Street to Harbor Way. The city also launched the "Real Change – Not Spare Change" campaign that discourages tourists and visitors from donating to the homeless. Instead, they are directed to give to a fund that is used by area organizations to provide services to the homeless. Most of the other resilient downtowns have similar image campaigns that aim to boost positive perceptions of the downtown and to encourage downtown living and patronage of downtown businesses.

Safety

Going hand in hand with changing the image of downtown is safety. Providing safety to downtown residents, customers, and visitors is a central goal of all of the downtown development organizations. When people feel safe in the downtown, they are more likely to live there and patronize businesses and events. The City of Middletown built its new police station directly on Main Street in the city's downtown, in part for security reasons. The location ensures the presence of police officers in the downtown throughout the day and night. Built in 1996, the 47,000 square-foot building was highly supported by the public as it was funded through a voter referendum at a cost of $9.9 million.

Downtown Visions, Wilmington's downtown organization, has a safety division whose goal is "to aid in crime reduction and thereby enhance public confidence in the security of Downtown Wilmington." To ensure that the downtown is safe, ten uniformed police officers are assigned to the downtown. The organization also deploys fifteen uniformed "Safety Ambassadors" throughout the downtown. The safety ambassadors first undergo training in public safety including first-aid and CPR and are equipped with a two-way radio system on their patrols to enable them to stay in touch with police officers.

The responsibility of the "Safety Ambassadors" is to report crime and nuisance activities to police officers for action to be taken. They are also the face of the community and help with directions and wayfinding, answer questions, and provide after-hour safety escorts when needed. In 2001, Downtown Visions also began a Video Partnership Program with the police department. In this program, cameras are installed at twenty-five vantage points around the downtown. The "Safety

Ambassadors" monitor live feeds to these cameras and identify problems that may be occurring in the downtown. Police officers are then alerted to act. Since the inception of the program, over 10,000 incidents have been reported to police and fire personnel and the program has helped to catch crime, locate missing children, and identify early stages of fires.

William Lucy, a Professor of Urban Planning at the University of Virginia and past president of Charlottesville's Planning Commission, attributes part of downtown Charlottesville's success to safety of the downtown environment. A telephone survey of 1,075 residents in the city by Meekins et al. in 2000 found that 96 percent of the respondents felt safe in the downtown. Lucy argues that there is a symbiotic relationship between safety and the success of retail businesses in the downtown:

> Safety would seem to have a reciprocal relationship with downtown success. Some feeling of safety was needed for downtown to succeed, on one hand. On the other hand, a successful downtown contributed to feelings of safety. Since nearly all shopping downtown occurred during the day, it seemed that safety there was adequate to support retail activity. Since restaurants, bars, and theaters downtown did well at night, and their success encouraged a growing number of similar enterprises, safety concerns seemed minor.
>
> (Lucy 2002, p. 29)

Concern over safety in downtown Santa Barbara has led the downtown organization to increase police presence in the district. Two police officers are assigned to the downtown to do "restorative policing" which involves making contact with the homeless downtown and getting them assistance with treatment services, as well as putting them in touch with their families. All of the other cities deploy police officers throughout the downtown to ensure safety.

Regulations

In resilient downtowns, historic preservation and design guidelines are enforced. Both are seen as integral to maintaining the character and quality of the downtown. However, redevelopment of underutilized and abandoned property is encouraged through modification of zoning and other regulations that often make it onerous to redevelop these properties.

The City of Wilmington revised its codes to speed up the permitting process and encourage the refurbishing of downtown buildings into mixed uses that also include residential housing (Sebens 2011). According to the city's Development Services Manager, Kaye Graybeal, the regulations for the CBD have been revamped to make it easier for developers to get their projects through the approval process. For example, a new development downtown only has to meet state water quality regulations, whereas elsewhere it has to meet both city and state water quality and quantity regulations. Height limitations downtown are much higher at 240 feet, as compared to other districts that are 80 feet. Additionally, developers in the downtown do not have to prepare a traffic impact study, which may be required for other areas in the city. These changes seem to be yielding dividends. Terry Espy, managing partner and project developer for one of the downtown projects, expressed satisfaction at the positive changes with the permitting and development process: "Before, it was so gray and confusing it was almost impossible for a developer to do it on their own. I saw a dramatic change" (Sebens 2011).

For years, housing development in downtown Santa Barbara consisted of large and expensive condominiums, starting at a minimum of $1.5 million per unit. These types of housing units have been beyond the reach of young professionals and most of the city's workforce. It is estimated that some 30,000 people commute each day to work in Santa Barbara because they cannot afford to live within the city boundaries. Explaining the reasoning for this rising cost of housing in the downtown, Steve Cushman, President of the Santa Barbara Chamber of Commerce, observed:

> The baby boomers are all starting to retire and are coming with a pocket full of money. They can pay cash for a million dollar condo and that's what's happening and is going to continue to happen because Santa Barbara is so popular around the world.
>
> (Schmidtchen 2008)

In 2003, the city organized a design charrette of volunteers from the Santa Barbara chapter of the American Institute of Architects to generate ideas for the development of affordable market-rate housing, catering to young professionals and the city's workforce. A total of $300,000 in volunteer time was committed by the fifty participants at the event. These affordable housing proposals, vetted by the public and city officials, were found to be acceptable and innovative. The design proposals have been embedded in the city's new General Plan, which now provides for the development of mixed-use, high-density housing to be built in Mobility Oriented Development Areas (MODA). To make it work, density standards and parking requirements have been relaxed for new development. "By eliminating the space developers must set aside for parking—roughly 300 square feet per parking space—the cost of land would presumably be reduced" (Welsh 2009).

The city, through its zoning ordinance and updated comprehensive plan, has made a conscientious policy shift to give priority to the development of smaller, affordable housing in the downtown (see Table 3.7). Earlier in 1989, city residents approved Measure E, a charter amendment to the city's municipal code that restricted non-residential development to no more than three million square feet over a twenty-year period. This was aimed at ensuring a housing/jobs balance in the city. Section 28.87.300 of the city's Municipal Code stipulates the allocation of such development as shown in Table 3.7.

The measure limits small additions to no more than 30,000 square feet annually and stipulates that procedures for allocating square footage under these categories be established by resolution of the City Council. Measure E was recently extended for another ten years.

One of the major hindrances to redevelopment of downtown property in the City of Greenville has been fragmented land ownership. To decrease this burden on developers, the city has engaged in land assembly and the streamlining of property ownership and title registration procedures to make property acquisition easier for developers.

Table 3.7 Priority projects and size of recommended development

Priority Projects	Square Footage
Approved Projects	900,000 sq. ft.
Pending Projects	700,000 sq. ft.
Vacant Property	500,000 sq. ft.
Minor Additions	Exempt
Small Additions	600,000 sq. ft.
Community Priorities	300,000 sq. ft.

Source: City of Santa Barbara (2009)

The city's zoning ordinance has also been updated to be more developer friendly. For example, the development of the Bookends, Riverplace, and the Edge at North Main condominiums did not need to go through the Planning Commission for approval because multifamily and high-rise multifamily residential units are permitted as conditional uses in the city's C-4 central business district. However, because they are new construction, they still had to comply with the central business district design guidelines and obtain a certificate of appropriateness from the Design Review Board. While the zones surrounding the CBD have height and density limitations, the city's central business district is zoned C-4 and has no height, use, density, or parking requirements. The intent is to promote a "unique, high-intensity mix of office, service, retail, entertainment, cultural, government, civic, and residential uses and encourage pedestrian-friendly development" (Sasaki Associates, Inc. 2008, p. 66).

The support from city government has helped boost residential construction in the downtown. Between 1992 and 2002, the City of Greenville witnessed $160 million in new residential construction. Additionally, $100 million in housing renovation took place in the city's historic neighborhoods (City of Greenville 2012). Much of this new development was in the form of condominiums and townhouses, although some apartments were part of the renovation as well. There are over 1,700 condominiums and apartment units in downtown Greenville. Of these 1,031 were built since 2000 (see appendix to this chapter).

In addition to these large lofts and condominium projects, almost every two-story building in the downtown has lofts and living space on its second floor, with retail on the ground level. These include the lofts above Venti, Bergamo, Mike's Subs, Giorgio Trattoria, and the old TD Waterhouse, among others.

Incentives

In addition to relaxing regulations, resilient downtowns also provide incentives to encourage redevelopment of downtown properties. The city of Wilmington provides several incentives, most notable of which is the city's Upstairs Program. A decade ago the City of Wilmington launched the Upstairs Fund that provides gap financing to enable vacant property owners to bring their properties back to productive use and to convert the upper floors into residential living spaces (see Figures 3.3 and 3.4):

Figure 3.3 A Wilmington downtown building before a facade improvement.

Credit: Downtown Visions and Main Street Wilmington, City of Wilmington, DE

> The Upstairs Fund is a program administered by the City of Wilmington's Office of Economic Development (OED) that is intended to stimulate the economic revitalization of Wilmington's downtown by providing incentives for comprehensive renovations of existing buildings with vacant or underutilized upper floors along the historic Market Street commercial corridor. The goal of the program is to facilitate development that will attract a diverse residential population and will contribute to a vibrant community with retail, entertainment, and food and beverage establishments.
>
> (City of Wilmington 2009, p. 2)

The program "encourages the conversion of upper-story space into affordable and market-rate housing units, giving preference to residential projects over other types of use" (City of Wilmington 2011, p. 34). In addition to providing residential development, the Upstairs Program stimulates economic development in the downtown. As of 2011, the city had spent $15 million on the Upstairs Project. In turn, funds are recouped through an expanded tax base.

Figure 3.4 A Wilmington downtown building remodeled with Upstairs Fund for upper-floor residential use.

Credit: Downtown Visions and Main Street Wilmington, City of Wilmington, DE

The Riverfront Development Corporation (RDC) and the Wilmington Renaissance Corporation (WRC) have also played a significant role in the redevelopment of downtown properties by acquiring and remediating brownfield sites to decrease the cost of development. Once ready, the properties are then sold to developers. This cost reduction has incentivized the development of Christina Landing and Justison Landing, two projects that were recently completed in the downtown riverfront neighborhood. State agencies also provided infrastructure improvements totaling $135 million; $50 million for the Christina Landing and $85 million for the Justison Landing project (Rolland 2006, p. 12).

In Chico, the city provides several incentives to developers for downtown housing development. Developers of mixed-use buildings in the downtown are given priority in the processing of their building permits. They may also receive density bonuses, deferral of any impact or permit fees, and flexibility with parking and landscaping requirements. Additionally, the city has assisted downtown developers of residential units with infrastructure upgrades at no cost to them. This has encouraged the redevelopment of several historic properties in the downtown into mixed uses. The redevelopment of the 1911 Waterland-Breslauer building is one such example. Located on Broadway and W. 4th Street in downtown Chico, the building was recently refurbished for office and retail space on the ground floor with the upper floor transformed into residential lofts (see Figure 3.5).

In Greenville, the city's downtown strategic plan recommended a series of actions that needed to be taken to increase downtown living and attract the target demographics. The city estimates that some 1,400 housing units will be built in the downtown over the next ten years. As a result, it recommended using "price

Figure 3.5 The Waterland-Breslauer building on Broadway and W. 4th in Downtown Chico was recently renovated into a mixed-use property and is used for retail and offices.

write-downs, public sector ownership of key sites, public parking development and other incentives" to decrease the cost of such development (Sasaki Associates 2008, p. 19).

Exemplars

Wilmington and Holland provide good examples of how communities have used incentives, regulations, and public–private partnerships to boost downtown housing development and increase the residential population in downtown. For Wilmington, we will discuss the development of the Shipley Lofts for the creative class; for Holland, we will discuss Midtown Village, a school building that was repurposed and converted to downtown housing for the elderly.

The Shipley Lofts

The development of the Shipley Lofts in Wilmington at 701 Shipley Street provides an example of the city's wise use of incentives to boost housing development that targets the housing needs of young professionals and the creative class. It also offers an example of the repurposing of a historic structure to meet the city's current housing needs. The building that is now the Shipley Lofts is a five-story structure that was originally designed by John J. Kennedy, a Wilmington Architect. The building is a nineteenth-century, commercial-style Gothic Revival architecture and was constructed between 1917 and 1919 for Beadenkopf, an investor. In 1919, it was purchased from Beadenkopf by the Foord & Massey Company to be used as a furniture showroom and warehouse.

The original buildings on the site were burned down by fire. Thus the rebuilt structure was designed to be fire resistant with steel beams, heavy timber, and plank floors. The Foord & Massey Furniture Company sold the building to Stern & Company in 1924. Later, in 1934, Sears, Roebuck & Company opened their downtown store in the building and remained there until 1950. Afterwards, the building was used by various businesses as office and retail space until 1964 when the offices of United Community Fund of Delaware, a non-profit agency, bought the building in 1993. The Saints Andrew and Matthew church purchased the building from United Way with the intent of converting it into housing for the homeless. Unfortunately, funding for the project did not materialize.

Then in 1997, an exploratory committee was formed by the church to identify and explore ways to redevelop and reuse the building. This led to the formation of the Shipley Village Community Development Corporation (SVCDC) in 1999. The goal of SVCDC was to redevelop the building for mixed use and to "create a vibrant community with a high quality of life and an environment that promotes economic opportunity through developing affordable housing and stimulating the presence of appropriate business, educational, cultural, social, and other amenities" (Saints Andrew and Matthew 2012).

It was at this time that Mayor Baker floated the idea of turning the building into a live/work space for artists with gallery space for the exhibition of their work on the first floor. This was in recognition of the growing artist community in the city. The Episcopal Church of Saints Andrew and Matthew leased the building to SVCDC for ninety-nine years with annual payments of $100,000 and a $400,000 note.

The total cost of redeveloping the building was $6.3 million, $400,000 of which was contributed by the city. The city's initial contribution was then used to leverage other sources of funding for the project. The developers received Historic Tax Credits of about $2 million, as well as Low Income Tax Credits of $2.5 million. Other contributions came from foundations ($400,000), a Delaware Community Investment Corporation loan of $636,648, and seller financing. The Ingerman Group, the non-profit wing of Saints Andrews and Matthew, Shipley Village Community Development Corporation, and MBI Development Company were partners in the redevelopment of the building.

The Shipley Lofts opened in March 2010 for occupancy (see Figure 3.6). Although the building is open to all tenants, the lofts were designed and built with visual and performing artists in mind. Each of the twenty-three loft apartments is about 886 square feet in size and has studio space, a living room, a kitchen, and a bathroom. The first floor of the building is devoted to gallery space and display area, so that artists can showcase their work. With this, a historic structure was transformed for use by the creative class, with ideas and financial support from the public and private sector.

Figure 3.6 The Shipley Lofts in downtown Wilmington, DE.

The Midtown Village Lofts

A study by Anderson Economic Group in 2008 identified the need for additional senior housing in Ottawa County, noting the City of Holland in particular as one of the communities in the county with such a need: "The over-65 age demographic is increasing faster than all others in the county, yet housing availability is limited" (Anderson Economic Group 2008. p. 6). Others have observed the low cost of living in Holland, along with the rich outdoor and downtown amenities, as an attraction for retirees:

> If you can survive the cold winters, Michigan is a great place to retire. Holland, Michigan is at the top of the affordability list with a median home price of $160,000, low real estate taxes and their low income and sales tax rates are 3.9% and 6%, respectively.
>
> (Corley 2009)

Young professionals are also attracted to downtown Holland. The *Holland Sentinel* narrated the story of a young professional couple, Sarah and Tyler McCoy, who moved downtown. They are both in their mid-twenties and used to live in Granville, MI, and commute to work in Holland, where Tyler works as an engineer at JR Automation and Sarah works in the career services office at Hope College. The couple credit the convenience and walkability of the downtown with "a good combination of city living and suburban conveniences for their decision to move downtown."

A commentary by the *Holland Sentinel* provides support for this young couple and others like them that are choosing to live downtown:

> Most people think of their home as a refuge from the hustle and bustle of the working world, but many are beginning to realize that refuge doesn't have to be two miles from the nearest store. They are looking for complete neighborhoods that serve many needs. The ultimate "mixed-use" neighborhood in this area is downtown Holland. The second-story lofts above Eighth Street shops are among the most coveted residences in our area, and downtown condos have continued to sell amid the real estate downturn.
>
> (*Holland Sentinel* 2009)

The City of Holland's Center of Centers plan outlines a program for the redevelopment of its central city neighborhood, including the provision of mixed uses, senior housing, space for artists' lofts, and housing for the creative class (City of Holland 2010). Several of the redevelopment projects involved the repurposing of old historic buildings for residential use. Midtown Village is one such project, which involved the transformation of a historic, abandoned school building into a downtown residence for the elderly (see Figure 3.7). The school embodies much of the community's history. It was built in 1923 and named after Egbert E. Fell, a superintendent of Holland schools from 1910 to 1945.

The Holland School district saw a drop in its student population, in the last two decades, necessitating the decommissioning and consolidation of some of its schools. Between 1997 and 2007, the number of students enrolled in preK–12 in the Holland School district decreased by 1,000 students from 5,500 to 4,500 students. According to Thomas Page, an administrator in the school district, the Holland School board made the decision to "economically right size" from thirteen buildings to eight buildings. The E.E. Fell High School was decommissioned and students were consolidated into the remaining eight buildings. Part of the rationale for decommissioning the school was to also control costs. As the building aged, it became expensive to maintain. It is estimated that the cost for replacing the school's windows alone would have required the school district to spend $600,000 in 2005. In addition, heating costs for the school district averaged $60,000 to $70,000 a year. There were also concerns with vandalism and the impact of the school's appearance on the downtown.

In 2006, the Holland Public Schools sold the E.E. Fell Junior High School and the Community Education building next door to Jubilee Ministries for $775,000 (Kloosterman 2009). Jubilee Ministries then contacted Dennis Sturtevant, CEO of the Dwelling Place, a non-profit community development corporation based in Grand Rapids, MI, to partner with them in the redevelopment of the school into elderly housing. Although Dwelling Place did not have a facility in Holland, it had a reputation in the region for transforming historic property into affordable housing. According to Dennis Sturtevant, the mission of Dwelling Place is to "provide quality affordable housing and supportive services for residents who need these services and to use the redevelopment projects as catalysts for neighborhood revitalization."

Figure 3.7 Midtown Village Apartments in Holland, MI.

Through the expertise of Dwelling Place, the building was redeveloped into Midtown Village Apartments, a thirty-unit residential complex for seniors. Located downtown, the apartments are in close proximity to city hall, the museum, library, and Centennial Park. For Dennis Sturtevant, the project is "really covering a desire and need that empty nesters have: that is, to age with dignity. They want to be able to age in place. If someone gets to a place where they need a caregiver, there is the flexibility to bring a family member in" (Peck 2011).

Located at 372 S. River Avenue, Midtown Village is a 61,000 square foot building. The apartments range in size from 1,100 to 1,400 square feet. It took Dwelling Place six years to complete the project. Because it is a historic building, the design had to be approved by several layers of local, state, and federal levels of government. For example, the replacement windows had to be approved by city, state, and national historic commissions before they were installed. A majority of the $9 million cost it took to refurbish the school came from federal low-income housing tax credits, state historic credits, state brownfield tax credits, a $207,000 Michigan State Housing Development Authority mortgage, and $4.7 million in federal stimulus money. The Bank of Holland is also a part-owner of the project through its purchase of $2.5 million in housing tax credits from the developer.

The historic features of the building have been preserved as much as possible. For example, there are "imperfections in the walls, trim and baseboards in the halls, original rounded windows, staircases and the River Avenue entry" (Manwell 2011).

Midtown Village is a high-quality, multifamily residential building. It has high ceilings and sky lights, motion detector lights, security cameras in the wide hallways, secure entry, a computer and exercise room, conference room, and upper-floor outdoor patio. Additionally, the development is LEED certified. The building meets federal "affordability" requirements, but is not low-income housing. Midtown Village Apartments opened in downtown Holland in October 2011 and is serving the housing needs of the elderly. Haworth, Inc., the founder of whom was a woodwork teacher in the school, donated all of the furniture in the building, thus maintaining the historical connection with the company's hometown.

Reflecting on the project, Dennis Sturtevant concluded: "To me it is not so much what we learned as what has been reinforced. There are always questions about cost containment but if you build to high quality, the building will be maintained longer and the residents and neighborhood will appreciate it more. If you need to redevelop a building, make it feel special so people's sense of place is impacted. Also consider the cost per square foot of the entire building not just the cost per dwelling unit and you will see that it is always a good investment."

Conclusion

Attracting and retaining a residential population downtown complements retail development and supports the growth of this sector. To succeed, cities must be creative in using regulations and incentives to support rather than stifle the redevelopment of existing buildings into residential uses. Safety must also be addressed to decrease both the perceived and the real concerns of residents' sense of security in the downtown.

 Please visit the companion website at http://routledge.com/cw/Burayidi for additional resources.

Appendix

Table 3.8 Downtown condominiums in the City of Greenville, SC

Existing Projects	Number of Units	Sale/Rent	Built 2000–2010
100 Court St Condos	42	S	42
109 N. Main St.	4	R	
123 S. Main St. (Old Meador's)	2	R	
155 River Place	36	S	36
224 E. Park Avenue	5	R	
233 North Main	17	R	17
38 Southland Place	10	R	
400 North Main	19	S	19
623 North Main	10	S	10
648 S. Main St.	8	R	8
Brick St. Lofts	8	S	8
Cauble Commons (100 N. Main)	9	S	
Cleveland Ridge (Oakland Ave)	10	S	
Commons at Hampton-Pinckney	15	S	15
Court Square (S. Main St.)	8	S	
Davenport	25	S	
Field House at West End	40	S	40
Greenville Summit	101	R	
Heritage Green Creekside	6	S	
Lavinia Ave Condos	10	S	
McBee Station–Apartments	197	R	197
McDaniel Green	41	S	
McDaniel Park (Knoxbury Terrace)	30	S	
McPherson Park (Poinsett Ave)	14	S	
Middleton Place	30		
Northgate Trace	47	S	
Park Heights (Univ. Ridge)	10	S	
Park Row (Bennett St)	8	S	8
Pendleton West–Single Family	18	S	18
Pendleton West–Townhomes	23	S	23
Poinsett Corners	81	S	81
Prevost Apts	12	R	
RiverHouse	10	S	10
The Bookends	30	S	30
The Brio	52	S	52

Existing Projects	Number of Units	Sale/Rent	Built 2000–2010
The Edge	50	S	50
The Lofts at Mills Mill	104	S	104
The Park Downtown	35	S	35
The Proctor Building	2	R	
The Richland at Cleveland Park	24	S	24
The Terrace at RP	27	S	27
The West End Cottages	13	S	13
Towers East	271	R	
University Ridge	48	S	
Village at Townes	36	S	36
Virginia Condos	16	S	
Wachovia Place	22	R	22
West Park and Townes	2	S	2
Ridgeland at the Park	42	S	42
Park Place on Main	7	S	7
McBee Station–City Homes	22	S	22
The Elements	20	S	20
The Brownstones (236 Rhett)	5	S	5
830 S. Main St. "Custom House" (corner of Wardlaw & S. Main)	8	S	8
River Walk Apartments	44	R	
Total Built:	**1,786**		**1,031**
Under Construction			
Bookends Phase 2 ("100 East")	48	R	
Total UC:	**48**		
Planned			
Rhett St. Apartments	100		
Apartments at Wardlaw/Rhett Streets	150		
Total Planned:	**250**		

CHAPTER 4

Courting New Immigrants

New immigrants can boost the residential population of downtown and near downtown neighborhoods. For this to happen, cities must show tolerance and acceptance of diversity. This is in line with the findings of a study of twenty-six communities by the Knight Foundation, which found "openness" of a community to be the greatest factor in people's attachment to place. The foundation defined "openness" by how welcoming a community is to different types of people, including immigrants, gays and lesbians, families with young children, and minorities. Openness was also found to correlate strongly with a community's rate of economic growth. Given this finding, the Foundation admonished communities to take active and visible measures to promote tolerance and diversity to make them "welcoming places for all groups" (Knight Foundation 2010, p. 17).

Similarly, Richard Longworth, a *Chicago Tribune* foreign correspondent for twenty years and now a senior fellow at the Chicago Council on Global Affairs, made waves recently with the publication of his book *Caught in the Middle: America's Heartland in the Age of Globalism*. In the book, Longworth made a strong and compelling case for attracting immigrants to midwestern cities to help rejuvenate their economies because:

> They not only bring jobs and skills. They bring global viewpoints, vital contacts with other nations, ethnic restaurants and neighborhood festivals, new art and different music. They make cities richer and more fun. Cities that are booming—New York, Chicago, Boston, Toronto, Denver, Portland, San Francisco, Atlanta—all have big and growing foreign-born population. Cities in trouble—Detroit, Cleveland, Pittsburgh, Baltimore—do not. Successful cities draw immigrants, which make them more successful yet.
>
> (Longworth 2008, p. 125)

The number of foreign-born residents in a community is a good indication of how accepting a community is of diversity. Immigrants tend to locate where other immigrants have settled. Tables 4.1 and 4.2 show the foreign-born population in the fourteen cities and their downtowns. Given that these are small cities, the number of foreign-born population that is settling in these communities is considerably high. Seven of the fourteen cities have a foreign-born population that reaches a double-digit percentage of each city's overall population, suggesting that immigration is a significant contributor to the growth of these cities. In Santa Barbara, for example, a quarter of the city's population is foreign-born. Many of the foreign-born population also reside in the downtown. In Middletown, over a quarter of the city's downtown residents is foreign-born; in Santa Barbara, it is 32 percent; in Santa Fe, it is 21 percent; and in Wilmington, it is 10 percent.

Table 4.1 Citizenship for the United States: city data

	Total City Population	US Citizens	Foreign Born Population	Percentage of City Population
Middletown, CT	47,349	41,111	6,238	13.2%
Wilmington, DE	71,437	64,858	6,579	9.2%
Greenville, SC	57,821	53,648	4,173	7.2%
Hendersonville, NC	12,900	11,254	1,648	12.8%
Charlottesville, VA	42,267	36,490	5,777	13.7%
Mansfield, OH	48,799	47,663	1,136	2.3%
Ripon, WI	7,686	7,273	413	5.4%
Holland, MI	33,708	29,799	3,909	11.6%
Lafayette, IN	66,148	60,888	5,260	8.0%
Fort Collins, CO	140,082	130,065	10,017	7.2%
Santa Barbara, CA	87,859	65,769	22,090	25.1%
Chico, CA	85,130	76,872	8,258	9.7%
Nacogdoches, TX	32,290	28,914	3,376	10.5%
Santa Fe, NM	67,588	58,177	9,411	13.9%

Source: U.S. Census: Compiled from Universe Total Population in the United States, 2006–2010 American Community Survey, 5-Year Estimates. American FactFinder. United States Census Bureau.

Table 4.2 Citizenship status for the United States: downtown data

	Total Downtown Population	Foreign Born Population	Percentage of Downtown Population
Middletown, CT	1,285	342	26.6%
Wilmington, DE	2,038	212	10.4%*
Greenville, SC	827	47	5.7%
Hendersonville, NC	2,078	94	4.5%
Charlottesville, VA	2,308	73	3.2%
Mansfield, OH	2,324	11	0.5%
Ripon, WI**	–	–	–
Holland, MI	7,909	558	7.1%
Lafayette, IN	806	59	7.3%
Fort Collins, CO	2,238	107	4.8%
Santa Barbara, CA	3,085	97	32.3%
Chico, CA	5,450	228	4.2%
Nacogdoches, TX	7,352	324	4.4%
Santa Fe, NM	359	75	20.9%

Notes

* The foreign born population for Census Tract 28 was used for the downtown as the Census Bureau did not report data for the foreign-born population for Block Group 1 of Census Tract 28 for the City of Wilmington.
** Too few cases at this level for data to be reported by Census Bureau for the City of Ripon.

Source: U.S. Census: Compiled from Universe Total Population in the United States, 2006–2010 American Community Survey, 5-Year Estimates. American FactFinder. United States Census Bureau.

New immigrants bring vitality to the cities' downtowns. They also become homeowners, help stabilize neighborhoods, and start new businesses that help grow the local economies. Izyumov et al. (2000) for example, found that:

> Within 20 years of arrival in the US, well over half (60.9%) of immigrants lived in owner-occupied housing in 1990. In fact, immigrants who have been in the US for at least 25 years actually achieve a higher homeownership rate than natives. Foreign-born persons who had arrived in the US before 1970 had a homeownership rate of 75.6% compared to native-born rate of 69.8%.
>
> (p. 13)

Restaurants, custodial services, retail establishments, and professional business services such as accounting, design, and high-technology firms are started by new immigrants. Table 4.3 shows the number of firms in cities with resilient downtowns and the proportion of these businesses that are owned by minorities. The City of Greenville, for example, had 9,371 firms. Of these, about 10 percent are minority owned. Table 4.3 shows 21 percent of all businesses in Santa Fe are minority owned. In Lafayette and Middletown, approximately 10 percent of all firms are minority owned. JoAnn Caddoo, Membership Coordinator for the Fort Collins Downtown Business Association, estimates that 10 percent of the city's 230 downtown businesses are owned by minorities.

Table 4.3 Minority-owned businesses in case study cities

City	Total Firms	Black-owned	American Indian-owned	Asian-owned	Native Hawaiian or Pacific Islander-owned	Hispanic-owned	Women-owned
Middletown, CT	2,958	3.5%	F	5.0%	1.3%	S	29.0%
Wilmington, DE	8,502	12.5%	0.4%	4.2%	F	2.3%	26.1%
Greenville, SC	9,371	5.3%	F	2.2%	F	2.2%	21.0%
Hendersonville, NC	2,346	2.7%	S	S	F	S	30.0%
Charlottesville, VA	4,917	S	F	3.3%	F	1.3%	25.8%
Mansfield, OH	3,741	S	F	3.2%	F	F	19.2%
Ripon, WI	394	F	F	F	F	F	36.3%
Holland, MI	2,829	4.3%	1.2%	F	F	3.6%	18.8%
Lafayette, IN	5,403	4.6%	S	S	F	5.1%	32.5%
Fort Collins, CO	14,925	0.6%	0.3%	1.9%	F	3.8%	29.3%
Santa Barbara, CA	14,003	1.2%	S	4.9%	F	S	27.4%
Chico, CA	7,478	1.1%	S	3.3%	F	6.4%	32.3%
Nacogdoches, TX	3,637	S	F	S	F	2.9%	19.6%
Santa Fe, NM	13,538	0.9%	2.8%	1.2%	F	16.1%	34.5%

Notes

F: Fewer than 100 firms

S: Suppressed; does not meet publication standards

Source: U.S. Census Bureau, State and County QuickFacts, 2007. U.S. Department of Commerce. United States Census Bureau.

In Holland, Luciano Hernandes, Ruben Juarez, and Ed Amaya are not only major players in the business community, but are also civic leaders. Luciano Hernandes, a Hispanic immigrant, started several firms in the community including Castex Industries, an embroidery business and TIGER Studio, established in 2000. TIGER Studio is a successful product and marketing design business that does customized industrial, graphic, and web design. The firm employs six people. In 2010, TIGER Studio won the minority business of the year award from the Holland Chamber of Commerce. Ruben Juarez, owner of Workforce Management, a firm also based in Holland but with offices in Grand Rapids and Wyoming, MI, specializes in recruiting and placing professional personnel in industrial, manufacturing, and professional service firms. The company has recruited and placed 1,500 people since its founding in 2007. In 2012, Workforce Management received the "Top Business" award from DiversityBusiness.com. According to DiversityBusiness.com, over 1,200,000 businesses in the United States had the opportunity to participate in the survey. Juarez's firm was chosen based on its annual gross revenue and business profile.

Three of the fourteen communities—Santa Barbara, Greenville, and Santa Fe—have Hispanic Chambers of Commerce. Of course, Hispanics have long and deep roots in Santa Fe and Santa Barbara, but these chambers facilitate networking opportunities for recent Hispanic immigrants as well. The Santa Fe Chamber lists more than seventy Hispanic businesses in the city, including firms in advertising and promotion, childcare services, utilities, transportation, real estate, and legal services. The mission of the Santa Barbara Hispanic Chamber of Commerce is stated as fostering "the economic vitality and prosperity of Small Business Owners and the Latino Business Community and to enhance the quality of life in the greater Santa Barbara area. We provide the opportunity for businesses to network and participate in the growing Hispanic business community" (Santa Barbara Hispanic Chamber of Commerce 2009).

A study by the Lusk Centre for Real Estate at the University of Southern California found that immigration will contribute as much as 82 percent of U.S. population growth between now and 2050, adding as many as 117 million people. As we have seen in Chapter 1, recent immigrants increasingly prefer to settle in small and medium-sized cities rather than in the large gateway communities. This provides small and medium-sized communities with an opportunity to boost both their overall and downtown populations. Painter and Yu (2005) analyzed census data from 2000 to 2005 in sixty mid-sized cities and found that these cities showed an average increase of 27 percent in new immigrant population, compared to that of the traditional gateway cities which saw a decline of new immigrants by 6 percent.

To capture this growing immigrant population, cities must provide the conditions that are conducive to attract them. In cities with resilient downtowns, tolerance and diversity are themes that are echoed by civic leaders in both the public and private sectors. In 2011, the City of Chico adopted one of the most aggressive diversity action plans of any city in the United States. The plan defines diversity broadly to include age, gender, ethnic heritage, sexual orientation, mental and physical abilities, and race. In the plan, the city states its goals for inclusivity and outlines specific steps and a timeframe for achieving these goals. The plan, published in both English and Spanish, states:

Diversity is constantly changing. When we recognize, appreciate and respect differences, we can work and communicate more effectively in governance and create a more unified and multifaceted community enriched through appreciating and understanding other's perspectives. The City of Chico Diversity Plan is a strategy to actively remove barriers and promote diversity within the city government and the larger community. The plan seeks to establish a climate for all individuals and groups to develop the trust and understanding to engage in city governance processes, influence decision making and access municipal services.

(City of Chico 2011, p. 3)

To achieve the goals of the diversity plan, the city committed itself to translate public directives into Hmong and Spanish, ensure public service announcements are multilingual, appoint a diversity coordinator, ensure that public art projects promote and reflect diversity, and provide an annual report on diversity in the city's workforce.

In 2009, then-Mayor Norris of Charlottesville unveiled a plan to increase workplace diversity in the city. He is quoted as saying, "We want to be known not just as a community that commits to talking about the difficult issue of race, but a community that also takes proactive steps to lead the way in improving conditions for all races" (Tenia 2009). He dubbed his initiative "targeted outreach program" and sought to partner with the University of Virginia to promote Charlottesville as a community of choice for minorities. This was to be accomplished through recruiting of recent graduates to the city, reaching out to mid-career professionals outside the city, and mentoring of minorities.

The city of Middletown describes itself as a "thriving and diverse culture appreciating community" (City of Middletown 2012b, p. 2). On January 3, 2012, Mayor Daniel Drew of Middletown signed into law the city's affirmative action plan that commits the Connecticut city to uphold and enhance diversity in an effort to ensure that people of diverse backgrounds are full participants in the city. The document made a distinction between "Equal Employment Opportunity," which it defined as providing all persons with the right to employment and advancement in the workplace based on their merit, ability, and potential, and "Affirmative Action," which is positive action to overcome the effects of past discriminatory practices against minority groups. In the affirmative action plan, the City of Middletown strives to:

Make good faith efforts that may be necessary in all aspects to ensure that the recruitment and hiring of underrepresented individuals reflect their availability in the job market, that the causes of underutilization are identified and eliminated, and that terms, conditions, and privileges of employment are equitably administered.

(City of Middletown 2012a, p. 1)

The proclamation went on to state that:

as our workforce becomes more diverse, we are challenged with the opportunity to find ways of enabling people of many different backgrounds to provide valuable contributions to the City of Middletown. It is not enough to simply increase diversity in the workplace; we must learn to respect and appreciate people from diverse backgrounds. When individuals communicate and work effectively with each other, affirmative action and the diversity within our workforce will mutually support an equal opportunity environment.

(City of Middletown 2012a, p. 2)

The private sector has also played a role in promoting inclusiveness in the city. Liberty Bank, headquartered in Middletown with thirty-seven locations in the state, has for the last ten years given a diversity award to individuals for their work in improving diversity relations in the bank's operations area. The Community Diversity Award was named after Willard McRae, former chairman of the Liberty Bank Board of Directors. McRae is also co-founder of the Middlesex Coalition for Children, the Middlesex Child and Adolescent Service System Program, and the Upward Bound Program at Wesleyan University. Liberty Bank President and CEO, Chandler Howard, made the following observation with respect to the award:

Our community today has many different faces ... many different voices. The Community Diversity Award was conceived to honor a few very special people who have led the way in bringing all those different voices into harmony. These are people who look at differences, and see opportunities. They experience the unfamiliar, and feel enriched by it. They listen to disagreements, and find common ground. Willard McRae is one of those special people.

(ICG Europe Limted 2009)

The award is presented each fall to recognize an individual "who has made a noteworthy and continuous contribution to his or her community in the area of diversity."

In 1994, the Middletown School Board in Connecticut approved a school diversity plan. This in itself would not be newsworthy except that a week prior, the largest school district in the region voted to reject a similar plan. Middletown's diversity plan passed with a seven to one vote. The board members cited the need to prepare students to work in an increasingly global and diverse workplace as the reasons for the vote (Nixon 1994).

In 2007, a group of business leaders in Western Michigan, where the City of Holland is located, released a report entitled "Strategies for a Culturally Competent Region." The report stresses the need for businesses and residents to be culturally competent, which enables the region to compete economically in the global environment. The report asserted that to be economically competitive, the region must attract, retain, and be accommodating to people of diverse cultures, backgrounds, races, and genders. The report notes:

In order to recruit and retain diverse workers, citizens and their families, it is critical to hear and respond to the beat of an ever changing population. A successful business climate and the welcoming ambiance of a culturally competent community will continue to draw workers with varied backgrounds and gifts. A successful business climate also fosters creativity, in the form of new products and innovation strategies for business growth. As businesses and communities diversify their populations, improved profits, opportunities, and reputations will lead to greater prosperity for our region.

(West Michigan Chamber Coalition 2007, p. 4)

The report outlined steps that communities and employers should take to develop cultural competency. For communities, the report recommended: i) the development of diversity programs at the workplace; ii) representation of the diverse community groups in its governance, especially on city boards; iii) recognition of persons who contribute to enhancing diversity in the region; and iv) promotion of diversity organizations. For employers, the report suggested they provide funding for employees to develop cultural competence, promote inclusivity, and provide mentorship programs for business leaders. In addition, firms should continuously make the business case for diversity in the workplace and ensure that their services and products appeal to a diverse population.

In the next section, we examine how cities with resilient downtowns have embraced diversity in their governance, promoted inclusivity in their programs and policies, and engaged in multicultural placemaking.

Governance

Civic leadership plays a vital role in promoting diversity and inclusivity in a community. New immigrants must feel accepted in the community in which they locate. Multicultural groups must feel safe, and eccentricity must be welcomed. Governance is not simply who holds elected office, but also whose voice counts when decisions are made. We will first look at the composition of those in elected offices, such as city council members. In addition to elected offices, we will examine the minority representation of other civic commissions, committees, and advisory boards formed by local government as these commissions, committees, and advisory boards provide a window to what these cities view as important voices in the governing process.

The composition of the elected government is perhaps the most visible statement a community can make about inclusivity. In this regard, all fourteen cities show considerable diversity on their city councils. Mansfield has nine members. Two of these positions are elected at-large; the rest are elected from wards. Two members of the council are women and two are African Americans.

Charlottesville's mayor, Satyendra Huja, is a native-born Indian. For twenty-five years, Satyendra worked as an urban planner in the city's Department of Planning and Community Development. Prior to becoming mayor, he was elected to the City Council in 2007 and re-elected in 2011 to serve a four-year term. Of the five council members, three are women. Additionally, the city manager is African American.

In Wilmington, the mayor and more than half of the City Council are African American. There are thirteen city council members, six of whom are African American. Two are women. Hendersonville's mayor, Barbara Volk, is female. At a retreat to discuss the city's strategic plan, Ron Stephens, a member of the City Council, made a poignant remark about what he considers to be important for the city: "Good government is inclusive—a place where everyone can participate and be included" (The Novak Consulting Group 2012, p. 3). Greenville has seven city councilors, five of which are female. Nacogdoches has five members on its City Council; one is African American and one is female.

All of the cities make room for representation of their diverse population, whether that diversity represents race, sex, ethnicity, or age. As shown in Table 4.4, besides elected office, several boards, commissions, and committees have been created by the cities to advise local government on matters of diversity.

Table 4.4 Committees and commissions related to diversity and inclusion

City	Committee/Commission
Middletown, CT	Youth Services Advisory Board Committee on People with Disabilities Senior Services Commission Human Relations Commission Affirmative Action Monitoring Committee
Wilmington, DE	Education, Youth and Families Committee Health, Aging, and Disabilities Committee
Greenville, SC	Youth Commission Minority Economic Development Institute, Inc.
Hendersonville, NC	Mayor's Committee on Disability
Charlottesville, VA	Commission on Children and Families Jefferson Area Board of Aging Sister Cities Commission Human Rights Commission ADA and ADA Advisory Committee Dialogue on Race
Mansfield, OH	Human Relations Commission Ohio District 5 Area Aging Advisory Board
Ripon, WI	None
Holland, MI	Human Relations Commission International Relations Commission Youth Advisory Council
Lafayette, IN	Commission on African American Affairs Commission on Latino and Hispanic Affairs Human Relations Commission Youth Council
Fort Collins, CO	Commission on Disability Human Relations Commission Senior Advisory Board Women's Commission Youth Advisory Board
Santa Barbara, CA	Access Advisory Committee Sister Cities Board
Chico, CA	Diversity Ad Hoc Committee
Nacogdoches, TX	Mayor's Committee on People with Disabilities
Santa Fe, NM	Mayor's Youth Advisory Board

Five of the cities have human relations commissions. These include Middletown, Lafayette, Holland, Mansfield, and Fort Collins. Like many of the other cities, the Mansfield Human Relations Commission is tasked with improving "communication, understanding and cooperation between all racial, ethnic and religious groups." Fort Collins' Human Relations Commission was established by local government "to promote the acceptance and respect for diversity through educational programs and activities, and to discourage all forms of discrimination based on race, religion, age, gender, disability, etc." For more than two decades, the commission has recognized individuals in the city who have made a difference in the lives of minority and disadvantaged residents through an annual award. The awards breakfast is attended by the city's mayor, members of the City Council, and civic leaders. Such a high-profile event is meant to showcase the importance the city gives to inclusiveness and acceptance of diversity.

In Holland, Magdalena Rivera was elected to the Holland School Board in 2011, the first Latina to be elected to the board. Al Sarano is head of the city's Human Relations Commission. The City Clerk, Ana Perales, is also a Latina. For many years, Luciano Hernandes served on the Holland City Council and the Ottawa Board of Commissioners. Roberto Zara is a member of the Neighborhood Advisory Committee.

Holland established an International Relations Commission in 1993 with the goal of promoting international and cross-cultural understanding and sensitivity in interactions within the community and abroad. In May 2009, the Commission helped organize the city's first Multicultural Connections, a celebration of diversity. In 1996, the Commission also helped to establish a Sister City relation with the city of Queretaro, Mexico. Through the Sister City program, both communities have promoted cultural understanding through tourism and cultural exchange visits. Since its formation, about nine delegations have visited Queretaro, and thirteen delegations from Queretaro have visited Holland. In 2008, Holland teachers visited Queretaro to set up an educational "e-pal" partnership to help bridge the cultural gap between the youth of the two cities. Several friendly games have also been played between the youth of the two cities in baseball, basketball, and football.

The cities of Santa Barbara, Charlottesville, and Hendersonville also have Sister City programs. Santa Barbara has seven Sister Cities on three continents, including Asia, South America, and Europe. The city's Sister City Board was formed in 1993 to promote friendship among people of different racial and ethnic backgrounds and to "bring about a better understanding of peoples of the world." Hendersonville has Sister City relations with Almuñécar, Spain, with a goal to "harness communication between the towns to promote tolerance of different values and ways of life." Charlottesville has four sister cities: Poggio a Caiano, Italy; Pleven, Bulgaria; Besançon, France; and Winneba, Ghana.

Of the fourteen communities, eight have a commission on youth issues. The purpose of these youth commissions is to ensure that the youth are involved in the governance of the cities and that the issues that affect this demographic group are given the attention they deserve by civic leaders. The Santa Barbara Youth Council, formed in 1994, provides an organized voice for the youth in the community. It advises the community on youth issues and engages them on civic matters. The purpose of the Holland Youth Advisory Council is to promote diversity education, showcase talents of the youth, and support young entrepreneurs.

Most of the cities define diversity broadly to include not only race and sex, but also disability, age, and sexual orientation. Four communities—Nacogdoches, Santa Barbara, Fort Collins, and Mansfield—have committees on disabilities. Three cities have committees on the elderly: Fort Collins has a Senior Advisory Board; Mansfield has an Aging Advisory Board; Middletown has a Senior Services Commission.

The City of Nacogdoches has a Committee on People with Disabilities, with eleven members serving two-year terms. The goal of this committee is stated thus:

> The Mayor's Committee on People with Disabilities envisions a community dedicated to the fullest possible inclusion of citizens at whatever level of ability they possess. The mission of the NMCPD is to keep the City Council advised of the living conditions and needs of people with disabilities in the City of Nacogdoches and to further opportunities for people with disabilities to enjoy a life of independence, productivity, and self-determination.
>
> (City of Nacogdoches 2012, p. 10)

Fort Collins is the only city with a commission dedicated specifically to women's issues. The purpose of the Fort Collins Women's Commission is to foster the participation of women in all decisions affecting women in the community.

With a growing non-English-speaking population, several of the cities are starting to provide their official documents in both English and Spanish to cater to the new immigrants. The City of Ripon publishes its calendar of events in both English and Spanish to cater to its growing Hispanic population. Some of the cities are also proactive in ensuring that all voices in the community are heard and that all groups are given the opportunity to participate in government. In 2010, the Charlottesville City Council started a community discussion series dubbed "Our Town Charlottesville" in which councilors hold town hall-style meetings in each of the city's neighborhoods. The goal of these meetings is to get as close as possible to ordinary citizens and "to remove as many barriers as possible so that voices previously silent to Council would be encouraged to attend and participate."

This program has increased resident participation in government and ensured that diverse voices and groups will be heard in the governing process. By all accounts, the program has been a resounding success. Writing about the first of the town hall meetings, the city's newsletter, *City Notes*, observed:

> City leaders wanted to start in neighborhoods whose presence had been under-represented in the past from Council meetings. The hope was to reduce the barriers that might keep parents, students, our older residents, and our poorer residents from attending city meetings. To address these concerns, city staffers provided dinner, childcare, and a very casual and accessible environment.
>
> There were loud voices, tears, handshakes and hugs, all a product of bringing City Hall to the neighborhoods to solve challenges together and make our city a better place to live. As at all of these meetings, a list was drawn up with promised changes, and city staff have been working through it. Hundreds

of participants—city residents, city staff and City Council—have devoted nine evenings to listen, challenge, answer, and commit.

(City of Charlottesville 2011, p. 1)

Charlottesville also holds an annual Neighborhood Leadership Institute where up to thirty residents are brought together to learn how they can more effectively participate in the governance of the community, starting at the neighborhood level. Participants learn skills in community organizing, effective communication, and collaboration. At the end of the program, participants work jointly on a community project in which they research a community problem and come up with action steps to address the problem. It concludes with a presentation of their findings to city leaders.

The City of Middletown has flattened its governance structure, making it easy for residents and business owners in the city to have access to civic leaders in the public, private and non-profit sectors. For over a decade the Middlesex Chamber of Commerce, with a membership of over 2,300, has held a monthly forum between its members, city leaders, and the general public. At such meetings public officials and business owners exchange information and get their questions answered. Members of the public are welcome to these meetings to ask questions or voice their concerns. Present at these meetings are the Chamber President, the city's mayor, heads of the major city departments including police, planning and community development, fire, health and water and sewer services, and parks and recreation. As many of the downtown businesses, especially restaurants on Main Street, are minority owned, this flattened organizational structure provides a less intimidating opportunity for recent immigrants to participate in decisions that affect them. The chamber has received several accolades for its work including the Vision 2000 Excellence Award from the NAACP, and the Governor's Laurel Award for Responsible Social Involvement.

Celebrating Diversity

Cities that cherish diversity provide visible signs of inclusion of other cultures in their landscapes. These include symbols, artifacts, festivals, street furniture, and art in public places. The Public Art program of Chico has a stated goal to "provide diverse and challenging employment opportunities for contemporary artists from all ethnic communities to ensure that a broad cultural heritage will be reflected in the community's public art collection" (City of Chico 2009). Not surprisingly, the city's public art is inclusive of the multicultural groups that make up the city's population. The artifacts of these groups are on display in public parks, government buildings, and prominent public places throughout the city. One of the most visible displays of public art is *Ancestor Gates*—four eight-foot gates that depict and celebrate the city's African American, Asian, Mexican, and Native American heritages. Located along Martin Luther King Jr. Parkway, *Ancestor Gates* is the work of several artists who used recycled material and engaged school children in telling the stories of the different ethnic groups living in the Chapman neighborhood. Figures 4.1 and 4.2 show *Ancestor Gates* by Jenny Hale (Lead Artist) and Robin Indar, David Barta, Amaera Bay Laurel, Paul Krohn, Stan McKetchin.

Figure 4.1 Native American arch inspired by feathers of the headdress worn on ceremonial occasions.

Credit: City of Chico, CA

Figure 4.2 African-American drum "Translated into a complex system of poly-rhythms and fluid dance movements."

Credit: City of Chico, CA

Public art is also a part of the urban fabric in Santa Barbara, where the works of several ethnic and internationally renowned artists are displayed throughout the city. An example is Luis Jimenez's *Spanish Dancers* on State Street in the city's cultural district. One of the strategic goals of the Santa Barbara County Arts Commission is to "promote Santa Barbara County as an international cultural arts destination and highlight regional cultural traditions, festivals, institutions, and venues working in partnership with the Conference and Visitor Bureaus in the County and the Downtown Organization in Santa Barbara" (Santa Barbara County Arts Commission 2009).

Some cities provide funding to enable minority artists to produce and showcase their work. Hendersonville administers the Grassroots Grants Program of the North Carolina Arts Council, which requires that 5 percent of the annual funding be allocated for minority and underserved artists. In Santa Fe, 2 percent of the cost of capital projects is dedicated to the acquisition of art. The city's Art in Public Places program was established in 1985 to "honor Santa Fe's unique historical and cultural heritage as well as reflect its present." The Art in Public Places Committee is responsible for reviewing and determining the location of such art in the city's public places.

Not only does public space in these cities feature "ethnic" art, but the performing arts are also used to educate the public about diversity. In an effort to showcase diverse cultures, several of the communities hold ethnic and international festivals as well. Each year, the City of Greenville hosts the Greenville Scottish Games, the Greek Festival, Oktoberfest, Hispanic Festival, A Day with India, Shinnehkai and Bon Japanese Festival, and World Tai Chi Day. The city holds an annual Community Pride celebration that is co-hosted by the faith community and civil liberties groups.

In Nacogdoches, the city has been celebrating a Multicultural Festival for the last twenty-five years. It is organized by the Sacred Heart Catholic Church and supported by local companies such as Cordova Construction Co., Jeffrey Cuevas-NRG Aquatic Physical Therapy, Oral & Facial Surgery Group of East Texas, LLP, and numerous individual philanthropists. At the festival, people can enjoy ethnic cuisines from the diverse groups in the community including Filipino, Indian, Italian, Polish, Mexican, and Burmese. Most importantly, the festival provides an opportunity for people to learn about the cultures of different ethnic groups that live in the city.

The Fringe Festival, celebrated in Wilmington, is an alternative to mainstream art festivals. Fringe festivals provide venues and opportunities for artists whose work would otherwise be considered too edgy and offbeat to be seen. The first Fringe Festival was held in the city in October 2009. The concept originated in Edinburgh, Scotland, in 1947, where alternative artists performed their acts outside of the Edinburgh International Festival. Despite its unorthodoxy, the Fringe Festival was welcomed in Wilmington by the city's leadership and community organizations. Mayor James Baker and the City Council supported the festival in its first year, with an $11,000 contribution. The festival has also been supported by local organizations including the Delaware Division of the Arts, Delaware Lottery, Spark Weekly, and Mobius New Media.

The website for the Fringe Festival describes it as, "innovative, thought-provoking and engaging. Fringe Wilmington challenges artists of all creative disciplines to explore the outer edges of their art in a supportive environment." In Wilmington, the Fringe Festival is a five-day multidiscipline juried event comprising different art forms including comedy, music, dance, magic art, photography, painting, and film.

Jeff Onore, a playwright and one-man performer of the "Slip and Fall Guy," described Fringe Festivals as "so fringe, so clever and so out of the mainstream. If you are eager to be exposed to something that's not force-fed through your all-powerful TV, the potential exists to be really startled by something great" (Cormier 2010).

The city's leadership has also openly welcomed the gay and lesbian community and supported the first Alt-Takes Festival, a GBLT festival in Wilmington. When I met with Mayor Baker at the majestic Hotel du Pont in downtown Wilmington for lunch, I was eager to know why the city adopted such an open-arms approach to the diverse groups that other cities have not. Now in his last year of a third and final term, Mayor Baker is the second African-American mayor of Wilmington. Prior to becoming mayor, he served for twelve years as a council member and was president of the council for sixteen years. His response to my question was stated as a matter of fact:

> As an African American I know about bias and what it can do. I know bias stifles creativity. We take advantage of every opportunity to speak to all groups

in the community. We embraced the gay community and see them as part of the panoramic tapestry of the city. We simply provided the gay community, like any other group, open access and let them know they are welcome.

The support of the Fringe and the Alt-Takes festivals by the city's leadership sends a strong message that in Wilmington it is okay to be different, iconoclastic, and unconventional. Onore, who is from Massachusetts, received a personal letter from Mayor Baker to let him know he was accepted at the festival and welcome.

Diversity Programs and Policies

Inclusive communities usually have formally adopted polices stating their positions on diversity. In some cases, there may be programs adopted or implemented by local government or the private sector to advance such a goal, even if it is not formally adopted by the city. In September 2008, a Charlottesville City Council retreat led to the identification of seven priority implementation goals for the city. One of the identified goals was to improve race relations. Thus was born the *Dialogue on Race* initiative, a community-wide endeavor to engage residents in a discussion of race relations in the city and to promote inter-racial understanding. In 2010, more than 700 residents participated in study circles on race. This led to the identification of several action items that the city is now in the process of implementing.

Holland has established a mentoring program for children of immigrant farm workers. The program enables children and families of immigrants in the city to receive academic and social support from volunteers, while at the same time enabling these volunteers to learn about the cultures of these immigrant families. Additionally, the city's diversity education program provides opportunities for residents to learn about the diversity and culture of different groups to help blunt ignorance and racism. An annual holiday potluck dinner is also organized by the Alliance for Cultural and Ethnic Harmony. As Marvin Younger, President of the Alliance for Cultural and Ethnic Harmony's board of directors stated, "People think of this community as just a Dutch community, but there is so much more here. This is a celebration of the diversity we have in Holland. This is a safe space for everyone, including families. We welcome everybody."

Another group, the Lakeshore Ethnic Diversity Alliance, works to rid the area of racial and ethnic prejudice through diversity education and advocacy. The alliance also works to provide equal educational access and opportunity for all residents. The organization administers diversity workshops for churches, government, civic groups, schools, the private sector, and non-profit organizations to educate them on diversity. Presentations at these workshops have included cross-cultural communication, the impact of stereotyping, workplace diversity, and adverse racism. Feedback from these workshops indicates the organization is making an impact on improving tolerance and diversity awareness. Some comments in regards to the workshops include:

> I realized, as a teacher, I have the responsibility to address comments from students and identify bias in materials.

I learned involvement in the community and advocacy is critical to break down walls that hate built by racism.

This experience has helped me continue to develop a sensitivity especially to the unconscious nature of racism ... My view of the urgency of doing something about racism and my personal responsibility has changed.

I realized there is a lot of local pain in the community that I have not personally seen or felt.

(Lakeshore Ethnic Diversity Alliance 2011)

Wilmington has the National Coalition of 100 Black Women, Inc., a non-profit advocacy group for black women. The goal of the organization is to empower women through education, through self-sufficiency for single mothers, and through job training, healthcare and voter registration so they can make a difference by influencing public policy. The organization has a mentoring program for young girls and women and has awarded more than $75,000 to beneficiaries through the Dr. Teresa Drummond Scholarship Fund. Additionally, the City of Wilmington has a Minority Business Opportunity Committee, which galvanizes public and private sector resources to support the development of minority businesses.

Charlottesville has two organizations that support minority businesses. The Chamber Minority Business Council was formed in 2012 to provide support for minority start-up businesses and to help existing ones flourish through "increased exposure and visibility." In Hendersonville, the Latino Advocacy Coalition promotes a just community for all. Most recently, the coalition is known to have fought to reverse laws that target illegal immigrants in the United States.

In recognition of the diversity of the city's population, Vision 2025 of Greenville County stated thus: "In 2025, Greenville County public and private sector leaders and residents welcome and integrate all its residents into a unified community whose diverse members and populations have full equality" (City of Greenville 2003, p. 33).

The City of Greenville has several organizations that provide a supportive platform for multicultural groups in the city. The Diversity Leaders Initiative, started in 2003 by the Riley Institute in cooperation with the American Institute for Managing Diversity, was established to honor community leaders who have made important contributions to enhancing diversity in the Greenville area. Each year, the Upstate Chambers and Riley Institute honor individuals and organizations that have enhanced diversity in the area. The Riley Institute also runs a Diversity Leaders Academy, which brings leaders from business, government, and the non-profit sector to reflect on diversity issues in the state. The classes meet four times a year and train participants to be advocates of diversity by providing them with skills to deal with diversity in the workplace.

In 2007, the Minority Economic Development Institute was formed in Greenville to assist in the education, training, and mentoring of minority-owned businesses. Through the Greater Greenville Chamber of Commerce, Project Advance provides mentoring for women entrepreneurs. The Business Women Action Committee and the Hispanic Committee provide opportunities for women and Hispanics to network. The committees also assist with mentoring and education of female and Hispanic business owners.

Greenville is also home to the International Center of the Upstate. The center's goal is to promote cross-cultural understanding and harmony and to welcome people from diverse backgrounds into the region so they can contribute to the development of the area. The center was started in 1998 by the City of Greenville, the Greater Greenville Chamber of Commerce, and Michelin North America in response to the needs of a diverse workforce that was being brought to the city by multinational corporations. Michelin's North American headquarters is located in Greenville. BMW also has a production facility in Greenville, where the company produces its sports utility vehicle. The International Center of the Upstate provides a welcome mat for international visitors and residents, organizes language classes and workshops on international and cross-cultural issues, serves as a liaison between local businesses and the international community, and organizes social events to help foreigners feel welcome. In 2005, the center received the Upstate Diversity Leadership Award for Outstanding Achievement in Promoting International Diversity. In 2006, it received recognition from Market Street Services for being "an excellent starting point for strengthening networks of immigrant entrepreneurs and professionals."

In Fort Collins, the "Not In Our Town" community-based organization fosters racial harmony by addressing the causes and effects of hate-motivated behavior. The organization staffs a hotline where people can report discriminatory practices. It also has prevention and response teams. The prevention team is responsible for implementing programs that address prejudice and discrimination. The response team acts on hate-related incidents. Likewise, Fuerza Latina, an immigrant group, was formed in 2003 to educate immigrants and promote human rights and fair treatment for immigrants. The group also has a hotline to help people who are being deported or detained for immigration-related violations. More importantly, Fuerza Latina works to educate the community and change laws that are detrimental to immigrants.

The Santa Fe Community Foundation has two initiatives that support Native American as well as gay and lesbian causes. The Lesbian and Gay Funding Partnership has made more than eighty grants to date totaling $368,765 to support counseling, safe space, teen suicide prevention, and mentoring of lesbian, gay, bisexual, and transgender persons. The Native American Endowment Fund, established in 1993, supports programs that enhance Native American heritage. It has provided funds to organizations for education, life skills training, health and violence prevention, and interpersonal skills development.

Since 1997, the Middlesex Chamber of Commerce has run an award-winning "Side Street to Main Street Business and Leadership Development Program." The program is funded by Aetna and provides sixteen weeks of four-hour training sessions for minority small business owners or potential business owners who have not had formal business training. The classes teach the participants how to write a business plan, research the market feasibility of a business idea, and learn financial management, as well as leadership and business skills. Over 170 minority participants have graduated from the program, many of whom have gone on to start their own business.

Additionally, the City of Middletown has several community programs that address the needs of minority and low-income youth. The Oddfellows Playhouse, a community theater, is one such example. The theater was started in 1975 by five

Wesleyan University students and now serves about 2,000 young people each year. The goal of the organization is to teach theater to the youth, to promote positive growth of young people through the performing arts, and "to offer opportunities especially to underserved and at-risk youngsters to promote the development of a genuinely multiracial, multicultural society." The organization also touts as one of its objectives, "breaking down barriers of racial, ethnic, and cultural isolation" among the youth. Forty percent of the students in the organization's programs are minority.

The Oddfellows Playhouse received the Middlesex County NAACP Community Service Award in recognition of the organization's role in the growth and development of the youth in the community. Larry McHugh, President, Middlesex County Chamber of Commerce, said of the Oddfellows Playhouse:

> It is important that our community celebrates the success of an organization like Oddfellows Playhouse. Their presence in our community makes this a place people want to live. Oddfellows provides a fun, healthy environment for our young people. They learn more than simply how to act—they learn how to live.
> (Pugliese 2010)

The organization is supported by contributions from the public, private, and non-profit sectors including Pratt + Whitney, Citizen's Bank, Middletown Community Foundation, Middlesex United Way, The Irving Kohn Foundation, J. Walton Bissell Foundation, Maximilian E. & Marion O. Hoffman Foundation, Inc., and the Connecticut Department of Education, among others.

Providing a Safe Place for Multicultural Groups

Cities that attract diverse populations are also places that support and provide safe public spaces where multicultural groups can gather. As shown in Table 4.5, these safe places can be specific to a particular group or generic to all groups in the community. Cities with resilient downtowns demonstrate such inclusivity.

The Fort Collins LAMBDA Community Center is one such location. The center, located at 212 S. Mason St., provides a place for gay, lesbian, bisexual, and transgender populations to meet and socialize. The center provides advocacy, education, cultural, and support services for the GLBT community. It has a youth drop-in room called Rainbow Alley that receives more than 750 visits a month. The center also has a hotline to provide legal and advocacy services to members.

The City of Wilmington provides several safe places for diverse community groups, the oldest of which is the El Centro Latino. El Centro Latino began in 1969 when Puerto Rican immigrants came to the city to seek job opportunities, particularly in tanneries. Many of these immigrants faced language and housing problems. To attend to these issues, they banded together to seek ways to address their needs. The meetings were initially held in the basement of the St. Paul Roman Catholic Church before moving to a house at 1202 W. 4th Street. Eventually the community raised enough funds to build a 30,000 square foot structure in 1990 at 403 N. Van Buren St. The center is supported by both public and private donors, especially community stalwarts such as Bank of America, JPMorgan Chase, DuPont,

Table 4.5 Gathering places for multicultural groups

City	Gathering Places	Focus
Middletown, CT	Middletown Senior/Community Center	Elderly
Wilmington, DE	El Centro Latino Cristina Cultural Arts Center Wilmington Senior Center	Hispanic Open but multicultural focus Senior citizens
Greenville, SC	Greenville Cultural Exchange Center	African American
Hendersonville, NC	Opportunity House	Elderly
Charlottesville, VA	Islamic Community Center American Turkish Cultural Center	Moslem Moslem
Mansfield, OH	Dewald Community Center	Faith-based Christian place
Ripon, WI	Senior Center	Elderly
Holland, MI	Children's Advocacy Center Latin Americans United for Progress Center	Youth Hispanic youth
Lafayette, IN	Hanna Community Center Bauer Community Center Faith Community Center	African American neighborhood Youth Christian faith-based
Fort Collins, CO	LAMBDA Community Center Northside Aztlan Community Center Fort Collins Senior Center Fort Collins International Center	Gay, Lesbian, Bisexual & Transgender Community Center Recreation Center Elderly Promote International Understanding
Santa Barbara, CA	Bronfman Family Jewish Community Center La Casa de la Raza Pacific Pride Foundation	Jewish community Hispanic GLBT
Chico, CA	Stonewall Alliance Center Del Oro Division – Salvation Army Community Center	GLBT
Nacogdoches, TX	Senior Center	Elderly
Santa Fe, NM	El Museo Cultural de Santa Fe Poeh Center The Nancy Rodriguez	Hispanic culture and learning center Native American Hispanic culture

United Way, Agilent Technologies, Wal-Mart, and Unison Health Plan. El Centro Latino has a budget of more than $2 million and employs more than eighty people. The center provides more than forty programs to members, including housing, skills training, advocacy, as well as alcohol and substance abuse rehabilitation programs.

Wilmington also has the Christina Cultural Arts Center (CCAC) and the Downs Cultural Center as safe meeting places for its diverse population. The Mission of CCAC (shown in Figure 4.3) is stated thus: "to make affordable arts education and multicultural programs accessible to children, teens and adults in a family environment" (Christina Cultural Center 2012). The Downs Cultural Center, located

Figure 4.3 Christina Cultural Arts Center, Downtown Wilmington, DE.

at 1005 N. Franklin St., runs theatrical arts programs with, and for, the elderly. The goal of the Downs Cultural Center is to create senior-friendly, multigenerational, and multicultural programs for seniors, recognizing that the arts can be a means for the elderly to stay active. Programs at the center are organized, performed, and enjoyed by the elderly and their families.

The Greenville Cultural Exchange Center was established in 1987 as a venue for historical reflection, education, and research. The center provides guided tours, exhibits, and resources that educate people on the city's diversity, especially the contributions of African Americans. The center was started by Ruth Ann Butler, a former history teacher in the Greenville County Schools, to collect and preserve African-American history. The center has a library, an exhibition space that showcases the works and achievements of African Americans, and a meeting space for professional associations.

The City of Charlottesville has several gathering places for multicultural groups in the area. These include the American Turkish Culture Center, the Charlottesville Masjid & Islamic Community Center, and Jefferson School African-American Heritage Center. A new Islamic Community Center has been under construction since 2008. The Islamic Society of Central Virginia purchased two-thirds of an acre on Pine Street near the University of Virginia for the new center. Despite concerns from some community residents, the city's leadership enthusiastically supported the project. As stated by Mayor Dave Norris, "This is a city of very rich religious diversity and tolerance. The Muslim community in the area had a small facility and the fact that they're now growing into a larger home bodes well for the health of our religious community here in Charlottesville" (Satchell 2008). The groundbreaking ceremony for the Islamic Center was attended by the mayor in a show of support.

The building of a new center became necessary, as the city has experienced an increase in its Muslim population, arising from an influx of immigrants from Bosnia, Albania, Afghanistan, Sudan, Somalia, Burma, Turkey, and Russia. The proposed center is designed to accommodate 225 worshippers and has a prayer area, library, six classrooms, a kitchen, and a multipurpose room. According to Khan Hassan, a board member, "We are part of the community. We want to expand our role and be as involved as we can in bringing social justice, in bringing opportunities for those less fortunate and in bringing opportunities for students and the young."

The Islamic Community Center is both a place of prayer as well as a gathering place for educational and social events for Muslims. The center provides education for its members on the Islamic faith, but also reaches out to the larger community. The Islamic Society of Central Virginia, which runs the center, sponsors several volunteer activities including adopt-a-highway, feeding of the homeless, and Habitat for Humanity home-building projects. "The Masjid and Islamic Community Center will also feature guest speakers and allow for open dialogues on current issues, with the aim of spreading the word of God and correcting the deformed image of Islam and Muslims in the U.S. and the West" (Islamic Society of Central Virginia n.d., p. 4).

El Museo Cultural de Santa Fe is housed in a 31,000 square foot former warehouse in the Railyard Neighborhood. The center has art galleries, exhibition space, and a theater for performing arts. The objective of the center is to provide a place where Hispanic culture is preserved and promoted. Emphasis is put on learning and doing, so its exhibits and lectures include workshops for hands-on education. Through the performing arts, the center seeks to educate the public about Hispanic art, culture, and ways of life.

Conclusion

Communities that want to grow their downtowns must be welcoming of diversity and of new immigrants. In cities with resilient downtowns, civic leaders understand the importance of accepting "unfamiliar" residents. These leaders make it a point to go on record as supporting diversity and tolerance. Because successful downtowns have become neighborhoods in high demand, many new immigrants may not be able to afford housing in the downtown. However, for cities with blighted neighborhoods in or near the downtown, immigrants can provide a boost to the redevelopment of these neighborhoods. This is evident even in some of the resilient downtowns.

 Please visit the companion website at http://routledge.com/cw/Burayidi for additional resources.

CHAPTER 5

Downtowns as Civic and Cultural Centers

Successful downtown redevelopment programs must include retention and expansion of civic and cultural amenities in the downtown as a major component of the program. This is not always a given. In some instances, public policies that are intentionally good may actually be detrimental to the health of downtowns. California's Senate Bill 1407 is a classic example. In 2008, SB 1407 was authored by then Senate President pro tem Don Perata, D-Oakland, to provide funding to renovate forty-one of the sixty-eight courthouses in California's thirty-four counties that had "critical or immediate needs." The bill, signed into law by Governor Arnold Schwarzenegger, came with a $5 billion price tag. The cost of rebuilding the courthouses is expected to be financed through revenue bonds, increased court fees, penalties, and assessments. On the surface, this is a welcome bill, as it will help to improve courthouses across the state that need to be rehabilitated. As stated by the Governor:

> Improving our state's aging court facilities has been an integral part of my promise to Californians to rebuild our infrastructure and increase public safety. This bill not only delivers on that promise to finance desperately needed construction projects, but it will also help create thousands of jobs for California workers.
>
> (California Courts 2008)

Some of the courthouses in California, like in several other states, are overcrowded and do not meet seismic and other safety and security requirements, especially in the post-9/11 era. *The Capitol Connection*, the newsletter of the State of California Court system, described the state's courthouses thus:

> There is inadequate assembly space, courtrooms and deliberation rooms; limited access for the disabled; inadequate separation of victims, defendants, and families in criminal cases; and unsecure hallways to prevent jurors from coming in contact with parties. Moreover, inadequate security places children, jurors, witnesses, litigants, visitors, and court employees at personal risk.
>
> (California Courts 2008)

Thus, SB 1407 is a welcome response to the problems of the state's courthouses. However, without a critical and reflective application, there is potential for this law to adversely impact downtowns. The new measure may be used by some communities as an opportunity to relocate their courthouses outside of the downtown and take advantage of green space. Often, these locations are viewed as less complicated to develop than rehabilitating older courthouses in the downtown.

Let's revisit Nevada City, a case that was mentioned in Chapter 1, to examine this situation further. The Judicial Council of California determined that Nevada City needed an 83,000 square foot courthouse with 210 parking spaces. The building required a 4-acre site at a cost of approximately $108 million. Due to its size and land needs for parking, it was initially decided to relocate the courthouse outside the downtown until residents spoke out against the new location. Mayor Reinette Senum is quoted by the *Nevada City Advocate* as saying, "This will be a terrible blow to our local economy if they move it out of the downtown. These blanket state policies don't help local economies" (Butler 2010).

Nevada City is not the only community facing a blanket application of this state law. Another case in point is the proposed relocation of the San Benito County courthouse in California. According to the Administrative Office of the Court, the old courthouse, located at the corner of 5th and Monterey Streets, is "in deplorable condition ... and incapable of meeting the region's growing demand for court services" (*Hollister Freelance* 2008). The new courthouse, which has been approved by the state to be located on Flynn Road, is estimated to cost $35.6 million and will be funded by court fees authorized through SB 1407. The Hollister Downtown Association (HDA), San Benito County Chamber of Commerce, and the local bar association have officially opposed the Flynn Road site, stating that such a move would reduce foot traffic to the downtown and affect downtown merchants: "We feel like taking the courthouse from downtown is the wrong thing to do and [it's] the wrong time to do it," said Rick Maddux, owner of Maddux Jewelry and President of the HDA. "It may save money initially but will lose money later on" (*Hollister Freelance* 2008).

Consequently, the HDA sent a letter to the California Administrative Office of the Court stressing the need to keep the court offices downtown. The public was also wary of the decision by the state to relocate the courthouse outside downtown. As stated by one resident: "My big fear is not that the court might leave downtown, but that after it leaves that other offices may follow." Another resident is quoted as saying, "I think in the short term, moving it will be pretty brutal. But in the long term, who knows?" (*Hollister Freelance* 2008).

California is not the only state where the relocation of civic and cultural facilities outside the downtown is controversial. In Georgia, the relocation of Habersham Courthouse in Clarksville has caused public controversy. It all began after the county commission purchased a 30 acre tract of land at a cost of $1.1 million in August 2008 outside the city limits for the new courthouse. This countered a state law that required county courthouses to be located within city limits of the county seat.

Assistant County Manager Jason Tinsley said that the current site of the courthouse was ruled out due to concerns over traffic, parking, and inadequacy of land for expansion (Gurr 2010). The opposition to the relocation of the courthouse is similar to that in California. As the *Gainsville Times* reported, the concern was over the negative impact on the downtown, due to the relocation of the court.

The paper quoted the former President of the Clarkesville Business and Community Association, John Lunsford, as saying that there are three things that can kill downtown activity: building a bypass, moving the post office, and moving the courthouse. According to him, the city hit all but one: "We've been bypassed, and we've moved the post office." Another resident stated, "To move the courthouse out of the City of Clarkesville, I just don't feel is wise … right now we need to focus on keeping the courthouse within the city to keep the vitality of Clarkesville alive as much as we can."

In the 1990s, Greene County, GA, identified serious problems with the county's courthouse, including non-compliance with the Americans with Disabilities Act. The building used window air-conditioned units for cooling in the summer and was heated by an old boiler. There was insufficient capacity to accommodate the spatial needs of the courthouse. The then Board of Commissioners of Green County decided to save the building. However, by the early part of the twenty-first century, it was decided to relocate the courthouse outside the downtown. Among the leaders who opposed the court's relocation was Laverne Ogletree, a probate judge who had been in office since 1982. Laverne argued that the courthouse is an integral part of the downtown and generates a lot of foot traffic that helps sustain downtown businesses. She wrote a letter to the Board of Commissioners, urging them to do further studies before moving ahead with their decision:

> As a person who has had the privilege to work in the courthouse since 1974, I know firsthand the time and effort that was put into the decision to keep our courthouse in downtown Greensboro in 1993. I am also aware of the concern for future growth, space needs and downtown parking. I know that those needs can be met without moving. A first step is to determine what the needs are and to determine how to satisfy those needs.
>
> (Dawson 2009)

Nationwide, battles are raging over the relocation of civic and cultural amenities outside downtowns. Civic leaders in resilient downtowns recognize the impacts of such relocation and have worked to retain these uses in the downtown. While some California communities were busy trying to find sites outside the downtown to relocate their courthouses, Santa Barbara did the exact opposite.

The current Santa Barbara criminal courthouse serves the south district of Santa Barbara County. The county is responsible for a number of caseloads including but not limited to domestic violence, probate and mental health cases, pre-trial hearings, family law, misdemeanors, small claims, infractions, felonies, and criminal arraignments. The county's court system comprises four facilities and eight trial courtrooms located in the City of Santa Barbara. These are the Santa Barbara Jury Services Building, the Santa Barbara Juvenile Court, the Figueroa Building, and the Anacapa Building. Two of the eight criminal trial courtrooms and a juvenile courtroom are located in the Santa Barbara Juvenile Court. Another courtroom is located in the Jury Services building which is used for juvenile dependency hearings, criminal trials, and traffic court trials. The Figueroa Courthouse and the Anacapa courthouse are both located in the El Pueblo Viejo Landmark District of the City of

Santa Barbara and do not currently meet the increased demand for judicial services, nor the county's security and parking standards (see Figure 5.1). The Projected Judicial Equivalents (PJEs), which estimate future courtroom and judicial workload needs, determined an increased need for both courtroom space and judgeships for the district. The assessment showed that the court is currently using 39,604 square feet of space, but will soon need 69,476 square footage of space, a deficit of 29,872 departmental gross square feet (DGSF).

Not only is the space inadequate, there are also issues and concerns over security, non-compliance with the Americans with Disabilities Act, and inadequate holding areas. In the Figueroa building, there are no security cameras in the courtrooms. There are no separate circulation areas for judicial officers, staff, and the public. Most disturbing for a community concerned with its image, in-custody defendants are moved across the street from the Figueroa Building to the Anacapa Courthouse for judicial proceedings. There is also an inadequate consultation area for attorneys and their clients.

To meet the increased demand for judicial services and safety, an assessment was conducted of the court facilities. The assessment ranked the Santa Barbara courthouse facilities as "immediate need" in the Trial Court Capital Outlay Plan, and is one of forty-one projects that are to be funded by SB 1407 revenues. The assessment report recommended the building of a new courthouse of 97,266 square feet, with eight criminal courtrooms and a parking structure that will meet the projected space needs and address security concerns of the existing court facilities. The new courthouse will also provide separate areas for the public, restricted areas, and secured circulation areas.

While the county and state were in agreement on the necessity of building a new courthouse, they did not agree on its location. The county proposed the

Figure 5.1 The Santa Barbara County Courthouse at 1100 Anacapa Street, Downtown Santa Barbara, CA.

acquisition of three downtown parcels of land: two parcels behind the Figueroa building, and one on Hayward Street for the courthouse location. The state frowned on this proposal, preferring instead to move the courthouse to a site outside of the downtown that would not require land assembly.

According to Gary Blair, Executive Officer of the Santa Barbara Courthouse, the county preferred to locate the new courthouse downtown, to prevent the bifurcation of the criminal courts from the civic courts. In addition, moving the courthouse out of the downtown would also separate the courthouse from most attorneys' offices, which are located downtown. Thus, according to Blair, the county's preference is to construct the new courthouse across the street from the historic courthouse and keep the courts (criminal and civil) in the downtown core. As described by Blair in a personal correspondence:

> It makes no sense to bifurcate the court system and relocate the new criminal building to some remote site in an industrial park or open space miles away when all of the attorneys have offices downtown and the business core is downtown. It would also be inefficient and more costly to bifurcate our court personnel since many are constantly going back and forth between our two buildings downtown on a daily basis. This includes court reporters, interpreters, records clerks, and back office staff.

The State Administrative Office of the Courts (AOC), the administrative arm of the Judicial Council, has the oversight responsibility for construction projects. It must deal with bureaucratic departments within the Executive Branch of state government in order to acquire properties that must be purchased for the construction of these new court buildings. This includes the Real Estate Division of the State Department of General Services (DGS), the State Department of Finance (DOF), and ultimately the State Public Works Board (PWB), which has the final approval authority to purchase the necessary land. The AOC generally favors buying a single parcel large enough to accommodate the building and the requisite parking.

The AOC repeatedly told Santa Barbara County that it was not acceptable to assemble several parcels of land for purchase. Notwithstanding that this often means relocation (and bifurcation of court operations) to a parcel of land that may be miles away from the downtown core of the city where courts have been historically centrally located, to the AOC this is a simpler and easier method. Assemblies of property for purchase require more coordination, especially when purchasing land from another government entity such as a county or a city, as opposed to purchasing from a private party who is often more motivated to sell. However, the negative consequences of moving out of the downtown core of a city can be detrimental to the city and to the court. The county argued otherwise and, in the end, the AOC agreed with Santa Barbara County to keep the courthouse downtown.

For decades, the First Judicial Circuit Court in Santa Fe has operated in a converted junior high school on the corner of Grant Street and Catron Street (see Figure 5.2). The courthouse serves Santa Fe, Los Alamos, and Rio Arriba Counties. In 2006, the county decided to build a new courthouse to accommodate the increased need for space and to improve security. Making the case for a new courthouse at a meeting of the Board of County Commissioners in November 2006, Joseph Gutierrez, Director of the Public Facilities Management Division, said:

> I don't want the Commission to lose sight of—I believe that's the second step of this process but it's also a priority of ours because there isn't a week that doesn't go by where we're moving somebody or rearranging an office, and it's just because we lack the facilities. So as we move forward with the court project, we're looking at a budget of $60 to $70 million. That's not strictly for the courthouse. That's for our second tier expansion on that.
>
> (Board of County Commissioners 2006, p. 45)

A "needs assessment" conducted for the county in 2004 determined that the building was half the size needed for handling the court's functions. Several potential sites were considered within and outside city limits. Sites considered included the former St. Vincent Hospital building, vacant land on the Santa Fe Indian School, a site at the rail yard, as well as a site at Las Soleras, south of the city limits. However, county commissioners directed County Facilities Manager Tony Flores to give preference to downtown locations (Grimm 2005).

Paul Campos, a Santa Fe County Commissioner, justified the need for a downtown location of the courthouse in this letter to the editor:

> The decision to place the courthouse downtown was influenced by a desire to benefit local residents with a centralized location, to augment downtown business with permanent courthouse staff and a constant flow of people into the area, and enhance the vitality of downtown as a hub of civic life. Downtown must be a place for all people of our community!
>
> (Campos 2008)

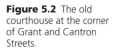

Figure 5.2 The old courthouse at the corner of Grant and Cantron Streets.

Chief Judge James Hall, who worked at the current courthouse for twelve years, was also quoted as saying: "I think it's very beneficial to have important community buildings located downtown to preserve the vitality of downtown for the local Santa Feans. You lose something if you pull public buildings from downtown" (Haywood 2007, A-1). When all was said and done, the Santa Fe County commissioners agreed to relocate the courthouse downtown at the corner of Sandoval Street and Montezuma Avenue (see Figure 5.3). The 2.4 acre site, located in what was a working-class neighborhood in the early to mid-twentieth century, will cost $55 million to build. It will be funded from the sale of bonds amounting to $25 million that was approved by voters in November of 2006. The additional cost will be supplemented with funds from a one-sixteenth-cent gross receipts tax.

During excavation on the chosen site, gasoline contamination was found, requiring the county to spend at a minimum $5 million to remediate the problem (Sharpe 2008). The State Department of the Environment had to remove more than 20,000 tons of gasoline-contaminated soil and extract 9,000 gallons of gasoline through a soil vapor extraction system. These unforeseen costs led some to suggest abandoning the site for less expensive locations outside the downtown. Phil Sena, one of the county commissioners, suggested locating the new courthouse at The Pavillion on the southwestern edge of Santa Fe. The owner of the site, Richard Cook of Espaola, was selling land at $6 per square foot, making it much cheaper to relocate the courthouse there than at the current site (Grimm 2010). Nonetheless, the county chose the downtown site due to the foreseen negative consequences it would have had on the downtown had another site been chosen.

At the County Commission meeting, commissioners voted unanimously to keep the courthouse downtown: "Commissioners expressed confidence that their actions to clean up the site were merited despite additional costs and delays, an idea echoed by District Judge Stephen Pfeffer, who thanked them for their continued efforts to keep the new courthouse downtown" (Grimm 2010, A-1).

Figure 5.3 The new courthouse under construction at the corner of Sandoval Street and Montezuma Avenue.

Public Facility Location in Resilient Cities

The examples discussed here bear testimony to the effects that civic and cultural facilities have on the health of a downtown. In addition to courthouses, the location of other government offices such as jails, city hall, police and fire stations, recreational centers, and post offices all have an impact on downtown's economic health. Eleven of the fourteen resilient downtowns are county seats, as shown in Table 5.1. While government has limited leverage in the location of private business, it has considerable power in deciding where public facilities are located.

Table 5.2 displays the number and types of government facilities located in the resilient downtowns. As shown in this table, these downtowns have a considerable number of governmental buildings. Leaders of cities in resilient downtowns work to retain and attract such civic and cultural uses to the downtown.

In 1961, Furman University and the Greenville Woman's College merged and relocated out of downtown Greenville. Years later, business leaders in the city convinced the state legislature of the need to locate the South Carolina Governor's School for the Arts and Humanities in downtown Greenville at the former site of the Furman Campus. The site now serves as a residential high school for the arts that offers talented and high-achieving high school students from across the state an opportunity to study arts in a nurturing environment. Both the city and the county of Greenville donated 8.5 acres of land at the former site for the new school. Following the city and county's commitments, the state dedicated $12 million toward a capital campaign that raised $14.5 million for building the school. In 1999, the Governor's School for the Arts and Humanities opened its doors to its inaugural class.

The city's downtown strategic plan recognized the importance of civic and cultural activities in the downtown. The plan thus calls for retaining these uses in the downtown:

> The purpose of this initiative is to keep government uses in Downtown Greenville. Government uses function as important anchors drawing employees and visitors to the downtown. Yet, downtowns across the country have been ill prepared and surprised to find government anchors leaving downtown to

Table 5.1 Selected communities and county seats

City	County
Charlottesville, VA	Albemarle
Fort Collins, CO	Larimer
Greenville, SC	Greenville
Hendersonville, NC	Henderson
Lafayette, IN	Tippecanoe
Mansfield, OH	Richland
Middletown, CT	Middlesex
Nacogdoches, TX	Nacogdoches
Santa Barbara, CA	Santa Barbara
Santa Fe, NM	Santa Fe
Wilmington, DE	New Castle

Table 5.2 Location of public facilities in resilient downtowns

City	Government Facilities Downtown
Middletown, CT	City Hall, Police Station, Metro Movies Theaters, Kid City Children's Museum, Community Health Center, Oddfellows Playhouse Youth Theater, The Russell Library, Greentree Art Center, State Courthouse, Fire Station, MAT bus depot.
Wilmington, DE	Federal Courthouse, City of Wilmington Offices, Library, Delaware Historic Society Offices, Amtrak Station, County Offices, State Government Offices, Convention and Visitors Bureau, Police Station, County Courthouse, Delaware Center for Contemporary Art.
Greenville, SC	City Hall, County Square (Greenville County Govt. offices), Federal Courthouse, Greenville County Courthouse, Municipal Court, Greenville City Museum, Bob Jones Museum and Gallery, Upcountry History Museum, Children's Museum of the Upstate.
Hendersonville, NC	Old and New County Courthouse, City Hall, Correctional Facility, Police Station, Library, Wingate University campus, Genealogy Museum, Mineral and Lapidary Museum.
Charlottesville, VA	City Hall, City Hall Annex, Transit Center, Recreation Center, Federal Courthouse, Police Headquarters, Discovery Museum, County Office Building, County Courthouse, City Courts, City and County Juvenile and Family Court, Regional Library, McGuffey Art Center, and Albemarle Historic Society.
Mansfield, OH	City, County, State and Federal Government Offices.
Ripon, WI	City Hall, Police Department, Ben Marcus Theater.
Holland, MI	City Hall, Ottawa County Courthouse and Jail, Holland Police Department, Civic Center, Post Office, Library, Transit Depot, Hope College, Window on the Waterfront.
Lafayette, IN	City: Lafayette City Hall, Central Fire Station, Street and Sanitation Depts. County: Tippecanoe County Courthouse, Tippecanoe County Office Building 1, Tippecanoe County Office Building 2, Tippecanoe County Public Library. State: Child Protective Services, Child Welfare, IMPACT, Vocational Rehabilitation Division of Indiana Rehabilitation Services. Federal: George E. Halliday USAR Center: Federal Courts, Downtown Post Office, FBI, US Marshalls Office, Labor Wage & Hour Division, Social Security Administration Building.
Fort Collins, CO	Larimer County. City of Fort Collins Building.
Santa Barbara, CA	City of Santa Barbara City Hall, City of Santa Barbara Public Works, Community Development and P&R Headquarters, County of Santa Barbara Administration, Santa Barbara County Courts/Courthouse.
Chico, CA	City Hall, Council Chambers, Post Office, Butte County Assessor's Office, Butte County Credit Bureau, City Fire Station #1.
Nacogdoches, TX	City of Nacogdoches, County Seat, Fire Station, Convention and Visitors Bureau, Police Dept. Headquarters, Fire Department Headquarters, County Courthouse, Texas State Senator Office.
Santa Fe, NM	State Capitol, State Office Buildings, Federal Courthouse, District Courts, County Administration Building, City Hall.

locations more convenient to suburban growth areas. Downtown Greenville must retain and attract government uses to protect its role as the civic hub of the metropolitan area.

(Sasaki Associates, Inc. 2008, p. 74)

To ensure the presence of government anchors downtown, the report charged the city's Department of Economic Development as follows:

A primary function of the City's Economic Development Department should be to monitor government agency activities and issues. The City should facilitate the development of the Federal Courthouse in the downtown and work with the County to develop an acceptable redevelopment plan for County Square while retaining the County's offices downtown.

(Sasaki Associates, Inc. 2008, p. 74)

Government buildings are not the only civic uses that need to be retained in the downtown. Some civic and cultural amenities are non-governmental in nature, but still play an integral role in downtowns. Such uses include sports stadia, performing arts centers, and theaters. In many cases, these civic buildings have typically been the catalytic projects that are used to jumpstart redevelopment of the downtown. The first anchor for revitalizing downtown Greenville was Greenville Commons. Built in 1982, Greenville Commons is a mixed-use structure with a convention center, hotel, and office complex. This anchor, in conjunction with others that followed such as the Peace Center, provided a catalyst for the development of retail, residential, and other activities in the downtown. Narrating the success of the city's downtown revitalization process, Sumo observed:

These catalyst projects have spawned other private developments, from the construction of new buildings like the RiverPlace, the largest private investment so far in downtown Greenville, to the rehabilitation of old buildings. Downtown revival has sparked interest in the preservation of many historical structures with fine architecture, which in turn has helped downtown set itself apart from the competition.

(Sumo 2007, p. 15)

The City of Mansfield's carousel project provides another example of how such civic amenities can boost downtown's economic health.

A Carousel Revives Downtown Mansfield, OH

Mansfield is a rustbelt city greatly impacted by deindustrialization like many other communities in this region of the country. The major employers in the city such as Westinghouse, an appliance manufacturer, Ohio Brass, and Tappan first downsized, then eventually were sold and moved out of the city. With the oil crisis of the 1970s, automobile sales suffered, as did demand for tires, thus affecting production at Mansfield Tire and Rubber Company. The business eventually closed its doors in 1978. Electrolux purchased Tappan Stove Company in 1979 and went out of business in

1992. The appliance division of Westinghouse was sold to White Consolidated. In 1990, both Westinghouse and the Ohio Brass Company moved out of the city. Thus, the loss of the manufacturing base had a detrimental effect on the city's economy.

Downtown Mansfield was hollowing out, as many businesses and middle-class residents vacated the downtown and central city for the suburbs and highway locations. In 1956, the West Park Shopping Center on Park Avenue West opened with much fanfare, marking perhaps the beginning of suburbanization of downtown businesses. By 1958, two other malls had opened outside the downtown. The first was the Johnny Appleseed Plaza that opened on Lexington Avenue, followed by the Mansfield Shopping Square Mall on Park Avenue West. Finally in 1968, as observed by Schaut, "the opening of Richland Mall was the final nail in the coffin for many of the downtown stores and the last major national chain store, Sears, moved from the square to the new mall" (2010, p. 80).

Needless to say, North Main Street, the major commercial route in the downtown, was severely impacted by these developments. By the 1980s, most buildings along North Main Street were abandoned. Many were vacant for so long that the utilities were shut off. In place of residents and businesses, North Main Street was taken over by vagrants, drunks, prostitutes, and the destitute. The situation got so bad that in 1984 when Bill Cosby came to the city for a performance at the Renaissance Theater, he could not help but remark on the deplorable situation he observed on the street. Cosby asked why North Main Street existed at all, since there were no vehicles, no people on the street, and all the buildings were boarded up. This comment is credited with awakening city leaders to the plight of the downtown and getting them to act. Shortly after Bill Cosby's visit in 1986, then Mayor Edward Meehan commissioned the North End Development Plan with a carousel as the centerpiece for the area's redevelopment.

The idea for a carousel was recommended by John Fernyak, who also suggested the formation of a non-profit organization to manage revitalization efforts for the blighted block on North Main Street. Fernyak hoped that a carousel would attract children and families to the area and help to spur revitalization efforts in what would later be called the Carousel District. However, the proposal for a carousel was not final, as Fernyak had to convince a skeptical public, city government, and the private sector that this would be beneficial in revitalizing the downtown. City Council had to commit to acquiring property on the block for the project through the power of eminent domain. Public funds had to be dedicated to clear the site for redevelopment. Finally, the private sector had to buy-in and contribute funding to the project.

Needless to say, there was much at stake when the City Council met on March 15, 1988 to discuss the "carousel idea." As Rex Collins, then President of the Richland Carousel District, observed prior to the meeting:

> The whole downtown redevelopment effort hinges on this vote. Local investors are prepared to take a major risk on an area that has sat dormant and decaying for years. If this doesn't go you're never going to see anyone come forward to redevelop it.
>
> (Futty 1988, p. 5-A)

Mayor Edward Meehan pledged support for the Carousel Plan, with the condition that it be coupled with private development of nearby property. In the end, the City Council voted to approve the carousel and devoted close to half a million dollars to acquire, clear property, and relocate businesses to make way for the development. In 1986, the Richland Carousel Park, Inc., was incorporated as a non-profit organization, and was charged with the responsibility of raising funds for the development and, eventually, for operating the carousel once it was completed. In 1988, City Council approved the 4th and Main Street Area Urban Renewal Plan, clearing the way for the City of Mansfield to acquire property for the redevelopment of the block. Once the land was acquired, it was sold to the non-profit Richland Carousel, Inc., for development.

Still, the public was skeptical of the carousel project. Residents wondered why City Council was spending money on a carousel when it could use the money to help retain many of the industrial businesses that were leaving town. Residents were in great need of jobs and believed another manufacturing plant would be far more beneficial than a "kiddie ride." Reflecting on the controversy, William Hartnett, President of Mansfield-Richland Area of Commerce, said:

> Had the carousel not been built and those dollars made available for other activities, you wouldn't have one company here that's not here. Do people think if we don't hire as many police officers, we would take that money and save a company?
>
> (*Carousel Journal* 1991, p. 3)

Other city residents suggested that rather than building the carousel in the downtown it should be located in one of the malls where there would be more people to ride it than in a deserted downtown. The running joke in Mansfield was that things got so bad on North Main the city had to call in the cavalry and what they got were thirty horses, four bears, four ostriches, four cats, four rabbits, two goats, two chariots, a lion, a zebra, and a tiger. This was in reference to the carved animals of the carousel. Few people gave the carousel project a chance to revive the neighborhood.

As said by Jack Pollock, the city's Economic Development Officer: "A lot of people just envisioned it as a merry-go-round. They have no vision as to what is really going in there. That area has been an area of bars and prostitution for years. They don't believe it can be cleaned up" (Futty 1991, p. 2).

Rex Collins, retired Chief Officer of Buckeye Bank, spearheaded fundraising for the development of the carousel. Collins was known in town for his "can do" attitude. He had previously led an effort to restore the Renaissance Theater and for the expansion of the Mansfield General Hospital. The group, which also included William Hartnett, President of the Mansfield-Richland Chamber of Commerce, was able to raise $1.25 million in private sector contributions.

In 1987, Carousel Works, Inc., of Bristol, CT, was contracted to hand carve the wooden carousel. The process took three years and was the first of such endeavors in the US since 1932. The work was inspired by Gustav Dentzel, a revered carver whose company created carousels from 1870 to 1928. As requested by Mayor

Meehan, private investment to restore the historic buildings in the downtown as part of the carousel plan also went full steam. In 1990, Engwiller Properties, Inc., invested $2 million to restore seven historic buildings on North Main Street, some dating back to the turn of the twentieth century. Today, the Carousel District has over thirty historic buildings that have been restored and are being used for professional offices, retail, and residential condominiums. As the *Carousel Journal* observed, "Developers believe it is fitting that a ride that flourished at the turn of the century is the centerpiece for an effort to revive a neighborhood that dates to that era" (*Carousel Journal* 1991, p. 1).

In 1991, the carousel opened to much fanfare in the city (see Figure 5.4). City leaders expected the carousel to draw about 30,000 people a year to the rides. To their surprise, the number of patrons who rode it on its opening weekend alone surpassed this expectation. Today, the carousel draws close to 200,000 riders a year and has been a resounding success, not only as a downtown revitalization strategy, but also as a business venture. As Lydia Reid, the former mayor of the city, rightly observed in 1996 of the Carousel District's success story:

> We took a red light district and converted it into the Carousel District. A vibrant downtown sends a message to businesses we are a prosperous community, a major player in the next century. If I drive through a downtown that's depressing, with buildings closed up, I am going to say, "This is a town on its last legs. If you see little on the streets it doesn't want to make you move there."
>
> (Ferenchik 1996, p. A-4)

Karen Sawyer, former director of the Mansfield Main Street Program, also added: "That carousel has become a magnet for families, for tourists and for area residents who finally decided they should come back downtown and see what's going on" (Hunt 1996, p. 7B).

The carousel project's success has been noticed by other communities around the country, as well as by professional organizations with an interest in center city revitalization. In 1994, Mansfield won first place in the Annual Downtown Revitalization Awards given by Downtown Ohio, Inc., a non-profit organization devoted to the revitalization of the state's downtowns. In 1996, the city was awarded a City Livability Award from the US Conference of Mayors at their annual meeting in Cleveland. The award honors mayors "for developing and implementing programs that improve the quality of life in American cities."

In addition to the restoration of historic property in the downtown, the carousel project has generated other spinoff activities in the neighborhood. Some educational institutions, such as Richland Academy of the Arts, opened on North Walnut Street. A Children's Science Museum opened in the restored building of the former Bing's Furniture Store on West 4th Street. Within two years of opening, over twenty businesses opened in and near the Carousel District and the number of downtown workers grew from 8,027 full-time and 983 part-time workers in 1991 to 8,700 full-time and 1,000 part-time employees two years later (*News Journal* 1994).

Figure 5.4 View of the carousel at the corner of 4th and North Main Street in downtown Mansfield, OH.

Credit: Downtown Mansfield, Inc.

In part because of the positive energy generated by the carousel project, the city has been able to retain most of its professional businesses in the downtown and attract new retail businesses to the Carousel District. Carousel-related businesses were also attracted to the district. For example, a carousel carving company, Carousel Magic, moved from Rexburg, ID, to Mansfield and located at 44 W. 4th Street with a showroom. The business hires craftsmen to design, sculpt, and build carousel animals.

Charlottesville's Downtown Mall

Charlottesville's downtown pedestrian mall provides yet another example of how city leaders have used a civic project to rejuvenate a city's downtown. But the mall's development is important for another reason: it is a good example of how quality placemaking can contribute to the revitalization of a declining civic space. Additionally, the pedestrian mall's development showcases the importance of collaboration between the public, private, and non-governmental sector in the redevelopment of downtown. In the following section, we will discuss how these principles were utilized and achieved in the development of the mall.

Background to the Pedestrian Mall's Development

The pedestrian mall in Charlottesville shows that downtowns can successfully provide a counterweight to the suburban pull if the right combination of civic improvements is undertaken. Like many other downtowns around the country, Charlottesville's downtown was suffering from business flight to the highway locations and the suburbs. The city's downtown was dying, the result of competition from the newly built Barracks Road Shopping Center and the construction of Interstate 64 in 1970, which diverted traffic away from the downtown. Between 1966 and 1970, the share of downtown's retail sales fell by 2.8 percent, while that for Barracks Road increased by 14.2 percent (Yellig 2006). City leaders decided to take action to address the decline of the downtown. City Council established a Central City Commission in 1971 for the purpose of addressing the deterioration of the downtown.

To put the mall project in perspective, it is important to briefly recount the history of planning in Charlottesville. Although the city was initially platted for settlement in 1762 by Thomas Walker, there was no official planning institution in the city until the mid-1930s. A zoning ordinance was adopted by the city in 1929. In 1934, the City Council established a City Planning Commission (CPC) that was composed of civic leaders with no official training in city planning. The city hired a professional consulting firm to assist in the preparation of the first Master Plan of 1955 to 1959. That responsibility fell on Harlan Bartholomew. A downtown redevelopment plan was a component of this Master Plan.

Harland was involved in the preparation of several city plans in the United States. In 1919, he founded Harland Bartholomew & Associates (HBA), an urban planning consulting firm. Harland served on the national Slum Clearance Advisory Committee and was influential in the development of both national housing acts: the Housing Act of 1937 and the Housing Act of 1949. Needless to say, he was an advocate for slum clearance. Harlan Bartholomew embraced Euclidean zoning and the strict separation of land uses. He saw density as a problem and a contributory factor to urban blight. In his Master Plans he privileged the automobile over other modes of transportation. As a result, his plans almost invariably included widening streets, ample provision of parking garages, and a looping highway around the downtown. HBA's proposals for redeveloping downtown Charlottesville thus embraced the policies of the urban renewal era, which could be summed up in the adage "clear and rebuild."

The firm's Master Plan for Charlottesville aimed at ensuring a more efficient traffic flow through the CBD. This was to be achieved by widening downtown streets, most specifically South Street, which was to be widened from 66 feet to 88 feet to accommodate increased traffic. The plan also called for connecting downtown streets to the nearby US 250 bypass and Interstate 64 to ensure a smooth traffic flow through the downtown. What Harland considered to be the messy and disorderly mixed-use development in the CBD would be replaced by separate use districts. Commercial uses would be segregated into superblocks and access to downtown would be enhanced by building parking garages. The Master Plan recommended the demolition of Vinegar Hill, a predominantly African-American neighborhood, to make way for street extensions and the development of suburban-style housing, parking garages, and shopping centers. When the urban renewal plan was implemented, some forty businesses were forcibly closed and over 500 people were displaced in Vinegar Hill.

The Birth of an Idea

The idea of creating a pedestrian mall was first broached in HBA's 1955 Master Plan for the city, but it was not until the early 1970s that the idea came to fruition. In the Master Plan for the city, HBA suggested the creation of a pedestrian-friendly commercial strip linking the west end of Main Street to Vinegar Hill. Harland's ideas were in conflict with many city leaders in the 1970s who opposed several Euclidean redevelopment principles advocated in his 1955 Master Plan. In the early 1970s, the city underwent a transformation of sorts. The first all-democratic City Council was elected. Also, the first woman ever to serve on the council, Jill Rinehart, and the first African American, Charles Barbour, were elected to the City Council. The new City Council was more sympathetic to neighborhood and minority interests than previous administrations.

Two new appointments were also made by the City Council in 1971. Cole Hendrix from Kansas City was appointed as city manager. Also, a new director of the Planning Department, Thomas Conger, was hired. Both of these new leaders were critical of the HBA plan for the redevelopment of the downtown, as it involved the traditional urban renewal approaches that both Conger and Hendrix believed would be detrimental to the downtown and adjacent neighborhoods. Rather than proceeding with the HBA's plan for the downtown, city leaders decided to bring in Lawrence Halprin to assist in preparing a new plan for downtown revitalization.

In the 1970s, Lawrence Halprin was a renowned landscape architect who had been a consultant in the redevelopment of urban landscapes throughout the country. He came to national prominence at the Seattle World's Fair in 1962 with his work on the adaptive reuse of Ghirardelli Square in San Francisco and his design of the Nicollet Mall in Minneapolis. Halprin was guided in his work by the everyday human experiences of the built environment. He designed his spaces to be of human scale and user friendly. In 1974, he was brought in as a consultant for the redevelopment of Charlottesville's downtown. Though HBA had proposed a pedestrian mall for Main Street, the firm's approach to revitalization differed significantly from that of the Lawrence Halprin plan.

In 1974, City Council approved a downtown revitalization plan on a 2–0 vote with development of a pedestrian mall as the centerpiece of the revitalization proposal. Three council members abstained because of conflict of interest. The mall would eventually cost $20 million to build. As described in the minutes of the City Council, the goal of the mall was multifaceted:

> The Council finds that the public safety, welfare, comfort, convenience, trade and industry will be served by the creation of a pedestrian mall in that portion of east main street lying between east seventh street on the east and first street on the west.
>
> (Charlottesville City Council Minutes September 16, 1974)

The Process

Halprin arrived in Charlottesville in 1973. Unlike HBA, whose Master Plan was for the entire city, Halprin was charged to prepare a redevelopment plan for only the downtown. City leaders wanted the project to be a joint venture between the public and private sectors, in particular downtown businesses. When Alvin Clements, Chairman of the Central City Commission, appeared before the City Council in 1973 to discuss the project, he made it clear that both sectors would share in the $140,000 cost of the design, half of which would be paid by the city and half would be paid by the business community (City Council Minutes January 16, 1973).

Halprin's process in the design of the mall utilized precedence and made use of, rather than worked against, the existing natural and built fabric of the downtown. In particular, he was guided by the work of Thomas Jefferson's design of the Academical Village for the University of Virginia. Jefferson's academic village had a core area, the lawn (a public square) around which other buildings and uses were located. Thus, the Academical Village was a live, work, learn, and recreational neighborhood. From this precedence, Halprin incorporated diversity and accessibility features in his design of the pedestrian mall to improve the vitality of the downtown. By doing so, his plan provided access by propinquity, whereas the HBA plan required access by the automobile.

In order to incorporate public opinion in the design of the mall, Halprin held several meetings, referred to as "Take Part Workshops." These workshops were based on previous "Experiments in the Environment" models that he developed with his performance artist/choreographer wife, Anna Halprin. These workshops led to the identification of sixteen goals for the redevelopment of downtown (Foley 2010). These goals included the provision of pedestrian-only areas, provision of live/work areas, a diversity of activities to interest different age groups, and the provision of cultural activities. Older buildings in the downtown were to be preserved and given new uses.

The project was not without its challenges and obstacles. The idea of closing off Main Street to automobile traffic to create a pedestrian mall did not sit well with some downtown business owners, who feared that such a move would further lead to a decline in their client pool. Thomas O'Mansky, owner of Young Men's Shop on West Main, unsuccessfully sued the city to prevent the closing of Main Street to traffic. Ironically, O'Mansky's store is one of the few original businesses that still remain on the downtown mall. Another vocal opponent of the mall was Lee Hoffman, the owner of an automobile service station who feared that the closing of Main Street would impact his ability to service automobiles. The process was also criticized for being less representative of the community. Of the thirty-two participants, nine were drawn from the Central City Commission, three were city council members and one was a designer.

Design Elements of the Pedestrian Mall

Design elements of the plan have been key to the success of the pedestrian mall (see Figure 5.5). These design elements were the provision of a variety of uses and experiences, the sharpening of a sense of place, the separation of auto and pedestrian traffic, and improved accessibility to the downtown.

Figure 5.5 Downtown
Charlottesville's
pedestrian mall.

Diversity of Uses

In a way, the term "mall" in reference to this public space is a misnomer, as it connotes a place of shopping. Charlottesville's downtown pedestrian mall is in reality a civic gathering place that is designed to be more than just a shopping venue. Early on in its design, it was recognized that the mall would not succeed as a stand-alone shopping place. As a result, it was designed to be a mixed-use district that would link it to different elements of the downtown and make it a community center. As the Pew Partnership noted, the pedestrian mall is a "public space that integrates commercial, residential, and civic use—a place where public and private, work and play, form and function are intimately and beautifully connected" (Pew Charitable Trusts 2010, p. 46).

Even at its conception, the mall was seen by community leaders as the catalyst but not the only element that would revitalize the downtown. At a special city council session in 1975, Mitchell Van Yahres, then Councilman, stated: "I believe it will be the beginning of the rejuvenation of downtown Charlottesville. Other things will have to happen or the Mall will fail" (Minutes of City Council special session 1975).

The Halprin plan was the antithesis of the HBA plan. Rather than creating a single-purpose exclusionary zone for shopping, Halprin included live/work housing to ensure 24/7 activity. Halprin also sought to preserve the character of the neighborhood by repurposing the historic buildings that existed in the older neighborhoods near the mall, including Market and Water Streets and 2nd Street West and 7th Street. As Foley observed:

LHA not only proposed prominent civic features linking the pedestrian mall with Vinegar Hill in the form of a plaza and public library, but they suggested the development of a mixed-use neighborhood that included a motel and convention center, offices and retail, and multiple-family residential buildings.

(2010, p. 118)

In addition to professional offices such as banking and legal services, the mall has a total of 1.5 million square feet of commercial space including retail, entertainment, and restaurants. The Omni Hotel provides an anchor for the east end of the mall. It is estimated that about 75,000 people stay in the hotel annually, bringing much needed foot traffic to the downtown. The amphitheater and ice skating rink also bring families downtown for community-organized events, who then patronize downtown businesses. A downtown historic district was created in the 1980s sparked by the renovation of a downtown building that had an all-glass facade. The historic district designation was adopted to prevent future such redevelopments and to maintain the character of the area. A Design Review Board was given the responsibility to review all building plans proposed for the district.

Separation of Auto and Pedestrian Traffic

Rather than separating uses, the Halprin plan separated modes of transportation, in particular, keeping pedestrian traffic away from the automobile. Main Street is 60 feet wide, with pedestrian corridors on each side and outdoor cafés in the center, shaded by giant willow oak trees. The rationale for separating pedestrian from automobile traffic was explained in the downtown Master Plan as follows:

Accommodating the automobile leaves little or no space for urban amenities. The acknowledged intrusion of the auto on the psychological environment occurs pell-mell. Accommodating the pedestrian interrupts the smooth flow of traffic. The recommendation to the City therefore is to separate the two, particularly in the more intense areas of downtown.

(City of Charlottesville in Herman 2010, p. 98)

Without the separation of pedestrian and automobile traffic, safety would have been compromised and pedestrian traffic minimized, resulting in lower patronage of downtown businesses. While downtown initially lost sales to the Barracks Road Mall at its inception, by 1994, sales at the downtown mall exceeded those for the Barracks Road by 30 percent (Lucy 2002, p. 14).

A Sense of Place

Steve Davies, Senior Vice President of the Project for Public Spaces, a non-profit design and planning group, explained the failure of pedestrian malls in *The New York Times* as follows:

Pedestrian malls in the United States have a troubled history. When many cities installed them in the 1960s and 1970s, little thought was put into what would happen in the reclaimed space. Lacking a clear purpose, these malls were often devoid of public activity and became empty spaces, which, at their worst, were consumed by crime and loitering.

(*The New York Times* 2009)

This was not the case with Charlottesville's pedestrian mall, as its design was carefully planned. The pedestrian mall provides a sense of place unlike no other in the city. This was achieved through a combination of intricate design elements. The first of these is the streetscape. From street pavement to the right of way width, the design is continuous and has no separation between sidewalk, gutter, and street. Storm water drainage is provided by an indentation along what would have been a street curb. Second, the eight block mall is laid with 375,000 red bricks, each measuring 12 inches by 4 inches. These distinguish the mall's floor from the nearby streets and surrounding walls of the buildings and give the mall an exceptional visual appearance. A third design element is the enhanced street walls. Fifty percent of the pedestrian mall has 60 foot oak trees that protect pedestrians from the elements of the weather. The first outdoor restaurants started in their shade near the Halprin-designed fountains, attracted by these two design features: trees and fountains. There is an ample provision of street furniture, such as planters, benches, and fountains that are specially designed to choreograph with the landscape of the downtown.

The Experience

By all indications, the mall has been a resounding success, so much so that other downtown merchants who were not initially included within the mall's boundaries requested an extension of the mall to include their stores. Furthermore, many of the merchants were willing to pay for the cost of this extension. Thus, although the mall started with only five blocks, it expanded within three years to seven blocks. As Herman observed, "Today, the pedestrian Mall at the heart of the central business district, or CBD, designed by Lawrence Halprin Associates from 1973–76, is bursting with life and activity in spite of the economic downturn of recent years" (Herman 2010, p. 80). Charlottesville's downtown pedestrian mall has succeeded where a hundred others around the country have failed. Its success is the result of a number of factors including the use of traffic-calming techniques, attention to placemaking, accommodation of a diversity of uses, and, most importantly, the vision and drive of civic leaders.

William Lucy, Professor at the University of Virginia and past president of the city's Planning Commission, attributes the downtown's success to:

1) persistent and effective investment in and maintenance of downtown by city government with occasional support by county, state, and federal governments, 2) frequent investment and reinvestment by scores of property owners and visionary entrepreneurs, 3) leadership on special projects and activities by a wide range of voluntary non-profit organizations, and 4) design sensibility by public and private sectors that has respected traditions and usually has sought good quality construction and reconstruction standards.

(Lucy 2002, p. 7)

Consistency of policy in downtown development also helped. According to Lucy, in the last forty years there have only been two years when there was not a democratic majority on the City Council. There have also been only three city managers in the city in that time period and the current city manager was hired only three years ago.

Civic uses are major attractions in the downtown. The Pavilion brings an average of 110,000 visitors per season. According to Kirby Hutto, General Manager of the Charlottesville Pavilion:

> The appeal of attending a Pavilion show is unique compared to many other venues that present national touring artists. Often at these other venues, you drive, park in a huge parking lot with no amenities, and enter the venue where you are captive to overpriced concessions. With the Pavilion, the economic benefits of its shows spill over to all the nearby businesses.
>
> (Hutto 2007, p. 9)

The Virginia Discovery Center, a science museum for children, has also attracted over half a million visitors since its opening in 2001. Additionally, the Paramount Theater, a 1,000-seat movie theater originally built in 1929, was renovated at a cost of $14 million in 2005. Live Arts, a community theater venue with 400 seats, was built in 2007 at a cost of $8 million.

Restaurants also bring people to the downtown. Lucy's study of activity in the downtown mall found that 250–300 patrons dined at outdoor seating on the mall (not including those dining in restaurants) at lunchtime each day from Monday to Friday. On Friday and Saturday nights, there were as many as three rotations of more than 500 each at any given time. During the free weekend concerts, he counted about 3,500 pedestrians that went through the mid-point of the mall per hour. Even after a street crossing was put in the mall to provide automobile access, Lucy counted a fifteen to one ratio in pedestrian to automobile traffic, with more pedestrians at the east end than at the west side of the mall.

When the mall began to face difficulties in the 1980s, an idea was hatched to boost downtown traffic by holding free weekly outdoor concerts called "Fridays After Five." In 1988, the first "Fridays After Five" concert was held at the east end of the mall, beginning a tradition of music, beer, and food. Together with the Saturday Farmers Market, thousands of people visit the mall and downtown during the weekends. There are now nine movie screens downtown, including The Regal and one at Vinegar Hill. The Jefferson Theater has been converted into a 500-seat music performance venue. In 1983, the city provided $9.5 million in funding to build a hotel and conference center. These funds were raised by levying a 3 percent meals tax and a 4 percent increase in the city's lodging tax. The latest development is the building of the 3,700-seat amphitheater by Coran Capshaw in 2005. The project cost $2.4 million and was supported with a loan from the Charlottesville Industrial Development Authority. The downtown mall now has 120 boutique shops, thirty restaurants, a movie theater, ice skating rink and numerous coffee shops. It is bookended on both sides by the Omni Hotel to the west and by the Charlottesville Pavilion to the east.

According to Lucy, the "effect of the mall is so pervasive that it has affected every aspect of city life." To him downtown's success can be measured in two ways: by property assessment and by the number of events and people in the downtown. In terms of property assessment, the highest value residential neighborhood is North Downtown, even though it is older and has extreme variation in house size. A study by Thomas (2011) found that property in the downtown neighborhood is valued higher than neighborhoods near the University of Virginia, which presumably are preferred residential neighborhoods in the city. North Downtown is valued at $289 per square foot compared to the next highest value neighborhoods at Barracks/Rugby, Lewis Mountain, and Venable neighborhoods, where property was assessed at $239, $259, and $263 per square foot, respectively.

Downtown has also become a civic gathering place for annual celebrations including the book festival, film festival, photography festival, vegetarian festival, and craft festival. The downtown also holds alcohol-free New Year's Eve celebrations, allowing families with children to gather downtown for this special occasion.

Charlottesville's downtown has become a commercial, social, and civic park and is "thriving, attracting residents who wanted to live within walking distance of the eight block Pedestrian Mall in the heart of downtown" (Lucy 2008, p. 5). The mall has won numerous accolades, in part, because:

> Compared to other landscapes designed by LHA, Charlottesville's pedestrian mall has endured most gracefully. The mall has weathered economic difficulties, myopic private interests, and various design permutations and proposals thanks to staunch advocates in the city government, like former City Manager, Cole Hendrix, and former city planner and current City Council member, Satyendra Huja, as well as active and involved residents.
>
> (Foley 2010, p. 128)

Importance of Civic Leadership in Downtown Renewal

The examples from Mansfield and Charlottesville show that while it is important to retain civic and cultural uses in the downtown, cities must also identify and build appropriate civic and cultural facilities to complement other uses in the downtown. The previous discussion also attests to the significance of proactive and persistent civic leadership and collaboration between public, private, and non-profit sector leaders in downtown development. As we have seen in these discussions, it is the initial public sector investment that provides the catalyst for leveraging private sector investment. Each of these cities has uplifting stories of this form of partnership.

When the City of Holland received the Main Street designation in 1984, a Main Street Organization was formed to implement the four strategies of organization, design, promotion, and economic development. In 1989, this organization was merged with the existing Downtown Development Authority (DDA) into the MainStreet/DDA. The new organization was charged with the responsibility for the redevelopment of the city's downtown. From the beginning, "Downtown property owners and City Council were convinced that the economic and historic revitalization of downtown depended on a grassroots approach that would involve the public and private sectors" (Seiter 1996, p. 1).

The Main Street Committee began its work by educating both the public, private, and non-profit sectors to take ownership in the downtown redevelopment program and projects. One of the major issues at the time was the paucity of infrastructure in the downtown, much of which had been in place for decades and needed improvement. Thus, the first task of the committee was to improve the aesthetics and quality of the downtown amenities. A streetscape program began in 1988 and was followed by the development of a downtown strategic plan dubbed "Broadening the Vision" in 1995. In the same year, the DDA held a charrette for the downtown Western gateway. This was led by the Grand Valley Chapter of the American Institute of Architects. The group brainstormed ways to improve the aesthetics and redevelopment of this district.

The entire project was a joint effort between the public, private, and non-profit sectors in the community. The city provided financial incentives to encourage the appropriate remodeling of downtown properties and adopted ordinances to protect historic property. The city contributed and continues to contribute toward the operating budget of the MainStreet/DDA. In addition, the city maintains over 20,000 flowers in the downtown and the downtown parking lots. The public sector also funded part of the cost of the snowmelt system that ensures ice- and snow-free streets in the winter.

The substantial investment by the public sector encouraged the private sector to step in and take responsibility for the development of GDP Park and Prince Park and to invest in building and business improvements. Riverview Group and Lumir Corporation invested over $20 million in their downtown properties. The private sector also contributed $2.1 million toward the street improvement program that was initiated by the public sector. Through a special tax on downtown properties, the private sector contributes close to $10,000 a year toward downtown projects (Seiter 2011).

Similar public–private partnerships are sustaining downtown redevelopment efforts in Wilmington. The Wilmington Renaissance Corporation, formerly Wilmington 2000, worked with the private sector to develop a vision for the development of downtown. Through the creation of the Downtown Improvement District, downtown businesses have imposed a tax assessment on themselves to fund the Clean and Safe Team and to enhance downtown security and beautification. A public–private effort has also resulted in major downtown redevelopment, including the 2002 renovation by the Buccini/Pollin Group of the former Dupont Company offices into downtown housing, office space and retail. The renovation of the Delaware Trust Building into upscale apartments also came to fruition from public–private partnerships.

Similar success stories of public–private partnerships are evident in Greenville. Here, these multisector collaborations funded the implementation of the city hall plaza at a cost of $45.7 million, with the private sector contributing $45 million of the cost and the public sector bearing the cost of demolition, environmental remediation, utility relocation, and the provision of public restrooms. Another example is the Greenville Commons project, which involved the collaboration of the city, the Greenville Community Corporation, Oasis Corporation, Camel Corporation, and Hyatt-Greenville Corporation. The public sector bore $10 million of the cost, while the private sector paid for the $24 million difference it took to implement the project. Public–private sector collaboration has not been limited to the provision of civic facilities. There are also examples of collaboration between these sectors in the provision of housing. At Mulberry at Pinckney, thirty-four single-family attached homes are being built with the Randolph Group at a cost of $4 million. At Pendleton West, fifty attached townhomes are being constructed in collaboration with the Randolph Group and Greenville Local Development Corporation at a cost of $11.4 million.

These success stories would not be told without the dedication and perseverance of the communities' civic leaders. It is these visionary civic leaders that took pride in their communities and refused to give up, even when the future looked bleak and a majority had already given up hope on the downtown. In the end, it is people that make a difference!

 Please visit the companion website at http://routledge.com/cw/Burayidi for additional resources.

CHAPTER 6

Historic Preservation and Heritage Tourism

Despite the deleterious consequences of many urban renewal programs that led to the demolition of countless historic buildings in central cities, many downtowns still have a rich concentration of heritage resources. These may be one-of-a-kind residential buildings, unique landmarks that help a city to tell its story of settlement and development, or distinctive civic buildings such as courthouses and churches. These historic resources provide an opportunity for cities to leverage heritage tourism for the development of their downtowns by increasing the daytime population in the downtown.

In 2009, the City of Muncie, IN, created a land bank with funding from the US Department of Housing and Urban Development (HUD). The land bank was the precursor to the identification of abandoned buildings in the city for either redevelopment or demolition. With the formation of the land bank, the city is able to receive abandoned property that the county has been unable to dispose of through tax sale. Not long after the land bank was formed, the city declared hundreds of buildings unsafe and ripe for demolition, many of them in the historic Emily Kimbrough Neighborhood. The neighborhood is in the East Central District of the City of Muncie and is named after Emily Kimbrough, who was raised at 715 E. Washington Street in one of Muncie's downtown neighborhoods. She gained fame as an author of several books including *Our Hearts Were Young and Gay* (1942), a *New York Times* bestseller, and *How Dear to My Heart* (1944).

In 2011, the city earmarked $340,000 of HUD funds for the demolition of at least two dozen abandoned and blighted properties. Several structures earmarked for demolition were located in historic districts that have been classified as "notable," "significant," or "outstanding" (Slabaugh 2011b). There was resistance from many in the community including faculty and students in the historic preservation program at Ball State University who discounted the city's reasoning that many of the historic structures had to be demolished because they were beyond repair. Because the city was using HUD funding for the demolition, it had to go through the Section 106 review process established in the National Historic Preservation Act. In addition to requiring public participation, federal agencies had to ensure that work funded through the federal government did not adversely impact historic properties, and if it did, to develop and sign a Memorandum of Understanding between the federal agency and the relevant bodies documenting how the adverse impacts would be mitigated.

The opposition to the mass demolition had limited success, as the city decreased the number of structures it targeted for demolition, saving some historic houses from the wrecking ball. One of the historic houses that was slated for demolition was a 120-year-old Victorian-style house located at 911 East Jackson Street. The house is owned by Lew Beyers, a graduate of Ball State's Architecture program who intended to fix up the property. Prior to purchasing the house, it had sat vacant for more than twenty-five years. As said by Beyers, "I looked at it and thought hey, this is a great old house, it's got a lot of nice architectural details and character. I thought if I could get it for the right price it seems like a decent investment as something I could work on over time and try to bring it back" (Purdom 2011). The city agreed to provide $244,000 in HUD funding to subsidize its renovation. With these funds, Beyers planned to put in at least $45,000 of his own money to bring it up to code and turn it into a two-unit rental property.

This preservation versus demolition conflict is one that is played out in communities across the country. This is especially so in the Midwest, where cities that once depended on manufacturing now have to deal with abandoned property following deindustrialization and loss of population from the central city. Because most historic property in cities is located in the downtown, decisions about preservation or tear down invariably affect the health of the downtown.

Historic Preservation in Resilient Downtowns

Successful downtown redevelopment programs include historic preservation as one key component of the redevelopment strategy. These communities pass ordinances to protect their heritage and use this heritage to market their distinctness to the outside world. In the broadest sense, historic preservation is about preserving, enhancing, and protecting a community's way of life and history. This includes not only the physical culture of the community such as buildings and artifacts, but also the non-physical elements such as the performing arts. Show me a community with a strong historic preservation ordinance and I will show you a community with a strong cultural heritage! Communities with weak connections to their historic heritage often devolve into generica. Such communities cannot differentiate themselves from others and have no way to market their uniqueness. Because the downtown is where most of a community's heritage resources are located, attention to protecting and enhancing a community's heritage translates into a care for the downtown.

Resilient downtowns are found in communities that expend significant resources, both human and financial, to protect their heritage. In such communities one typically finds a plethora of public, private, and non-profit organizations that take on the responsibility of heritage protection and ensure the downtown's health. Such organizations include those formed by the public sector such as landmark and historic preservation commissions, as well as private and non-governmental organizations formed by private citizens that champion heritage preservation as their cause.

In resilient downtowns, attention is also given to the symbolic and organizational relationship between heritage preservation organizations and the tourism promotion bodies in the city. Symbolically, the office of the downtown manager, historic preservation, and the convention and visitors' bureau are located downtown and, in many cases, in the same building. This facilitates a close, working relationship between the organizations.

Organizationally, the downtown development manager, the director of the convention and tourism bureau, the historic preservation officer, officers of non-profit agencies involved in downtown redevelopment, and heritage preservation staff should all work across organizational borders and serve on one another's board of directors. This aids in having open communication and information sharing between all organizations. It also ensures that policies and programs reinforce rather than work against each other.

Resilient downtowns differ from others in that they follow three fundamental yet profound steps in linking historic preservation to heritage and cultural tourism. The first step is identification and appreciation of their historic and cultural heritage. The value of a historic structure as perceived by these communities goes beyond their market or economic value. It is the intrinsic value of the property that counts. This is in acknowledgement of the fact that using the economic valuation for historic property would render many of them economically indefensible for public investment. As the City of Charlottesville explains with respect to protecting its historic resources:

> The value of preservation in Charlottesville can be measured both in qualitative and quantitative terms. Safeguarding the heritage of the City promotes pleasure, education, and a sense of well-being among its citizens. Protecting the city's unique resources also fosters civic pride, contributes to an understanding of the City's past, and serves as a guide for future development.
>
> (City of Charlottesville 2012)

The City of Middletown also explains the rationale for its design guidelines as follows:

> Middletown is greater than the sum of its parts. It is a 350-year-old, traditional New England, Connecticut River Valley community, with a rich history and proud heritage. It possesses a unique downtown, a vital business community, and a rich stock of natural resources and preserves. These qualities are shared qualities, and their perpetuation requires a shared effort. To preserve and protect the history, heritage, and aesthetic resources that together form much of the quality of life in our city, the citizens of Middletown, both directly and through their duly appointed representatives and officials, have produced this document as a framework and reference point for reviewing projects proposed in commercial and downtown areas of the city.
>
> (City of Middletown 2002, p. 4)

In addition to appreciating their heritage, communities with resilient downtowns take measures to protect their heritage. Such strategies usually include "carrots and sticks," with the carrots being tax incentives and subsidies and the sticks being penalties and fines. Finally, because these communities take care to preserve their heritage and the quality of their cultural resources, they are proud to share them with the rest of the world in the form of heritage tourism promotion. We discuss these three steps with examples from the resilient downtowns.

Resilient Downtowns Recognize and Value Their Heritage

The first step is recognition of the importance that historic resources contribute to a city's well-being. This often starts with an inventory of the city's historic resources. For example, between 1977 and 1979, the Greater Middletown Preservation Trust conducted a survey of the city's historical and architectural resources. The goal was to provide a list of historic resources in the city that would provide the basis for preservation planning. The Trust identified the most significant historic district in the city to be the downtown, "particularly those areas presently zoned B-1 and mixed use" (The Greater Middletown Preservation Trust 1979, p. 145). The survey led to an inventory and classification of the city's historic buildings into several types including Center-Chimney colonial, Georgian, Federal, Greek Revival, Italianate, Gothic Revival, Builders, and Queen Anne.

Middletown is not alone. Cities with resilient downtowns have a large proportion of their historic buildings located in the downtown. Table 6.1 shows the number of historic structures in the resilient downtowns that are on the National Register of Historic Places. Because these communities value their heritage, they are willing to go through the laborious process of getting the properties listed on the National Register to ensure that they are preserved for posterity. The appendix to this chapter also provides the names of these historic buildings. At least a fifth of the historic structures in these cities are located in the downtown. Four of these communities—Fort Collins, Chico, Holland, and Nacogdoches—have more than half of their historic structures located in the downtown. This bears testimony to the care and protection that these cities have for their heritage. While other cities saw a decimation of their historic buildings in the urban renewal era, cities with resilient downtowns protected these properties from destruction.

Table 6.1 Number of historic structures on the National Register of Historic Places in city and downtown

City	Number of Structures Downtown	Number of Structures Citywide	% Structures in the Downtown
Middletown, CT	7	30	23
Wilmington, DE	38	111	34
Greenville, SC	17	39	44
Hendersonville, NC	63	613	10
Charlottesville, VA	20	65	31
Mansfield, OH	16	46	35
Ripon, WI	3	13	23
Holland, MI	6	9	67
Lafayette, IN	11	29	38
Fort Collins, CO	15	26	58
Santa Barbara, CA	9	27	33
Chico, CA	7	13	54
Nacogdoches, TX	13	20	65
Santa Fe, NM	15	47	32
All cities	**240**	**1088**	**22**

Note
Boundaries of downtowns determined by census tracts defined in Chapter 2.

Source: National Park Service, National Register of Historic Places, U.S. Department of Interior. Retrieved June 1, 2011, http://nrhp.focus.nps.gov/natreghome.do?searchtype=natreghome

As the list of names in the appendix to this chapter indicates, these historic structures help the communities to tell their history and also serve as national treasures. A Republican who wants to learn about the origins of his or her party may want to visit the Little White Schoolhouse in downtown Ripon. This building is considered the birthplace of the Republican Party and where organizers of the party first met (Brown 1854/1978). The Republican Party was formed from a coalition of several groups that opposed the Kansas-Nebraska Bill, introduced in 1854 by Senator Stephen Douglas to extend slavery beyond the Missouri Compromise. In response to this bill, people of various party affiliations congregated in the Little White Schoolhouse on March 20, 1854 to protest the bill. As Earle Bovay, one of the leaders of the movement recalled, "We went into the little meeting, Whigs, Free Soilers, and Democrats. We came out Republicans, and we were the first Republicans in the Union" (City of Ripon 1969, p. 137).

The Little White Schoolhouse is a simple, unadorned structure located at the southeast corner of Blackburn and Blossom Streets in downtown Ripon (see Figure 6.1). The building is described as "a small one-story frame building sided with clapboards and painted white, a typical one-room schoolhouse in appearance. The only architectural ornamentation of note consists of a paneled single front door framed by simple pilasters carrying an entablature. In front of it is a small, square, open porch with two plank steps leading up to it" (City of Ripon 1969, p. 139). While small, the building has significance to both the Republican Party and the City of Ripon. Its preservation helps the city to tell its contribution to the formation of one of the major political parties in the United States.

In Middletown, the St. Luke Home for the Destitute and Aged Women is located at 135 Pearl Street and has been preserved as a civic and national historic property. This late Victorian-style house provides a place of respite for fourteen women. It is a three-and-half-story brick building and is described as having two bay window piers that:

> Flank the front entrance, capped off above the roof line by a gable-roofed dormers. Decorative elements such as the wrought iron fence, ivy on the façade, and quoin-like brick projections on all corners add a picturesque quality to the building.
>
> (City of Middletown 2005, p. 53)

The building is significant in the social history of Middletown. In the mid-nineteenth century, the daughter of a prominent family in the city became homeless and had to be sheltered in an almshouse. Upon hearing of her condition, Mrs. Williams, the mother of Bishop Williams, rented the upper floor of an old house on Cherry Street to house the woman and two other women who were in a similar situation. Later, the house was purchased by a group of churches in the community and used to house destitute women. Eventually it came under the management of the Episcopal Church, which hired someone to take care of the residents. It was at this time that it gained the attention of the state legislature. In 1865, the legislature incorporated the building. The act of incorporation stipulated that the "trustees shall be seven in number, and shall always be clergymen and laymen in either protestant church in

Figure 6.1 The Little White Schoolhouse, Ripon, WI. Considered the birthplace of the Republican Party.

the City of Middletown, and some clergymen in the Protestant Episcopal church shall be president of the board of trustees" (J.H. Beers & Co. 1884, p. 63). This facility was originally located in an old house at the corner of Pearl and Lincoln Streets, but an endowment from the Holy Trinity Church in 1892 enabled the city to build a new house at its current location. The house is a testimony to the benevolence of the City of Middletown's residents. It is a statement that no homeless person will be left behind.

Such are the buildings that have contributed to making these places living histories embodied in their heritage. Downtown Greenville is recognized as the jewel in the crown of the city's heritage. The city has long been recognized as a leader in historic preservation and has made this the bedrock of the downtown's revitalization strategy. Four of the city's log cabin buildings, constructed in the 1800s, are listed on the National Register of Historic Places. These include Governor Middleton's House, the Fountain Fox Beattie House, the Elias Earle Town House, and the Josiah Kilgore House, now home to the Greenville Garden Club.

Other downtown structures registered on the National Register of Historic Places include the Imperial Hotel, Greenville City Court, and the Stradley and Barr Dry Goods Store. In the 1990s, several buildings were restored to accommodate the Peace Center, including the Gunter Theater, the former Coach Factory, the former

Huguenot Mill, and the former mayonnaise factory known as Wyche Pavilion. Additionally, the Westin Poinsett Hotel, built in 1925, was restored. Greenville's historic preservation efforts won the city South Carolina's Honor Award for historic preservation.

Charlottesville's history is greatly reflected in its architecture. The city's history is closely tied to Thomas Jefferson through Monticello, which was dedicated in 1924. The dedication of the site revealed the public's interest in experiential tourism. It also showed the public's curiosity in learning about the life, principles, and philosophy of the former president. The public display board in downtown Charlottesville was erected by the Thomas Jefferson Free Speech Center as a tribute to his fight for freedom of expression. His plantation attracts thousands of visitors each year and although it is several miles away, the downtown has profited from it. The Monticello Hotel was built in 1926 to bring tourists downtown and is considered a part of Monticello history, although it has now been converted into condominiums.

The courthouse in downtown Charlottesville is a nationally recognized historic structure. This brick, two-story structure was the center around which the settlement grew. Originally constructed of wood in 1762, it served as the capital of Virginia in 1781 and was used by Thomas Jefferson and Monroe for their law practice. It also served as a meeting place for four religious denominations in the city. This is a valuable heritage resource worth preserving.

The City of Santa Fe takes pride in its history, art, and architecture. The downtown, which is a national historic district, is where the plaza, the Palace of the Governors, and the original capitol building are located. Built in 1610, the capitol building is the oldest public structure in the United States. The Plaza of the Villa Real de la Santa de San Francisco de Assisi was built in 1610 by Governor Pedro de Peralta and was designated a national historic site in 1960. The Palace of the Governors houses the New Mexico History Museum and is the vending location for authentic Native American art.

West of the Plaza is the adobe Santuario de Guadalupe, which was built between 1776 and 1796. It is the oldest shrine to Our Lady of Guadalupe. Loretto Chapel, built in 1873, is located on Old Santa Fe Trail. It features a loft staircase that makes 360-degree spiral turns without any side support. Legend has it that St. Joseph, the patron saint of carpenters, sent a carpenter to build the staircase and then mysteriously disappeared without payment.

The City of Nacogdoches has recognized, valued, and preserved its cultural heritage. This is reflected in the number of historic houses and structures that have been preserved in the city's downtown. Of particular interest is the work of one of the city's prolific architects, Diedrich Rulfs. After emigrating to Nacogdoches in 1880, Rulfs became a famous Texas architect who designed more than fifty structures in Nacogdoches, Garrison, San Augustine, Crockett, and Lufkin. In Nacogdoches, he designed many houses that are now part of the historic fabric and folklore of the city's downtown. Rulfs designed houses for many of the city's famous and most influential residents including Judge Stephen W. Blount and Laura Blount. The Laura Blount and Judge Stephen W. Blount houses, built in 1896 and 1897, are located at 821 North Street and 310 North Mound, respectively (Nacogdoches CVB n.d.). Rulfs also designed Tolbert Hardeman's house at 408 Mound Street and many of the city's historic churches including the Christ Episcopal Church (1902) at the corner of Mound Street and Starr Street, and the Zion Hill Baptist Church (1914) at 324 North Lanana Street.

Also well preserved in downtown Nacogdoches is the Sterne-Hoya House Museum and Library, which is part of the El Camino Real National Historical Trail. It is said to be the oldest frame house of historical significance that is still on its original site. It is furnished with original items donated by the Hoya family and depicts its occupancy at the time of the Texas Revolution. Sam Houston, a hero of the revolution, was baptized in this house. The Durst-Taylor Historic House and Gardens is a wood-frame house built in 1835. It is the second oldest house in the city. The house and its gardens depict life in the state in the 1840s and take visitors to a simpler time in the city's history.

The efforts of community leaders in Fort Collins led to the preservation of several historic buildings in the city's downtown. These include the C&S Freight depot transit center, the renovation of the Northern Hotel into mixed-use retail and affordable housing for seniors, and the rehabilitation of the Opera House and its conversion into a one hundred-seat theater that is now managed by the Downtown Development Authority.

There are eleven historic districts in the City of Wilmington. The city treasures its historic resources and is cognizant of the importance of these resources to the city: "City Historic Districts are designated most often in response to the concerns of area residents interested in preserving the character of their neighborhoods and protecting their historic resources, capturing the essence of Wilmington's past for future generations. Additionally, preservation plays an important role in maintaining the economic vitality of the City as a whole" (City of Wilmington 2003, p. 53).

As we have seen, the history of these cities and their downtowns is closely tied to their architectural and cultural heritage. Although recognition of this heritage is important, cities of resilient downtowns go a step further by protecting this heritage through a combination of local ordinances, incentives, and institutions formed specifically with the goal of safeguarding this heritage.

Resilient Downtowns Protect Their Heritage

Resilient downtowns protect their heritage through i) city ordinances, ii) financial incentives and penalties, iii) human resource support, and iv) a collaborative and integrative organizational structure.

The City of Middletown used Section 8-2 of the Connecticut General statutes on Village Districts to protect the distinctive historic character of the downtown neighborhood between Wesleyan University and Main Street from alteration, and as a result, protected it for posterity. The ordinance regulates new construction as well as the reconstruction, and rehabilitation of property in the district, design and placement of buildings, use of paving materials, and building elements. All such modifications must go through the city's Design Review Preservation Board for vetting before they are approved. The district also limits the area to one- and two-family residential uses. With special permission, daycare centers, libraries, and churches may be allowed (City of Middletown "Section 39D").

The city has also adopted design guidelines that provide standards for the alteration and modification of buildings in the downtown. The design guidelines state:

> As Middletown's historic center, the Downtown Middletown area is the most aesthetically sensitive of all the design review areas. Buildings of special historical value are concentrated here, the city's retail, financial, and government centers are located here, and for outside visitors who visit "Middletown," it is this area in particular that they most frequently come to and take away impressions of when they leave.
>
> (City of Middletown 2002, p. 6)

Santa Fe's Historic District Overlay Ordinance, enacted on October 30, 1957, is the second oldest historic code in the United States and predates the National Historic Preservation Act of 1972. The leadership of the city decided in the early 1900s to use the Santa Fe adobe-style buildings with flat roof pitches, roof drains, and projecting vigas as the guiding historic style for all buildings in the city's downtown. Newer construction is required to be harmonious with historic buildings by using similar materials, color, proportion, and general detail so that the dominating effect is that of adobe construction. The Historic Preservation Division of the city is charged with preserving the "character of Santa Fe by effectively administering the Historic Districts and Archaeological Districts ordinances and by educating the public about historic preservation." In addition, the historic preservation office provides development review for building modifications and all new development to ensure that they conform to the downtown's historic fabric.

The City of Santa Fe has a fifty-year rule that classifies structures in the historic district into three categories: all structures built prior to 1961 that have little or no alteration are considered historic; contributing historic structures are over fifty years old and have had some alteration but have not lost their historic quality; non-contributing structures, though old, have been altered enough to lose their historic integrity. Over 6,000 buildings, some 20 percent of the city, has some form of historic preservation protection. Additionally, there are five thousand contributing structures in the city's historic districts. Building heights in the downtown are limited to five stories and cannot be taller than the Cathedral Basilica of Santa Fe.

David Rasch, the city's Historic Preservation Officer, noted that one of the reasons for enacting the city's historic preservation ordinance was to show appreciation for the city's past and to help promote tourism. The city's 2005–2025 Comprehensive Plan affirmed the significance of historic preservation for Santa Fe, noting that it promotes "a harmonious outward appearance" that will "preserve property values and attract tourists and residents alike." The protection of historic structures also provides economic benefits to owners and craftsmen. Repairs to historic structures are typically completed by certified restorers. Thus, the policy ensures employment for people in the preservation trade.

As an incentive, the city's designation of a property as historic qualifies the owner to receive up to $25,000 in state tax credits. This can be written off their state income taxes. An annual awards dinner is also held to recognize property owners that have used exemplary and innovative remodeling and renovation techniques to rehab their buildings.

The City of Wilmington uses a combination of incentives, regulations, and penalties to protect its historic properties. The city has a tax abatement program that provides financial assistance for remodeling commercial property within the historic district. The State of Delaware's historic preservation tax credit program "allows owners of commercial or residential property to reduce their income tax liability by a percentage of the costs they incur rehabilitating historic buildings" (Maloney 2009). The Delaware Preservation Fund "provides financial assistance to owners of historic properties in the form of mini-grants and rehabilitation loans" (Preservation Delaware 2012). Perhaps the most effective incentive for historic preservation is the city's facade improvement program. This program is supported with contributions from banks and local corporations. Downtown Visions, the organization that manages the Business Improvement District runs the program.

In 2011, the facade improvement program provided $25,000 to qualified property owners for each building facade that faces a street. Downtown Visions identified 276 downtown commercial buildings that needed improvement. The organization works with the Delaware Historical Society to ensure that the restoration of historic buildings is authentic. Also, all restorations of historic property must go through the city's Design Review and Preservation Commission. This ensures that improvements retain the original historic elements of the buildings, "which have a much longer life-span than new construction and are ideal for small, independent businesses" (Downtown Visions 2011, p. 9).

Property owners have typically used the facade improvement funds for installing new awnings and display windows and for improvement to pedestrian-level lighting (see Figures 6.2 and 6.3). For property owners that are not able to pay the required matching funds, Downtown Visions works with First State Community Loan Fund, a non-profit community development financial institution, to assist them in securing financing at affordable rates.

The city adopted a vacant property registration ordinance in 2003 that requires property owners to register property that has been vacant for more than forty-five days with the city. There are several goals of the ordinance. One is to decrease the aesthetic impact of vacant buildings on neighborhoods. The second goal is to ensure that property owners are accountable for maintaining their buildings (many of which may have historic value): "It is intended to encourage owners of vacant properties to immediately fix up the property or to sell the property to an individual or an agency that will make the property attractive for sale or rental" (City of Wilmington 2011a). An annual fee is assessed on vacant property owners for each property that sits vacant for more than a year. The fee increases with the length of time that the property has been vacant and ranges from $500 to $5,000.

Since implementation of the ordinance in 2003, long-term vacancy rates (defined as property that has been vacant for more than ten years) in the city have decreased by 51 percent. In 2003 there were 142 properties listed as long-term vacant properties. By 2011 this dropped to ninety-six properties. The city also issued close to $1.1 billion in rehabilitation permits to property owners since the inception of the program. Table 6.2 shows the number of vacant properties that are

Figure 6.2 The Pana 700 block before facade improvement with funds from the Upstairs Program.

Credit: Downtown Visions and Main Street Wilmington, City of Middletown, DE.

Figure 6.3 The Pana 700 block after facade improvement with funds from the Upstairs Program.

Credit: Downtown Visions and Main Street Wilmington, City of Middletown, DE.

listed with the city and the length of time that they have been vacant. At the end of 2011, there were 1,444 vacant properties. Of these, 753 were eligible for fee assessment, meaning that they had been vacant for more than one year. Also, 328 of the properties were on the vacant property list for the first time. Most property owners choose to fix up their properties rather than pay the fee to keep them vacant. Reflecting on ten years of the program, Mayor Baker observed:

> The Vacant Property Registration Fee Program continues to send a powerful message to negligent property owners that Wilmington will not allow these property owners to diminish the quality of life in our neighborhoods. The battle to rid the City of property owners who keep their properties vacant through purposeful negligence is never ending, but one that is well worth a consistent and sustained effort in order to revitalize City neighborhoods.
>
> (City of Wilmington 2011)

The program has withstood court challenges and has now been replicated in other cities such as Revere, MA, Salisbury, MD, and the cities of Altoona, Reading, and Carbondale in Pennsylvania.

In 2009, the city also passed a Public Nuisance Properties legislation in which property owners are assessed a fee on a point scale for each time the city takes an action against a property. For example, a call to a property that results in an offense involving a weapon is assessed eight points, but a violation of a sanitation ordinance is only assigned one point. A building is classified as a nuisance when it accumulates twelve points in a six-month period or eighteen points within a twelve-month period. At this point, the Commissioner of Licenses and Inspections can close the property, suspend, or revoke any licenses for operating the business or trade in the building and/or issue a summons to the property owner. If the property owner refuses to follow the order, he or she is subject to a fine of $1,000 for the first offense, $2,500 for the second offense, and $5,000 for the third and subsequent offenses. These penalties are meant to prevent property owners from neglecting

Table 6.2 Number of vacant property registered with the City of Delaware since 2003

Month	Less Than 1 Year	1–2 Years	3–4 Years	5–9 Years	10+ Years	Totals
Jan 03	352	348	292	235	142	1369
Jan 04	461	333	287	233	141	1455
Jan 05	481	356	163	265	143	1408
Jan 06	304	393	146	251	127	1221
Jan 07	373	326	134	184	119	1136
Jan 08	332	341	146	143	117	1078
Nov 09	350	410	145	136	87	1128
Apr 10	531	287	202	167	89	1276
Jan 11	246	785	233	174	77	1515
Nov 11	566	472	185	149	72	1444

Source: City of Wilmington (2011).

their property and to ensure a quality built environment for city residents. They also have the effect of protecting historic property from wanton abandon and neglect.

In Fort Collins, the revitalization of the downtown resulted from the need to protect historic buildings from the state bulldozer. In the 1980s, there was a proposal to do a major realignment of U.S. Route 287 that would have caused the destruction of many of the historic buildings in the downtown. This precipitous event galvanized the community and started the process of downtown revitalization. Visionaries such as Gene Mitchell led the effort to preserve the downtown historic buildings and turn Old Town into a pedestrian-friendly plaza. In 1982, voters approved the creation of a Downtown Development Authority (DDA), a public non-profit agency, and charged it with the goal of helping to revitalize the downtown by using public funds to leverage private investment. The DDA provides financial incentives to encourage development and redevelopment in downtown Fort Collins with a $5 million tax levy on downtown property. The city provides matching funds of up to $5,000 through a zero-interest loan program for the exterior rehabilitation of landmarks and historic property. Another $900 in design assistance is provided to enable property owners pay for the services of design professionals in rehabilitating historic properties. The city's latest downtown strategic plan recognizes the importance of historic preservation: "Downtown Fort Collins is the vibrant heart and soul of this community, with a history and neighborhood fabric warranting preservation and enhancement" (City of Fort Collins 2006, p. 3).

In 1981, Fort Collins also adopted design guidelines and formed a Landmark Preservation Commission to review exterior alterations to landmark structures in the city's historic districts. The design guidelines state as follows:

> These guidelines are a set of design concepts that direct design alternatives and indicate the range of approaches to yield results that are compatible with the character of the Historic District. The guidelines are not intended to unreasonably restrict creativity. They are instead intended to protect the district from designs unsympathetic to the existing historic character … The Old Town Historic District must be protected from changes that will erode its historic integrity, so that it can be held in trust for future generations to enjoy.
>
> (City of Fort Collins 1981, p. 1)

In Fort Collins, as in many other resilient downtowns, there are typically more than one organization that take on the responsibility of historic preservation and downtown redevelopment. At least four organizations play this role in Fort Collins. The DDA is responsible for advising community leaders on planning and development of the downtown. As previously mentioned, it has the authority to levy a $5 million tax and issue tax increment bonds for downtown's development. The Landmark Preservation Commission is responsible for historic preservation. The city also has a volunteer organization, the Historic Fort Collins Development Corporation, which is dedicated to the preservation of Fort Collins' historic resources. The Downtown Business Association (DBA) promotes and provides services to downtown businesses. The organization also puts on a number of public events such as the NewWestFest, a music show, to draw people to the downtown.

Symbolically or out of practicality, the DDA, DBA, and the Convention and Visitors Bureau are all located in the same building at 19 Old Town Square. The executive officers of these organizations sit on one another's board meetings. Table 6.3 lists the different organizations with responsibility for downtown development in the city.

The 2006 Downtown Strategic Plan calls for the creation of an alliance of all the downtown organizations to ensure efficiency in operations. As described in Fort Collins Downtown Strategic Plan, "The Alliance is envisioned to allow DDA and DBA officers to meet in a more formal way to determine overall vision and policies for downtown, thereby elevating the organizations' clout and influence" (City of Fort Collins 2006, p. 26).

Beet Street, one of the downtown non-profit organizations, promotes public and performing arts in the downtown. The organization is responsible for placing the much admired and ubiquitous pianos in the downtown and organizes artists to paint transformer boxes to make them more aesthetically pleasing. Lately, the organization has taken on the task of restoring "ghost-signs" in the city.

As shown in Figures 6.4 and 6.5, ghost signs are painted wall signs that over time have been painted over or have lost their luster from harsh weather. The restoration of these signs "is intended to provide a means of determining the significance of the city's extant painted wall signs and provide suggestions for the preservation and interpretation of these historic advertisements" (City of Fort Collins 2007, p. ix). The signs also help to restore a sense of place for the downtown where most of the wall signs were painted.

By all indications, the designation of historic properties in Fort Collins is having a positive effect on the downtown. A study for the Colorado Historic Foundation compared property values in Old Town Fort Collins, a designated historic district, to property values in non-historic districts. The study found that after Old Town's

Table 6.3 Fort Collins downtown development organizations

Name	Activities
Convention and Visitors Bureau	Marketing and promoting downtown Fort Collins Coordinating Downtown Events
Downtown Development Authority	Advises community leaders on planning and development in the downtown Uses TIF funding to stimulate redevelopment in downtown
Downtown Business Association	Advocates for development in Downtown Fort Collins Produces programming and events downtown
Historic Fort Collins Development Corporation	Private non-profit organization with interest in historic preservation
Landmark Preservation Commission	Reviews redevelopment proposals affecting historic property to ensure authenticity of remodeling and preservation of historic elements of buildings
Beet Street	Promoting the arts in downtown, especially "Arts in Public Places"

Figure 6.4 Owl Cigar sign at 113 College Avenue in downtown Fort Collins.

Source: City of Fort Collins (2007), p. 6

Credit: City of Fort Collins, CO.

Figure 6.5 Coca Cola Sign Rehabilitation Project.

Source: City of Fort Collins (2011), p. 1

Credit: City of Fort Collins, CO.

designation as a historic district in 1979, property values grew 721 percent by 2003, compared to a 423 percent rise for properties in the undesignated comparison area (Clarion Associates 2005).

Like other cities with resilient downtowns, the City of Greenville also established design guidelines for the central business district and for its seven historic districts. Also characteristic of resilient downtowns, there is more than one organization responsible for the health of downtown. In Greenville, this includes the Arts in Public Places Commission and the Design Review Board. The Arts in Public Places Commission was formed with the responsibility of recommending sites for the placement of art in the downtown to enhance public spaces. The Design Review Board, as the name implies, reviews proposals for the exterior modifications of buildings and structures to ensure that they conform to the architectural features of the historic districts.

The City of Santa Barbara was one of the first cities in California to embrace historic preservation for protecting its identity. In 1922, the Community Arts Association and the Architectural Advisory Committees were formed in the city with the objective of assisting in the beautification of the city and protecting the city's architectural heritage. This was followed by the formation of an Architectural Review Board in 1923.

Following California State legislature's passage of a bill allowing local governments to adopt historic districts, Santa Barbara enacted an ordinance in 1959 creating a historic district for El Pueblo Viejo (The Old Town). This district had an area of sixteen blocks around the old Presidio and protected all of the historic adobe buildings from demolition. The historic district was further extended north to include the Santa Barbara Mission. The following year, the City Council formally adopted an ordinance that specified architectural restrictions in the district, prohibiting its destruction. The rationale for designating El Pueblo Viejo as a historic district was stated as follows:

> The purpose of El Pueblo Viejo is to preserve and enhance the unique heritage and architectural character of the central area of the city which developed

around the Royal Presidio, founded in 1782, and which contains many of the city's important historic and architectural landmarks. In addition to the preservation of landmarks, the cohesiveness of the area is achieved by regulation of architectural styles used in new construction, as well as review of the exterior alterations of existing structures.

(Historic Landmarks Commission and City Council 2009)

Following the designation of the El Pueblo Viejo as a historic district, an Advisory Landmark Committee and a Historic Landmarks Commission were formed in 1960 and 1993, respectively. The city also adopted a Historic Structures Ordinance in 1977. All of these organizations were charged with the responsibility of reviewing projects in the El Pueblo Viejo Landmark District for consistency with the character of the district and to help preserve the historic character of the neighborhood.

The Santa Barbara Trust for Historic Preservation (SBTHP) was established in 1963 by Pearl Chase to help restore and preserve the history of Santa Barbara. Since its founding, the non-profit organization's primary task has been the restoration of the Santa Barbara Presidio, the last fortress in California that was built by the Spanish in 1782. The Presidio occupies one block in downtown Santa Barbara and lies at the intersection of Santa Barbara and East Canon Perdido Streets. At its establishment, the Presidio was used as a government headquarters and a military post, as well as the staging ground for protecting residents from enemy attacks. Several of the city's original structures and buildings were preserved including El Cuartel, the second oldest historic building in the State of California. Also preserved by the efforts of Pearl Chase and the Santa Barbara Trust for Historic Preservation is Casa de La Guerra that dates from 1819. These are relic reminders of the city's Spanish heritage. Other buildings of the era that have been preserved for posterity are the Pico Adobe, a one-room building at 920 Anacapa Street that was built for the Pico family, and the Hill-Carrillo Adobe at 11–15 East Carrillo Street that was built in 1825–1826 by Daniel Hill for his wife Rafaela Ortega. This building is said to be the first house in Santa Barbara to have a wooden floor.

A second historic district was created in 1977 as the Brinkerhoff Avenue Landmark District. This district developed in the late nineteenth and early twentieth centuries and is named after a local physician, Dr. Samuel Brinkerhoff. A guide to Santa Barbara's historic property explains the city's historic preservation program this way: "Santa Barbara, founded in 1782, is world-renowned for its history and specialized architecture. Its citizens have devoted years of attention to protection and recognition of these attributes" (Days 1984, p. 1).

As the oldest town in Texas, Nacogdoches has preserved its heritage through incentive grants and regulation. As a result, the heritage sector has become an important marketing resource for the community, especially its downtown. The design guidelines for Nacogdoches summed up the rationale for adopting the city's guidelines:

Preserving our community's heritage has become increasingly important to residents and property owners as loss of historic resources continues and neighborhood character erodes. Many citizens recognize that buildings from our past help define our identity for the future. In this sense they serve an important social function … preserving historic buildings helps to enrich the cultural diversity that the community offers its residents and visitors.

(City of Nacogdoches 1991, p. 1)

Since 1989, the city has awarded an average of $25,000 annually in historic preservation grants to property owners to help with the rehabilitation of historic properties. The funds for these grants are raised from a hotel occupancy tax. To date, as much as $2 million worth of projects have been funded through the program. Tax abatements are also provided to property owners to encourage building improvements. For example, the city is now considering providing property owners with up to $500 in permit reimbursement for the cost of obtaining sign permits. As part of the Main Street program, property owners also benefit from professional design assistance in remodeling their property.

To further protect historic property, the city has a demolition by neglect provision in its historic preservation code that serves as a deterrent to property owners from allowing their property to deteriorate and turn to blight. The code states:

No owner or person with an interest in real property designated as a landmark or included within a historic district shall permit the property to fall into a serious state of disrepair so as to result in the deterioration of any exterior architectural feature which would, in the judgment of the historic landmark preservation committee, produce a detrimental effect upon the character of the historic district as a whole or the life and character of the property itself.

(City of Nacogdoches 2012)

The city's commitment to the downtown and the protection of its heritage can be seen in the number of organizations and individuals that are involved in this endeavor. The city has a historic preservation officer, a downtown manager, a downtown business association, a historic landmark preservation commission, and five districts on the National Register of Historic Places. Additionally, the city has a convention and visitors bureau all working together to protect the city's historic resources and to promote development of the downtown. The city's efforts at historic preservation were rewarded with the 1st Ladies of Texas Treasure Award for historic preservation.

The City of Charlottesville has several properties that are listed on the National Register of Historic Places. The city enacted an Architectural Design and Control Ordinance in 1959 and established a "restricted design district" for thirty-three buildings in the Court Square area. In 1973, a Historic Landmarks Commission was created to identify historic properties in the city and propose historic districts for the community. This led to the adoption of a Historic Preservation Ordinance in 1976. A Historic Preservation and Architectural Control District in Charlottesville was created in the same year, covering much of the downtown. The architectural styles in the downtown historic district include Greek Revival, Colonial Revival, Gothic Revival, Queen Anne, and Italianate styles. The city's website states that, "the city's historic preservation program strives to preserve these resources that represent the individuals, events, trends, and designs that formed the city's history and environment" (City of Charlottesville 2012).

In 1985, concerns over alterations and demolition of buildings in the downtown mall led to the formation of the Downtown Architectural Design Control District (ADCD) and the Downtown Board of Architectural Review to guide development in the downtown. It is the responsibility of the Board of Architectural Review to ensure that changes to these buildings do not violate the historic character of the district. Charlottesville also has a Historic Resources Committee which was formed in 1998 to "promote and help develop the historic resources of the community." The city acknowledges the important role that historic preservation plays in attracting tourists to Charlottesville. From this recognition, the city created the Entrance Corridor Review Board and charged it with the responsibility of enhancing the visual appearance of the twelve major tourist entry points to the city. In 1993, the city established a Revolving Loan Fund to provide low interest loans to property owners for rehabilitation, maintenance, and remodeling of historic properties.

Resilient Downtowns Share Their Heritage

Because of the wealth of cultural and heritage resources in resilient downtowns, visitors and tourists flock to them to see and experience these sites. Thus, tourism is a growth industry in resilient downtowns. A study conducted in 2010 for the Fort Collins Convention and Visitors Bureau showed that one of the major tourist destinations in the city is the downtown. The survey found that more than 40 percent of visits to the city were tourism related and the top three reasons for visiting the city were for vacation (27%), visiting family and friends (22%), and outdoor recreation (21%). Most of the visitors were drawn to the activities in Old Town (Loomis and McTernan 2010).

The Convention and Visitors Bureau (CVB) works closely with the other downtown organizations to promote the downtown to visitors. For example, the CVB is responsible for marketing, promoting, and coordinating downtown events and for maintaining a community events calendar. The CVB also assists other organizations with data on visitor demographics, so these organizations can better target and market their activities.

Downtown Fort Collins can be experienced by foot or by bike. The CVB provides visitors with a walking tour brochure, enabling visitors to enjoy over twenty historic gems in the city on foot. The walking tour provides tourists with the opportunity to learn the history of the McPherson Block, erected in 1884 with its ornate pressed metal cornice, the Whitton Block built in 1905, and the Northern Hotel that has been restored with an art deco facade. Those who prefer touring on bicycle can choose from over one hundred bicycles at the bicycle library in Old Town Square. These can be rented for a week at a time.

The arts and heritage resources are a centerpiece of the City of Greenville's tourism industry. In 2007, when the city retained the services of Tourism Development International (TDI) to promote the tourism industry, the downtown and the city's historic resources were regarded as the lynchpin of the plan. The *Tourism Product Development Concept*, produced in 2007, recognized the city's heritage as the catalyst for promoting tourism and increasing visitor spending, noting that "Greenville's Unique Selling Proposition is its Downtown, which can rightly be described as a 'southern gem'" (Tourism Development International 2007). In particular, the firm recommended that Heritage Green be developed into the catalyst for downtown tourism promotion based on its wealth of historic resources:

> The Greenville Cultural Quarter will involve the modification of, and development of additional facilities to, the present Heritage Green. In the short term, the goal will be to transform what is a collection of facilities that are presently disconnected from visitor routes into a vibrant, integrated historical and cultural quarter; and, in the longer term, the aim is to instill a sense of place into the area.
>
> (Tourism Development International 2007, p. 2)

A tourist that was interviewed in the TDI study put it aptly: "You have to work on what is indigenous to Greenville." It can be argued that much of what is unique to Greenville is in the city's downtown. An earlier study by Randall Travel Research identified Greenville's downtown as "the magnet/top attraction." The report noted the importance of tourism to the city's economy, observing that the city receives $779 million a year in visitor spending and that business trips account for half of the nights spent in hotel rooms. The report established a goal of increasing visitor spending to $3 billion and creating 38,000 new tourism-related jobs by 2015.

Tourism was identified as early as the 1920s as a major asset in the development of Santa Fe. This was reinforced by Fred Harvey, who popularized adventures in the west to easterners. Tourists from the east came to Santa Fe to experience the pueblo architecture and Native American cultures of the southwest. Santa Fe is a major beneficiary of heritage tourism and this sector accounts for approximately 40 percent of the local economy. People visit downtown Santa Fe for its architecture and historic heritage. Without historic preservation, there would be little or no tourism industry in the city. As McWatters (2007) put it:

> The Santa Fe Style ...was not simply intended to produce a reflection of the romantic City Beautiful movement. In fact, it had a quite practical purpose: to use architectural preservation and, perhaps more importantly, restoration to stimulate tourism and reverse economic decline.
>
> (p. 88)

A survey of visitors to Santa Fe by the Convention and Visitors Bureau in 2010 found that most people visited the city for leisure (76.4%). Tourists cited the city's art shows, Indian market, scenic beauty, historic sites, authentic experience, museums, art galleries, cuisine, and architecture as the reasons for their visit. On average, visitors spent five nights in the city and about $2,216 each during their stay, patronizing and purchasing artifacts and enjoying the city's culture (Santa Fe Convention and Visitors Bureau 2010).

Keith Toler, Executive Director of Santa Fe's Convention and Visitor's Bureau, acknowledged that the bureau uses the city's rich historic resources to tell the story of the authenticity of Santa Fe's culture. According to him, the city attracts thousands of visitors each year and of the 6,000 paid sleeping rooms, 1,500 are in the downtown. Some of the biggest tourist attractions in Santa Fe are the city's museums: the George O'Keefe Museum, the Museum of Fine Arts, the Institute of American Indian Arts Museum, the Museum of International Folk Art, the Wheelwright Museum of the American Indian, and the Museum of Spanish Colonial Art are all located in the downtown.

Santa Barbara has capitalized on its rich cultural and historical heritage to promote tourism as an economic development sector. A 2008 study of tourism's impact on the community rightly noted that:

> Santa Barbara is a center for historic architecture, most notably as the locale of the Santa Barbara Mission. This has inspired much subsequent development in the distinctive Spanish Colonial or Mission style throughout the region and especially in Santa Barbara's downtown commercial district, from shops and restaurants to government facilities, private office buildings and cultural venues.
>
> (CIC Research, Inc., and Lauren Schlau Consulting 2008, p. 44)

The tourism industry is a major sector of Santa Barbara's economy, and the city's heritage resources are central to the success of its tourism sector. An economic impact study completed by CIC Research, Inc., and Lauren Schlau Consulting of Los Angeles in 2008 for the Santa Barbara Convention and Visitors Bureau and Film Commission found 5.7 million people visited the city in 2008. Tourists stayed an average of 1.4 days, generating 7.7 million total visitor days and spent on average $79 a day in the city. The study also found that half (52%) of all tourists to Santa Barbara visited the downtown (see Tables 6.4 and 6.5). If one adds the visits to Santa Barbara Paseo Nuevo (21.2%), Santa Barbara Museum of Art (9.1%), the Maritime Museum (8.5%), the Santa Barbara Mission (8.5%), and the Santa Barbara Natural History Museum (2.4%), then 84 percent of all visits to the city were heritage related (see Table 6.5). Spending for admissions to these attractions alone—local tours, museums, theaters—totaled almost $30 million. When the total direct ($612 million) and indirect impacts (about $796 million) are considered, spending by tourists on heritage-related resources amounted to over a billion dollars each year. That is a huge contribution to the city's economy. To capture this interest in the city's heritage resources and better coordinate and manage tourism in the city, a Tourism Improvement District was recently created. It will be funded with a $0.50 to a $1.00 county-wide room tax on hotel stays.

The City of Nacogdoches is a stop on the El Camino Real National Historical Trail that stretches from Crocket, TX, through Nacogdoches to Natchitoches, LA. The trail, which has existed for more than 300 years, is also known as the King's Highway and provides several educational stops at major historic sites along the way. In Nacogdoches, the Stone Fort Museum is one of these historic stops along the highway. Another historic site on the highway is the house of Sterne Hoya, the leader of the Texas Revolution.

A survey of visitors to the City of Nacogdoches showed that most visitors were drawn by the heritage experience that the city provided. As Brian Bray, Historic Preservation Officer for the city, wryly stated in a personal interview, "Without

Table 6.4 Santa Barbara, CA visitor demographics

Measure	Total Countywide	City of Santa Barbara	County of Santa Barbara
Total visitors*	8,242,500	5,684,000	5,286,300
Average length of stay—all visitors (days)	2.4	1.4	2.6
Total visitor days	19,444,500	7,741,900	13,652,600
Average daily spending per person	$83.98	$79.06	$71.61
Total annual direct visitor spending	$1,589,760,000	$612,100,000	$977,700,000
Direct spending ratio	100.0%	38.5%	61.5%
Total direct + indirect visitor spending**	$2,164,530,000	$795,730,000	$1,368,800,000

Notes

*Santa Barbara City and Santa Barbara County visitors and visitor days cannot be added to equal the Total Countywide as some visited both areas. However, Santa Barbara City and Santa Barbara County spending can be added to equal the Total Countywide.

**Indirect total spending results by multiplying city direct spending by a 1.3 multiplier and county direct spending by a 1.4 multiplier.

Source: CIC Research, Inc., and Lauren Schlau Consulting (2008), p. 25.

Table 6.5 Venues visited by tourists in Santa Barbara, CA

Specific Venue	Total	Area Visited	
		City	County
All respondents	1587	1044	911
SB Downtown/State Street	34.9%	51.9%	31.3%
SB Wharf/Pier	33.4%	48.9%	25.3%
Santa Barbara Paseo Nuevo	21.2%	32.0%	19.6%
Santa Barbara Zoo	20.4%	32.3%	7.2%
Santa Barbara Museum of Art	9.1%	14.3%	9.3%
SB Harbor/ Maritime Museum	8.5%	12.7%	5.9%
Santa Barbara Mission	8.5%	12.7%	7.2%
Santa Barbara Natural History Museum	2.4%	3.6%	3.0%
Other	2.1%	3.5%	3.3%
None/No other purpose	36.8%	4.1%	58.5%

Source: CIC Research, Inc., and Lauren Schlau Consulting (2008), p. 25.

historic preservation there will be no downtown Nacogdoches." The city's downtown boasts a number of art galleries, museums, and historic statues which embody the city's heritage.

Nacogdoches' Convention and Visitors Bureau, as well as the other heritage organizations, work hand in glove to promote the downtown's uniqueness to outsiders. ShopNacfirst is a local program that encourages residents to consider patronizing businesses in Nacogdoches before shopping elsewhere. It is a cooperative effort between the Nacogdoches County Chamber of Commerce and the Main Street program. The annual Texas Blueberry Festival is held in the downtown and attracts as many as twenty thousand people each year. The festival provides the city with the opportunity to market the downtown to visitors. More than half of those attending this festival come from over 100 miles away. The Convention and Visitors Bureau also funds the purchase of flowers and light posts that are used to smarten up the downtown.

Perhaps in recognition of Charlottesville's rich heritage resources, the Thomas Jefferson Venture (TJV) program was launched to promote heritage tourism in the community. TJV was started by persons and organizations from the public, private, and non-governmental sectors to promote the region's economic competitiveness. Heritage tourism was identified as a sector in which the area has a competitive advantage. Tourist sites such as historic buildings, museums, and battlefields, in which the area is well endowed, are major tourist attractions. The research showed 37 percent of golf vacationers also visited historic venues during their stay in Virginia. Downtown Charlottesville has become a tourist site in its own right.

According to the Greater Wilmington Convention and Visitors Bureau, downtown Wilmington has the highest concentration of tourism in New Castle County. The city identified several organizations, including the Wilmington Renaissance Corporation, the Riverfront Development Corporation, and the Mayor's Office and charged them with the mission of telling the city's story, with a tagline to match: "Wilmington … In the Middle of it All."

To some, the revitalization of downtown Wilmington has occurred primarily because of the growth of tourism in the last twenty years (Bowen 2011). Within the downtown and near downtown neighborhoods, the city has preserved its history in the built environment. Market Street is the birthplace of the city. A stroll through Market Street is a step back in time to when most of the city's residents worked and lived downtown. At 605–606 Market Street is the building with a "C" on its second-floor facade, denoting the former Crosby and Hill Department store. The restored twenty-three-story Chase-Manhattan building, located at 1201 Market Street, is the tallest structure in the city. A restored federal townhouse also survives with much pride on 721 Market Street. Art deco structures built in the early twentieth century are located along this street, as is the Delaware History Museum at 504 Market Street. The museum displays exhibits of Delaware's rich cultural and economic history. Willington Square with a central green area houses six historic buildings that were relocated to the 500 Block of Market Street in 1976 to save them from demolition. They include the Cook-Simms House of 1778, the Coxe House of 1801, the Jacobs House of 1748, and the Jacob and Obidiah Dingee house of 1771.

Wilmington's Old Town Hall was the center of government and social activities leading up to the early twentieth century. It is now owned and operated by the Historical Society of Delaware. The DuPont Theater, built in 1913 with a capacity of 1,252 seats, is said to be the "oldest continuously operating legitimate theater in the country." The theater was designed by Charles A. Rich and was the brainchild of civic leaders such as J.J. Raskob, Pierre S. du Pont, and R.R.M. Carpenter. When it faced imminent closure in 1928, the Wilmington Chamber of Commerce rescued it with financial support from the public. The DuPont Company assumed management of the theater in 1946 and celebrated its one hundredth season in 2012. Renowned performers ranging from John Barrymore, Audrey Hepburn, Patty Duke, Joel Gray, and Kathleen Turner, among others, have graced this theater with their performance.

Conclusion

Downtowns have a wealth of historic resources. This heritage should be preserved first and foremost for its intrinsic value. However, these historic resources also provide an opportunity for cities to attract people to the downtown and contribute to its revival. There is a reciprocal relationship between historic preservation and heritage tourism. Because of growing interest in experiential tourism, communities that protect their historic and cultural resources can use this to reap the benefits of the growing market for heritage-related travel. The revenue that is derived from tourism can be used to further protect and enhance the heritage resources of the communities. In sum, heritage tourism is one more resource that cities have to revitalize their downtowns. Cities with resilient downtowns are vanguards of this strategy.

 Please visit the companion website at http://routledge.com/cw/Burayidi for additional resources.

Appendix

Table 6.6 Downtown structures and districts on the National Register of Historic Places

Middletown, CT (Census Tract 5416)

Church of the Holy Trinity and Rectory	381 Main St. and 144 Broad St.
Main Street Historic District (Middletown)	Roughly Main St. between College and Hartford Ave.
Old Middletown High School	Pearl and Court Streets
Saint Luke's Home for Destitute and Aged Women	135 Pearl St.
U.S. Post Office	291 Main St.
Washington Street Historic District	Roughly bounded by Washington, Terrace, and Vine Streets
Captain Benjamin Williams House	27 Washington St.

Wilmington, DE (Census Tract 2)

Brandywine Park	Roughly bounded by Augustine, 18th, and Market Streets and Lovering Ave.
Braunstein's Building	704–706 N. Market St.
Crosby and Hill Building	605 Market St.
Delaware Trust Building	900–912 N. Market St.
Delmarva Power and Light Building	600 N. Market St.
Jacob Dingee House	105 E. 7th St.
Obidah Dingee House	107 E. 7th St.
Zachariah Ferris House	414 W. 2nd St.
Foord and Massey Furniture Company Building	701 N. Shipley St.
Gorvatos'/McVey Building	800 N. Market St.
Grace United Methodist Church	9th and West Streets

Charles Gray Printing Shop	11 E. 8th St.
Max Keil Building	712 N. Market St.
Max Keil Building	700 N. Market St.
Lower Market Street Historic District	Market St.
Masonic Hall and Grant Theater	818 N. Market St.
Louis McLane House	606 Market St.
Old Customshouse	516 N. King St.
Old First Presbyterian Church of Wilmington	West St. on Brandywine Park Dr.
Old Town Hall	512 Market St.
Old Town Hall Commercial Historic District	Roughly bounded by 5th, N. King, 6th, and Shipley Streets
Phillips-Thompson Buildings	200–206 E. 4th St.
Reynold's Candy Company Building	703 Market St.
Rockwood	610 Shipley Rd
Rodney Square Historic District	Buildings fronting Rodney Square at 10th, 11th, Market, and King Streets
St. Joseph's Catholic Church	1012 N. French St.
Charles Schagrin Building	608 N. Market St.
Starr House	1310 King St.
Torbert Street Livery Stables	305–307 Torbert St.
Henry Townsend Building	708 N. Market St.
Trinity Episcopal Church	1108 N. Adams St.
U.S. Post Office, Courthouse, and Customhouse	11th and Market Streets
West 9th Street Commercial Historic District	111–320 W. 9th St., 901–909 N. Orange St., 825–901 N. Tatnall St.
Wilmington Club	1103 N. Market Ave.
Wilmington Savings Fund Society	828 N. Market St.
Wilmington WYCA	501 W. 11th St.
Woodward Houses	701–703 West St.
F.W. Woolworth Company Building	839 N. Market St.

Greenville, SC (Census Tract 2)

American Cigar Factory	E. Court St.
Carolina Supply Company	35 W. Court St.
Chamber of Commerce Building	130 S. Main St.
Christ Church (Episcopal) and Churchyard	10 N. Church St.
Davenport Apartments	400–402 E. Washington St.
Downtown Baptist Church	101 W. McBee Ave.
First National Bank	102 S. Main St.
Gilfillin and Houston Building	217–219 E. Washington St.

Greenville County Courthouse	130 S. Main St.
Greenville Gas and Electric Light Company	211 E. Broad St.
Imperial Hotel	201 W. Washington St.
Pettigru Street Historic District	Pettigru, Whitsett, Williams, Manly, E. Washington, Broadus, Toy, and Boyce Streets
Poinsett Hotel	120 S. Main St.
Reedy River Falls Historic Park and Greenway	Both banks of the Reedy River from the falls to S. Church St.; also roughly bounded by S. Main St., Church St., and Camperdown Way
Stradley and Barr Dry Goods Store	14 S. Main St.
John Wesley Methodist Episcopal Church	101 E. Court St.
Working Benevolent Temple and Professional Building	Corner of Broad St. and Fall St.

Hendersonville, NC (Census Tract 9312)

Clarke-Hobbs-Davidson House	229 5th Ave. W.
Aloah Hotel	201 3rd Ave. W.
Grey Hosiery Mill	301 4th St.
Henderson County Courthouse	1st and Main Streets
King-Waldrop House	103 S. Washington St.
Main Street Historic District	Main St. between 6th Ave. E. and 1st Ave E., also roughly N. Main St., 2nd Ave. W., W. Allen St., N. Washington, and 1st Ave. E.
Reese House	202 S. Washington St.
Lenox Park Historic District	Roughly bounded by Allen, Spring, and S. Whitted Streets, and Southern Railroad
Smith-Williams-Durham Boarding House	247 5th Ave. W.
West Side Historic District	Roughly bounded by 5th Ave. W., Washington St., 3rd Ave. W., and Blythe St.

Charlottesville, VA (Census Tract 10)

Abell-Gleason House	521 N. First St.
Albemarle County Courthouse Historic District	Courthouse Square and surrounding properties
Armstrong Knitting Factory	700 Harris St.
Carter-Gilmer House	802 E. Jefferson St.
Charlottesville and Albemarle County Courthouse District	Roughly bounded by Park, Water, Saxton, and Main Streets
Delevan Baptist Church	632 W. Main St.
Hotel Gleason/Albemarle Hotel, Imperial Café	617–619 W. Main St.
Thomas Jonathan Jackson Sculpture	Jackson Par bounded by High, Jefferson, and 4th Streets, and Albemarle County Courthouse
Jefferson School, Carver Recreation Center, and School Site	233 4th St.

Martha Jefferson Historic District	Includes parts of Lexington, Locust, and Grove Avenues, E. High, Maple, Sycamore, Poplar, and Hazel Streets
King Lumber Company Warehouse	608 Preston Ave.
Robert Edward Lee Sculpture	Lee Park, bounded by Market, Jefferson, 1st, and 2nd Streets
Marshall-Rucker-Smith House	620 Park St.
William H. McGuffey Primary School	201 2nd St.
Patton Mansion	1018 W. Main St.
Paxton Place	503 W. Main St.
Peyton-Ellington Building	711 W. Main St.
Pitts-Inge	331–333 W. Main St.
Ridge Street Historic District	200–700 Ridge St.
Judge William J. Robertson House	705 Park St.

Mansfield, OH (Census Tract 31)

BissmanBlock	193 N. Main St.
B.F. Bissman House	458 Park Ave. W.
City Mills Building	160 N. Main St.
First English Lutheran Church	53 Park Ave. W.
Hancock and Dow Building	21 E. 4th St.
Mansfield Savings Bank	4 W. 4th St.
Mansfield Woman's Club	145 Park Ave. W.
May Realty Building	22–32 S. Park St.
Mechanics Building and Loan Company	2 S. Main St.
Richland Trust Building	3 Park Ave. W.
Ohio Theater	136 Park Ave. W.
William Ritter House	181 S. Main St.
St. Peter's Church	54 S. Mulberry St.
Soldiers and Sailors Memorial Building and Madison Theater	36 Park Ave. W.
Stewart Towers	13 Park Ave. W.
Voegele Building	211 N. Main St.

Ripon, WI (Census Tract 416: Blocks 3000, 3017, 3018, 3019, and 3021. Census Tract 415: Blocks 2015, 2025, 2026, and 2027)

Baptist Church	133 East Fond De Lac St.
Little White Schoolhouse	Southeast corner of Blackburn and Blossom Streets
Watson Street Commercial Historic District	Roughly bounded by Watson St. from Seward to Jackson St., and Jackson and Scott St. from Watson to Blackburn

Holland, MI (Census Tract 249)

Holland Historic District	11th, 12th, 13th Streets, Washington, Maple, and Pine Streets
Holland Downtown Historic District	Roughly 9th from east of College to River Ave., from 9th St. to north of 8th St.
Isaac Cappon House	228 W. 9th St.
Thomas and Anna Morrissey House	190 W. 9th St.
Holland Old City Hall and Fire Station	108 E. 12th St.
Third Reformed Church of Holland	110 W. 12th St.
Benjamin Van Raalte House	1076 E. 16th St.
Kremers House	12th St. and Central Ave.

Lafayette, IN (Census Tract 6)

Big Four Depot	200 N. 2nd St.
Downtown Lafayette Historic District	Roughly bound by 2nd, Ferry, 6th, and South Streets
Ellsworth Historic District	Roughly bounded by Columbia, the Norfolk Southern railroad tracks, Alabama, 7th, South, and 6th Streets
Centennial Neighborhood District (part of)	Roughly bounded by Union, 3rd, 4th, Ferry, and 9th Streets
Marian Apartments	615 North St.
Mars Theater	11 N. 6th St.
St. John's Episcopal Church	315 N. 6th St.
Tippecanoe County Courthouse	Public Square
Upper Main Street Historic District	Roughly bounded by Ferry St., 6th St., Columbia St., and the Norfolk Southern railroad tracks

Fort Collins, CO (Census Tract 1)

Anderson Peter House	300 S. Howes St.
Armstrong Hotel	259 S. College Ave.
Avery House	328 W. Mountain Ave.
Baker House	304 X. Mulberry St.
Jay H. Bouton House	113 N. Sherwood X.
Fort Collins Armory	314 E. Mountain Ave.
Fort Collins Post Office	201 S. College Ave.
Montezuma Fuller House	226 W. Magnolia St.
Kissock Block Building	115–121 E. Mountain Ave.
Laurel School Historic District	Off U.S. Route 287
McHugh-Andrews House	202 Remington St.
Mosman House	324 E. Oak St.
Old Town Fort Collins	Roughly bordered by College and Mountain Ave., Willow, and Walnut Streets

| Opera House | 117–131 N. College Ave. |
| T.H. Robertson House | 420 W. Mountain Ave. |

Santa Barbara, CA (Census Tract 9)

El Paseo and Casa de la Guerra	808–818 State St., 813–819 Anacapa St., and 9–25 E. de la Guerra St.
Janssens-Orella-Birk Building	1029–1031 State St.
Anadalucia Building	316–324 State St.
Faith Mission	409 State St.
Rafael Gonzalez House	835 Laguna St.
Santa Barbara County Courthouse	1100 Anacapa St.
Santa Barbara Presidio	Roughly bounded by Carrillo Garden, De la Guerra, and Anacapa Streets
U.S. Post Office—Santa Barbara Main	836 Anacapa St.
Virginia Hotel	17 and 23 Haley St.

Chico, CA (Census Tract 10)

Allen-Sommer-Gage House	410 Normal St.
Silbertstein Park Building	426, 430, 434 Broadway
South Campus Neighborhood	Bounded by W. 2nd, Normal, W. 6th, and Cherry Streets
Southern Pacific Depot	430 Orange St.
St. John's Episcopal Church	230 Salem St.
Stansbury House	307 W. 5th St.
Chico Midtown Station	141 W. 5th St.

Nacogdoches, TX (Census Tract 9509 and 9510)

Eugene H. Blount House	1801 North St.
Stephen William and Mary Price Blount House	310 Mound St.
Old Cotton Exchange Building	305 E. Commerce St.
Durst-Taylor House	304 North St.
Hayter Office Building	112 E. Main St.
Roland Jones House	141 N. Church St.
Nacogdoches Downtown Historic District	Roughly bounded by Southern Pacific railroad tracks, Banita Cr., Pilar, Mound, Arnold, North, and Hospital Streets
Old Nacogdoches University Building	Washington Square
Old Post Office Building	206 E. Main St.
Southern Pacific Railroad Depot	500 W. Main St.
Washington Square Historic District	Roughly bounded by Houston, Logansport, N. Lanana, E. Hospital, and N. Fredonia Streets

Woodmen of the World Building	412 E. Main St.
Zion Hill Historic District	Roughly bounded by Park St., Lanana Cr., Oak Grove Cemetery, and N. Lanana St.

Santa Fe, NM (Census Tract 4)

Barrio de Analco Historic District	Roughly bounded by E. De Vargas and College St.
Fort Marcy Officer's Residence	116 Lincoln Ave.
Federal Building	Cathedral Place at Palace St.
Don Gaspar Bridge	Don Gaspar Ave. crossing over the Santa Fe River between Alameda and E. De Vargas Streets
Digneo-Valdes House	1231 Paseo de Peralta
Alfred M. Bergere House	135 Grant Ave.
New Mexico Supreme Court Building	23 Don Gaspar Ave.
Palace of the Governors	Palace Avenue at Santa Fe Plaza
Santa Fe Historic District	Roughly bounded by Camino Cabra, Camino de las Animas, W. Manhattan Ave., S. St. Francis Dr., and Griffin St.
Santa Fe Plaza	Santa Fe Plaza
Scottish Rite Cathedral	463 Paseo de Peralta
Second Ward School	312 Sandoval St.
Spiegelberg House	237 E. Palace St.
Pinckney R. Tully House	136 Grant Ave.
U.S. Courthouse	Federal Plaza

CHAPTER 7

Designing Resilient Downtowns

Placemaking is an important component of downtown revitalization. It is the art of transforming public space into quality environments. This is accomplished through an understanding of local culture and people's aspirations, and utilizing the assets of the community to create public spaces that work for the users of such spaces. While community input is necessary to the creation of quality public space "so is an understanding of a particular place and of the ways that great places foster successful social networks and initiatives" (Project for Public Spaces 2009).

Successful downtowns are places where care has been taken in the redevelopment of the public spaces, where attention has been paid to the details of design. Mary D. Hirsch, Downtown Development Manager for the City of Greenville, describes it this way:

> We design our downtown first and foremost for people. Everything from the sidewalk design to the public plazas to the building edges to the outdoor cafés, the spaces must work for people instead of cars. While our Main Street is open to vehicular traffic, the streetscape design carefully balances people and cars.
>
> (Hirsh 2011)

In Kevin Lynch's classic work *The Image of the City* (1960), he identified the physical elements that are important to people's perception of the built environment. According to him, the key to designing quality places is "legibility," in that people should be able to form a mental map of the city that helps them to better understand and navigate their way through it. To be legible, Lynch recommends that cities should have five elements. These include paths, edges, districts, nodes, and landmarks. Paths are the circulatory systems of the city that enable people to get around. Streets, sidewalks, and trails constitute the paths of a settlement. Edges are the physical boundaries created by geographic features such as mountains, rivers, and lakes. Districts are those areas of a settlement that have clearly definable and unique characteristics such as historic buildings or housing designs of particular features. Nodes are the focal points in the city such as intersections of major streets or vistas. Finally, landmarks are particular locations or objects that assist in wayfinding. These may be monuments, parks, or plazas.

In my study of the fourteen resilient downtowns, I identified the following design features that enhance the quality of place: i) they have a point of arrival; ii) their boundaries are clear and easy to recognize; iii) they are designed to be accessible;

iv) there is a sense of place in the downtown; and v) the downtowns provide a variety of rich experiences. Because of these features, the resilient downtowns are recognized and celebrated as quality places. Let us consider each of these features in turn.

Resilient Downtowns Have a Point of Arrival

All of the resilient downtowns have a design feature that provides an exclamation point, an announcement that one has arrived in the downtown. This design feature serves as the "watering hole" where the public meets on both formal and informal occasions to socialize and catch up on the local gossip of the day. This point of arrival is usually a public square, plaza, or public park usually with a monument(s) and/or fountain to embellish the aesthetics or significance of the place. In Wilmington, for example, this is at Rodney Square, and in Chico it is the Chico City Plaza (see Figures 7.1, 7.2, and 7.3). Table 7.1 lists the civic spaces and points of arrival in each of the resilient cities. In Santa Fe, the Plaza and Palace of the Governors announces that one has arrived at the downtown core. In Nacogdoches, the Plaza Principal is the community gathering spot and was included as a design element at the time the settlement gained status as a town in 1779. Antonio Gil Y'Barbo established his government headquarters in a house north of the square. In the early days of the community's settlement, Plaza Principal was used as a market, as well as a gathering place for political and social events. Although the plaza has lost many of these functions today due to the location of the former federal post office building in the center of the square in 1917, it still serves the role of welcoming visitors to the city. The post office has been converted into the Visitors Information Center. There is no better way to know that one has arrived in the downtown than to be welcomed by a smiling resident volunteer at the center.

The point of arrival in downtown Holland is Centennial Park, located at 250 Central Avenue. Originally the community's marketplace, it has continued as the site where most of the community's civic and cultural events are held, including the annual Tulip Time Festival. The Veterans Memorial and the statue of the city's founder, Albertus C. Van Raalte, are located in the park.

Not all points of arrival were incorporated into the early layout of these cities. Charlottesville's pedestrian mall, built in the 1970s, and Wilmington's Rodney Square at 11th and N. Market Street are examples of public spaces that are relatively new. In the 1920s, John Jacob Raskob, famous for building the Empire State Building in New York City, led the creation of the square in downtown Wilmington to honor Caesar Rodney, an American revolutionary leader. The square provides a public gathering space for downtown office workers, is a venue for music performances, and is a place of relaxation. It would have less of a purpose were it built in a residential neighborhood.

As landmarks in Kevin Lynch's nomenclature, these points of arrival help with orientation and wayfinding but, most importantly, they are significant in creating a downtown identity. In his travel blog, writer Luis E. Estrada (2008) points to the significance of these "points of arrival":

Figure 7.1 Rodney Square in downtown Wilmington, DE.

Figure 7.2 Chico City Plaza in downtown Chico, CA.

Figure 7.3 Palace of Governors in Santa Fe, NM.

Because I did not really know where I was going once I reached Santa Barbara, I just targeted the area with the most prominent landmark that I could find. So it was that I stumbled upon the Stearns Wharf when only a few of its establishments had opened for business and just a few people were walking and jogging in it, or fishing from it.

He goes on to say:

When I left the courthouse, I had a more "visual" understanding and amazement about how California evolved from a humble "frontier" land into the place with such an immense cultural influence on the rest of the world. But I did not know that the best was to follow. Suddenly, as I was following the suggested "Red Tile Tour" path, I was pulled 200 years back in time! I ran into the remains of the Santa Barbara Presidio, built by the Spanish Crown around 1782.

Without the wharf and the courthouse, Estrada's perceptions and orientation might not have been as vivid as he describes in his travel blog.

These points of arrival are actively used on a daily basis. By their very nature they invite the public to wander. I arrived in Holland on a Sunday afternoon and walked about the downtown. At Centennial Park, I noticed several people enjoying the

Table 7.1 Points of arrival in resilient downtowns

City	Points of Arrival
Middletown, CT	Union Park (South Green)
Wilmington, DE	Rodney Square
Greenville, SC	Piazza Bergamo, Falls Park on the Reedy, Shoeless Joe Jackson Plaza
Hendersonville, NC	Public plaza, mid-block public areas
Charlottesville, VA	The pedestrian mall
Mansfield, OH	Central Park, Richland Carousel Park
Ripon, WI	The Village Green
Holland, MI	Centennial Park
Lafayette, IN	Relocated Big 4 Depot and Reihle Plaza, Tippecanoe County Courthouse
Fort Collins, CO	Old Town Square Oak Street Plaza
Santa Barbara, CA	De la Guerra Plaza, SB County Courthouse, Paseo Nuevo Mall
Chico, CA	Chico City Plaza
Nacogdoches, TX	Plaza Principal
Santa Fe, NM	Plaza of the Governors

summer's afternoon breeze on benches in the park. A young man stopped to rest after what I suspected was several hours of a bicycle ride. A couple held hands as they stood beside the water fountain. Another couple was seated at a bench near the statute of Van Raalte. The following Monday, I saw several people taking their lunch break at the park. A young family was running around, chasing their little girl as she giggled. This is the value of these points of arrival. They dictate no action other than providing a place for people to simply be and, as a result, they enliven the downtown. The young man who was taking a break from his bike ride will likely patronize one of the downtown pubs for a beer. The couple that was spending time with their daughter may stop to buy a drink or grab a meal at one of the downtown restaurants.

Humans are gregarious beings. We are attracted to other people and want to be with the crowd. As people gather at these points of arrival, they not only attract others but also help to keep the downtown safe by providing "eyes on the street." Thus, points of arrival serve many functions other than providing legibility for the downtown.

Resilient Downtowns Have Recognizable Boundaries

Resilient downtowns have well-defined boundaries that are easily decipherable. The borders are defined either by geographic features or accentuated by design (see Figures 7.4 and 7.5). Because many of the resilient downtowns have preserved their historic architecture, this has also helped to define the downtown character. A well-defined downtown is important for policy and aesthetic reasons. From a design perspective, having clear downtown boundaries enables the city to identify its gateways and to highlight these with landscaping and directional signs. From a policy perspective, defined downtown boundaries enable city leaders to target subsidies and other programs to the beneficiary area and to track progress over time to determine whether revitalization strategies are working. When a community's redevelopment authority provides financial incentives to downtown businesses, the authority ought to be able to determine if these incentives have a positive impact on business recruitment and retention within the geographic boundaries of the downtown. This is impossible if the downtown boundaries are indistinguishable from the rest of the city.

Aesthetically, a well-defined downtown helps to create a visual identity and allows for the enhancement of gateways that lead to the downtown. Ripon is an example of a city with a resilient downtown that has used this design feature to obtain desired results. Much of Ripon's historic downtown buildings have been restored and their brick architecture helps to set the downtown apart from the rest of the city. The city also adopted urban design guidelines to ensure that the uniqueness of its downtown is maintained. The downtown design manual provides a guide to downtown property owners in four areas: gateways, downtown places, areas of opportunity, and downtown connections. With respect to the gateways, Ripon is enhancing the entry points to the downtown through improved signage, streetscaping and building orientations "that delineate the edges of the downtown and clearly establish the character of the downtown district" (Ripon Historic

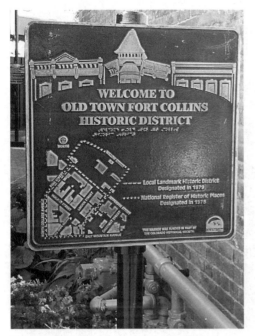

Figure 7.4 Marker to help identify the historic downtown in Fort Collins, CO.

Figure 7.5 A welcome sign at a gateway to downtown Hendersonville, NC.

Preservation Commission 2008, p. 33). Guidelines for downtown places suggest ways for improving the quality of place in the downtown by bringing out the uniqueness of each place and its functionality. Downtown connections are meant to improve wayfinding through directional signs. Areas of opportunity are adjacent downtown neighborhoods that are to be developed and appropriately linked to the downtown to complement its functions.

Some cities use "branding" to distinguish the downtown from other neighborhoods. One such community is Lafayette. Because of the fluidity of the central business district (CBD) that stretches from West Lafayette to Lafayette, the city has designated three districts within the CBD and promoted each through branding (see Figure 7.6). Each district is given a logo for advertising and all other forms of communication about the district including street signage. As stated by the city, "In an increasingly competitive environment, it is important that we put a recognizable face on the three distinct districts that comprise the downtown areas of Lafayette–West Lafayette" (City of Lafayette n.d., p. 1).

One of the districts is the Wabash Riverfront Area, which lies on both sides of the Wabash River. The Wabash Riverfront district stretches from River Road in West Lafayette through 5th Street in Lafayette. This district is not only the government center for Tippecanoe County but also home to a variety of retail and professional service businesses. In addition, several retail areas in West Lafayette are included in the Wabash Riverfront district such as Wabash Landing, River Market, and Levee Plaza. The second district is Chauncey Village on the West Lafayette side of the river, reaching from River Road up to the edge of the Purdue Campus at the Grant Street intersection. It is characterized by student-oriented retail and restaurants,

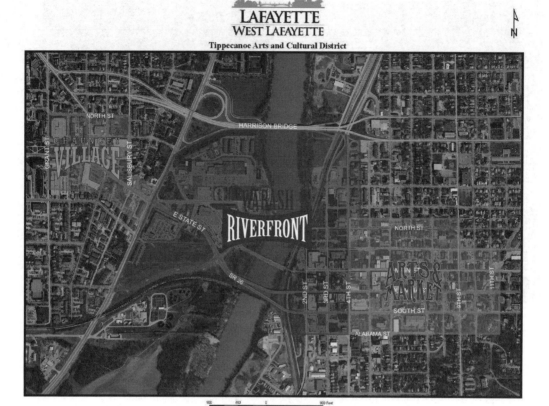

Figure 7.6 The three districts of Lafayette–West Lafayette branded for easy recognition.

Credit: City of Lafayette, IN.

although the district also has a broad consumer appeal. The historic downtown district is labeled the Arts & Market Area district. It is located in downtown Lafayette and stretches from 5th Street through 11th Street. This district is characterized by a concentration of historic buildings, local retail, a farmers' market, galleries, and entertainment. The three districts serve distinct purposes and have unique characteristics. The branding of each of the districts is meant to provide a visual image of their distinctness.

In 2006, the Wilmington Renaissance Corporation retained the services of The Vincent Group to help identify priorities for the redevelopment of the downtown. The firm held several focus group meetings and conducted a survey as part of its research study. When participants were asked to define the downtown's boundaries, they had different conceptualizations: some equated downtown with the central business district and the Market Street corridor; others defined the downtown boundaries as stretching from the Brandywine to the Christina River; still others thought of the downtown's boundaries as extending to Trolley Square and Union Street. This led The Vincent Group to conclude that:

Downtown is not clearly defined, according to the many different descriptions given by professionals, existing residents, and others interviewed for the study. The lack of clarity about where downtown starts and stops hinders efforts to market the area. While the lack of a clearly defined image permits the excitement of riverfront development to influence the overall perception of the downtown, the area also becomes associated with unrelated neighborhood-level problems.

(The Vincent Group 2003, p. 42)

The firm suggested that the city should use branding to market and distinguish the downtown physically and in the minds of residents. Subsequently, the Preservation Initiatives, the Commonwealth Group, the Buccini/Pollin Group, the Wilmington Renaissance Corporation (WRC), and downtown business leaders came together to create a conceptual framework for identifying and marketing the various districts in downtown Wilmington: "The lower end of Market Street has been renamed the LoMA Design District in hopes to attract the creative class, unique retail and restaurants as well as design-related businesses" (Wilmington Renaissance Corporation 2009, p. 3). The objective of this branding is to give areas in downtown an individual identity and to promote the three "Cs" of i) creativity, by attracting young professionals to the neighborhoods, ii) commerce, to make the districts the choice locations for niche business, and iii) community, to attract the creative class to live and work in these neighborhoods.

There is no mistaking the boundaries of downtown Santa Fe. The downtown is demarcated geographically by the Paseo de Peralta. Within its boundaries are the many art galleries. In fact, Santa Fe has the third largest art market in the United States (Visual Arts 2011). The city lives up to its reputation as the "City Different," especially so in the downtown. As early as the 1912 plan, there was a requirement to "maintain and enhance the character of the downtown to ensure that new buildings and building additions are consistent in harmony with surrounding buildings in terms of architectural style, height, pedestrian scale and design at the street level" (City of Santa Fe 2007, p. 6). This unique architectural style is primarily of "Spanish-pueblo revival" and "Territorial revival" (Visual Arts 2011). Visitors and residents appreciate the unique adobe-style architecture that has been well preserved in the city's downtown through enforcement of one of the strictest and oldest historic preservation ordinances in the country.

There are five recognizable districts in Mansfield's CBD. These districts have distinguishable features that are also accentuated visually by the city through banners and in the city's marketing and advertisement campaign. The five districts are i) the Square, ii) the Carousel district, iii) the Renaissance Theater district, iv) the Industrial flats, and v) the downtown residential district. The Square is the core of the downtown which features a central park around which several historic buildings are located. Some of these include the Richland Bank, First United Methodist Church, City Hall, the County Courthouse, and the former Reed's Department Store. The unifying feature of the Carousel district is the carousel that was built in the 1980s. Following its completion, several historic buildings were also restored in and around the Carousel district, especially along 4th and Main Streets, providing retail space and upper-floor residential units.

The Renaissance Theater is the core around which the Theater district is organized. The theater is a unique landmark and an entertainment destination located along Park Avenue West. This district has a distinct character with wider streets and a mix of building types. It is where the Holiday Inn and Park Place Hotel are both located.

The Industrial Flats district features old industrial buildings and warehouses. It lies north of the commercial area and at a lower elevation than the surrounding neighborhood. The Downtown Residential district is primarily a residential district that is located to the west and north of the square and consists primarily of historic older housing stock.

In Middletown, the city has distinguished the downtown from the rest of the city through signage and design features. The downtown market area plan, developed for the city by Mullin Associates in 1996, recommended the segmentation of the downtown into three main districts with clear identities for each area. These districts are the North End, the Central Core, and the South End. The North End lies north of Washington Street, the Central Core is the major downtown retail area and civic district and is bound by Washington Street to the north and College Street/Dingwall Drive to the south, and the South End stretches from College Street/Dingwall Drive to the north to Union Street in the south.

Later, the city conducted a slogan and logo contest and selected the best entries for use in downtown advertising and correspondence. Hence, "Middletown: It's All Here?" was born. In 2010, the Downtown Business Association (DBA) retained the services of a consultant to help prepare a wayfinding guide to improve navigation and provide clearly defined entrepôts for the downtown:

> Eight gateways at entrances to the city will point to areas of interest such as Main Street and the riverfront. Parking signs will point out hard-to-spot parking lots that are behind buildings. And visitors will be shown how to get to the city's downtown.

> (Vahl 2010)

Downtown Holland differentiated itself through streetscaping, which began in 1988. Brick pavers, period street furniture, landscaping, and design improvements were used to sharpen downtown's image. This was revisited in 1990 in the city's downtown strategic plan, "Broadening the Vision," which analyzed and identified downtown's priority areas for development, enhancement, and improvements over a five- to ten-year period. In 1995, the Downtown Development Authority (DDA) hosted downtown's first design charrette for the Western Gateway to help sharpen its distinctness. Other downtown redevelopment projects which the city is using to differentiate and provide singularity for the downtown are the Northern Gateway and Window on the Waterfront Park.

Holland's revitalization efforts have created a downtown that has maintained its historic integrity while building its economic base. Downtown stakeholders have worked together to retain existing businesses, recruit new ones, and develop upper-story housing with appropriate ground-floor uses. Design incentives have been revamped to fit users' needs and encourage continued investment in the downtown. Holland's public–private partnerships have ensured downtown's historic preservation through installation of public amenities that fit the downtown's character and encourage use and maintenance of the existing building stock. In addition, the DDA's Design Review Board (DRB) was established in 1993 and is now charged with sign approvals, murals, awnings, and special projects such as installation of downtown's wayfinding signage program and historical building plaques.

In the 1970s, Hendersonville redesigned its main street from four lanes to a two-lane serpentine street to slow traffic and increase safety and accessibility. Because of the street re-alignment, drivers entering the downtown are alerted to slow down and to recognize that they are entering a distinct area that is different from other neighborhoods in the city.

Resilient Downtowns Are Accessible

Resilient downtowns are accessible by different modes of transportation. While most cities give pre-eminence to the automobile, resilient downtowns accommodate all transportation modes. In them, the pedestrian, cyclist, and driver are all comfortable navigating the downtown because conflict is minimized through a multimodal transportation design system. As Forsyth and Krizek observed with respect to accommodating cyclists, it is important to provide:

> Routes where cycling is uncomplicated enough to permit cyclists to spend time viewing the scenery. Or, it might involve focusing routes where the level of detail of the context is such that it can be easily perceived from the speed of a bicycle—less detail needed than for a pedestrian, but more than for a motorist. Another key dimension—often absent in planning—is the degree to which a network links key urban places, important to different types of people, in a way that can contribute to public space use, vitality, and legibility.
>
> (Forsyth and Krizek 2011, p. 535)

Downtown Fort Collins is a very walkable district that is designed to cater not only to the automobile but also to pedestrians and bicyclists (see Figure 7.7). Although the major arteries through the downtown such as College and Mountain Avenues are wide, the city has done a marvelous job in taming traffic to accommodate different modes of transportation. College Boulevard is a divided road with a center lane devoted to parking, decorative street lights, and landscaping. Restaurants, kiosks, and outdoor cafés beckon pedestrians to wander and take a seat to enjoy outdoor dining. Bicycle lanes are clearly marked on the shoulders of downtown streets. Bicycle racks are also provided and crosswalks are painted or textured with colored bricks to ensure pedestrian safety. It is the only downtown in my travels that has bowls of water at strategic locations along the sidewalks so dogs can quench their thirst when they are on a walk with their owners. Walkability, safety, convenience, and aesthetics are the guiding principles of the redesigned downtown in Fort Collins.

Perhaps the reason these downtowns are so accessible is because of their compactness. This facilitates foot traffic, an essential ingredient for supporting downtown retail. Since customers can easily walk from one end of the downtown

Figure 7.7 Downtown
Fort Collins caters to
different modes of
transportation. In this
picture, a clearly marked
bicycle lane designates
right of way for bicycles.

Credit: Kinzelman Kine
Gossman Design and
Painting.

to the other, it eliminates the need for driving. Thus, the downtowns of these
communities are very much pedestrian friendly. Accommodating the pedestrian is
not just good design, but is also good for business. As shown in Table 7.2, most
of the resilient communities (ten of them) have a downtown area that is 2 percent
or less of the city's total land area. Greenville has a relatively large downtown of
1,118 acres; however, it only represents 6 percent of the area of the entire city. By
comparison, Ripon has the smallest downtown of 22 acres, representing 1 percent
of the city's total area.

Not surprisingly, all of the resilient downtowns have identified "walkability" as
an essential component of their downtown revitalization strategy. Charlottesville
attributes the success of its downtown to the creation of "a pedestrian mall
thirty years ago." The Design Manual for the City of Ripon's downtown implores
property owners to take the needs of pedestrians into consideration: "The design
of the building should help make the street enjoyable, visually interesting, and
comfortable. Individual buildings should be integrated with the streetscape to bring
activity within the building in direct contact with the people on the sidewalk" (Ripon
Historic Preservation Commission 2008, p. 34).

Corresponding with the objective of enhancing accessibility, the resilient
downtowns score high in walkability, achieving 80 or higher (see Table 7.3). The
most walkable of these downtowns are Chico, Charlottesville, Hendersonville,
Middletown, Santa Fe, and Santa Barbara, all of which score a 95 or above and
are designated "walker's paradise." Most striking is the difference between the
walk score for the resilient downtowns and that of their cities. For example, while
downtown Lafayette's walk score is 82, or "very walkable," the city's walk score is
43, or "car dependent."

Table 7.2 Size of downtown in comparison to city size

City	Size of Community (acres)	Size of Downtown	Size of Downtown as Percentage of Community
Middletown, CT	27,200	27	0.1%
Wilmington, DE	33,280	271	1%
Greenville, SC	17,280	1,118	6%
Hendersonville, NC	4,561	46	1%
Charlottesville, VA	6,450	60	0.9%
Mansfield, OH	19,136	184	1%
Ripon, WI	2,668	22	1%
Holland, MI	11,014	723	7%
Lafayette, IN	17,789	640	4%
Fort Collins, CO	34,100	580	2%
Santa Barbara, CA	26,240	850	3%
Chico, CA	21,120	68	0.3%
Nacogdoches, TX	16,192	179	1%
Santa Fe, NM	28,643	390	1%

Source: Data obtained from a survey of downtown managers of resilient downtowns by author.

Table 7.3 Walk score for cities

City	Downtown Score	Downtown Rating	City Score	City Rating
Charlottesville, VA	98	Walker's Paradise	63	Somewhat Walkable
Chico, CA	97	Walker's Paradise	54	Somewhat Walkable
Fort Collins, CO	85	Very Walkable	44	Car-Dependent
Greenville, SC	82	Very Walkable	52	Car-Dependent
Hendersonville, NC	95	Walker's Paradise	55	Somewhat Walkable*
Holland, MI	88	Very Walkable	52	Somewhat Walkable
Lafayette, IN	82	Very Walkable	43	Car-Dependent
Mansfield, OH	89	Very Walkable	40	Car-Dependent
Middletown, CT	98	Walker's Paradise	41	Car-Dependent
Nacogdoches, TX	85	Very Walkable	40	Car-Dependent
Ripon, WI	91	Walker's Paradise	47	Car-Dependent**
Santa Barbara, CA	98	Walker's Paradise	67	Somewhat Walkable
Santa Fe, NM	97	Walker's Paradise	51	Somewhat Walkable
Wilmington, DE	86	Very Walkable	67	Somewhat Walkable

Notes
* City walk score for Hendersonville is an average of scores taken from the north, south, east and west parts of the city.
** City walk score for Ripon is an average of scores taken from the north, south, east and west parts of the city.

Source: Walk Score. Retrieved April 2012, http://www.walkscore.com.

The City of Greenville attributes the walkability of the city's downtown to its design: "In order to make it vibrant and a place where people want to be, it must have a variety of spaces for shops, offices, restaurants, residential condos, and more." Main Street has been reconfigured from four to two lanes with wide sidewalks. Parallel parking was removed and decorative light fixtures, parks, and fountains were installed to transform downtown into a pedestrian-friendly neighborhood.

In 2002, the City of Middletown adopted design guidelines to serve as the framework for the redevelopment of its downtown and surrounding neighborhoods. The document stipulated that redevelopment should be geared towards: i) creating an active and comfortable pedestrian environment; ii) giving emphasis to creating proximity and views to the river; and iii) providing a streetscape that is inclusive of such elements as lighting, landscaping and pavement structure (City of Middletown 2002, p. 7).

Resilient Downtowns Provide a Sense of Place

In Kevin Lynch's other classic book, *Good Urban Form* (1981), he writes:

> Most people have had the experience of being in a very special place, and they prize it and lament its common lack. There is a sheer delight in sensing the world: … A good place is accessible to all the senses, makes visible the currents of the air, engages the perceptions of its inhabitants. The direct enjoyment of vivid perception is further enlarged because sensible, identifiable places are convenient pegs on which to hang personal memories, feelings, and values. Place identity is closely linked to personal identity. "I am here" supports "I am."
>
> (p. 132)

Resilient downtowns foster a sense of place due to the attention that is paid to detail in their design. Consequently, they provide a unique experience for residents and visitors that is unparalleled elsewhere in the community. In this sense, the downtowns serve as the "third space" that complements people's place of residence and place of work.

Downtown Santa Barbara makes a permanent impression on the visitor. There are at least three ineradicable features of the downtown. These are the experience of walking along redesigned State Street, the downtown's exquisite public spaces (plazas and alleys), and the city's unique Spanish-Moorish architecture. Twenty-two adobe-style, red tile roof buildings lie within twelve blocks of the downtown from Ortega Street in the south to Anapamu Street to the north, State Street to the west, and Santa Barbara Street to the east. All of the buildings are designed in the Spanish-Moorish style of architecture that is characterized by white walls, arches, domes, courtyards, and decorative tiles.

The Santa Barbara County Courthouse, which was designed by William Mooser III, is considered one of the most beautiful courthouses in the country. Its 85-foot bell tower provides visitors with a picturesque view of the city. The Santa Barbara Public Library and the Santa Barbara Museum sit next to the courthouse. Other memorable buildings include the Carrillo Adobe, the Casa de la Guerra, and El Cuartel adobe, the residence of soldiers who guarded the western Presidio gate, and the second oldest building in California. The Hill-Carrillo adobe has the city's first wooden floor. All of these distinctive buildings and architecture are uniquely Santa Barbara.

The city also has several exceptional public alleys and plazas (see Figure 7.8). Plaza de la Guerra is a centrally located "public courtyard" where the first city council met in 1850. The plaza is flanked by City Hall and the Santa Barbara News-Press. Presidio Avenue is the oldest street in Santa Barbara and La Arcada plaza, an outdoor mall, is lined with restaurants, shops, art galleries, and boutique shops. The plaza is accessible from State Street and Figueroa Street and is embellished with public art and fountains. La Arcada provides a pleasant stroll even if just for sightseeing. Other attractive public places in the city include Paseo Nuevo and La Cumbre plaza.

State Street is the heart of downtown Santa Barbara. It runs from the Stern's Wharf north for about a mile and half all the way to the heart of the downtown and is designed with the pedestrian in mind. As one approaches the downtown from the beach, the sidewalks are purposely widened and the street narrowed, thus forcing traffic to slow down. Main Street is lined with interesting architecture. Coffee shops, fine dining, antique shops as well as "mom and pop" specialty shops dot the street. You can shop till you drop or people-watch on benches provided alongside the street. The people-watcher is treated to an eclectic blend of people from famous people with million dollar houses in nearby Montecito to homeless people and surfers taking a break from the beach. There is always energy and vibrancy on State Street.

Fort Collins' downtown provides a sense of place at Old Town Square and in the downtown alleys. Trimble Court and Tenney Court connect College with Town Square, and Mountain Avenue with the Civic Center parking structure. The plaza and

Figure 7.8 Paseo Nuevo in downtown Santa Barbara, CA.

alleys are vibrant pedestrian spaces that stamp memories in the mind of the visitor. These alleys were aesthetically revamped in 2006 by the Downtown Development Authority to feature pedestrian-scale lights, planters, hanging baskets, flower pots, and street furniture (see Figure 7.9). The Art in Public Places program adorns the alleys with children's drawings using different themes for each alley. Typical themes include sustainability and the history of the city.

Working with local artists and non-profit groups, the Art in Alley's project used transformer cabinets as the canvas for artists. Over fifty transformer boxes have been painted in the process, transforming dull and unattractive boxes into picturesque work of art that now adorn the downtown. "Pianos About Town" also engaged artists to paint murals on pianos that are placed in downtown public locations. The pianos are moved around to different locations. Part of the thrill is to first find a piano and then play it (see Figure 7.10).

In Greenville, the "Mice on Main" is a unique approach to bring families to the downtown. It is a scavenger hunt where mice are hidden in several places on the nine blocks on Main Street. Children are then given clues to find them. This provides a fun activity for the entire family. The Liberty Bridge is another distinctive feature of Greenville's downtown. This "floating" bridge was completed in 2004 at Falls Park

Figure 7.9 An alley in downtown Fort Collins with hanging baskets, flower pots, and brick pavement.

Figure 7.10 A piano is provided in an alley in downtown Fort Collins, CO.

and provides stunning views of the city. The bridge has received many accolades for its design. In 2005, it was awarded the Arthur G. Hayden Medal for outstanding achievement in bridge design, engineering, vision, and innovation.

Furthermore, as Mary Douglas Hirsh put it, the City of Greenville has invested heavily in the arts and entertainment sector knowing that:

> People seek unique experiences to enhance their quality of life. Everything from "Shakespeare in the Park" during the summer to the annual "Fall for Greenville Festival," Greenville's events encourage people to come downtown, to get out of their cars, and to walk around and enjoy their experience. It helps that Greenville's climate is mild most of the year for these outdoor activities. Additionally, Greenville's emphasis on the arts is evident by the community's support of its annual "Artisphere" event held each spring and the growth of artist studios throughout downtown.
>
> (Hirsh 2011)

If you want the experience of walking the original red bricks that were used for street paving in a downtown, you need not go farther than downtown Nacogdoches (see Figure 7.11). From North Street to Mound Street, downtown Nacogdoches provides an easy stroll along the original red bricks that were used in paving the "Oldest Town in Texas." In between, one can take in the many art galleries that provide visitors with selections from handmade items to antique collectibles. Conveniently located in the heart of the downtown is the city's Visitor Center. Once inside, you are greeted by a welcoming group of volunteers that run the center and are happy to narrate stories of the uniqueness of the community and its many significant downtown buildings. A self-guided tour takes visitors to interesting sites and buildings within easy walking distance. Immediately south of the Visitor Center is the

Figure 7.11 A red brick street in downtown Nacogdoches, TX.

Plaza Principal. From there you can wind your way north with stops at the Sterne-Hoya House Museum and Library, Oak Grove Cemetery and from Zion Hill Baptist Church to the Indian Mound. This site is the resting place of the earliest inhabitants of the City of Nacogdoches. If you visit in the summer, you can participate in the annual Texas Blueberry Festival that attracts thousands of visitors to the downtown each year. Thereafter, you can take a stroll along the Lanana Creek Trail, a 2.5 mile trail that will take you from the downtown to the Stephen F. Austin State University.

Downtown Holland is unique in its functionality. To experience this, one needs to visit in the winter. The downtown has the largest municipally owned snowmelt system in the country. Over 405,000 square feet of snowmelted streets, sidewalks, and parking lots make it one of the most fascinating downtowns. The initial snowmelt system, developed by a Swedish firm, was installed in 1989 at a cost of $1.1 million as part of a streetscape beautification program. It melts an inch of snow per hour. The 250,000 square foot snowmelt system circulates warm water through 60 miles of 1 inch orange plastic pipes arranged every 6 inches under the street surfaces and sidewalk brick pavement. About 1,500 gallons of "condensate" cooling water per minute are pumped through 12 inch pipes to 3 inch pipes and then to the 1 inch plastic pipes. The system was updated in 2005 to double its capacity at a cost of $1.5 million, with an additional 12 inch transmission line from the city's power plant to the downtown. Between 2005 and 2007, approximately 155,000 square feet of additional area was added to the snowmelt system in the downtown. Together, the snow melted area now stretches from the east end of 8th Street to 12th Street and serves the Museum, City Hall, Centennial Park, and the Herrick District Library. The 2005 expansion also included the snowmelting of the parking deck and parking lot behind the Police Court complex on 8th Street which covers over 50,000 square feet.

Hendersonville has preserved its traditional downtown and Main Street has been transformed into a beautiful tree-lined avenue complete with brick planters. A stroll down Main Street surrounds one with sounds of classical music, exquisite seasonal plantings in a hometown setting of boutiques, numerous antique and clothing shops, and an old-fashioned pharmacy, in addition to benches on which to sit and people-watch. Few downtowns have remained as beautiful, vital, and alive as historic downtown Hendersonville. The streets bring history to life and the best of yesteryear into the excitement of today.

Santa Fe's downtown offers a unique experience to visitors. The city has developed a reputation for the fine arts and has attracted artists and writers for decades, dating back as far as the 1920s (Ettenson & Ettenson 2010). The city was once the home of popular artists Georgia O'Keefe and Alfred Stieglitz. Today, artists of different genres call the city home and the city continues to be recognized for its arts and culture. Hundreds of art galleries showcase a variety of styles and mediums, from traditional Native American crafts to glass art and photography. Several museums in what is appropriately dubbed Museum Hill offer an opportunity for people to learn about the history and culture of Santa Fe.

Resilient Downtowns Have a Variety of Land Uses and Activities

Successful downtowns have a mix of uses to ensure vibrancy throughout the day and night. The importance of diversity in cities was persuasively argued in Jacobs' seminal book *The Death and Life of Great American Cities* (1961) in which she made the observation that cities need to have "a most intricate and close-grained diversity of uses that give each other constant mutual support, both economically and socially" (Jacobs 1961, p. 14). The design of the resilient downtowns mitigates downtown's image as a mono-functional, unsafe, uninteresting, and bland district. In Chico, several buildings along Main Street were redeveloped into vertical mixed-use buildings that included residential units on the upper level. For example, the City's 1910 municipal building at 441 Main Street was restored in 2009 and now houses a downtown police station. Similarly, a prominent historical building at 240 Main Street that was once a department store has been restored and renovated for office use upstairs and retail use on the ground floor. Public space in downtown Chico has also been revamped. Chico City Plaza, the city's 138-year-old public space occupying a square block in the center of downtown, has been redesigned and reconstructed. It continues to serve as the central gathering place for residents.

The City of Greenville epitomizes the ideal mix of uses that has transformed the downtown into a healthy place. The downtown is approximately 1.75 square miles in area with a mix of residential, commercial, and civic and cultural uses. Downtown Greenville boasts ninety-five restaurants and ninety-one retail establishments (City of Greenville 2010).

Close to two thousand residential units have either been completed or are under construction in the city's downtown. For example, Wachovia Place, an infill development in the downtown, provides a healthy mix of street-level retail and twenty-four luxury apartments. Also generously provided in Greenville's downtown are parks and plazas that provide gathering places for people to enrich the social lives of the community. The redevelopment of Greenville's West End neighborhood exemplifies the creative reuse and redevelopment of an old industrial site into a mixed-use area. In 1994, the city renovated the Alliance Cotton Warehouse into the West End Market that now houses several shops and restaurants. Complementing this redevelopment is the West End Field Ballpark, the home of the Greenville Drive baseball team. These anchors have transformed the neighborhood into a destination for both shoppers and tourists. Another major feature of the city's downtown is the Fall Park on the Reedy, a public garden in the city's downtown developed at a cost of $70 million. This development also features a state-of-the-art pedestrian bridge, amphitheaters, greenways, and a botanical garden.

Mixed-use development is the hallmark of downtown Middletown and the city's design guidelines actively promote such uses:

> While acknowledging that some land uses are clearly incompatible, current planning practice also recognizes that mixed use development—especially in downtowns—best supports the functions of daily life: employment, recreation, retail, and civic and educational institutions. Such mixes foster vibrant, interesting communities.
>
> (City of Middletown 2002, p. 13)

The city encourages downtown living, recognizing that "residential uses tend to soften the edges of a strictly retail district while retail can benefit from a local customer base of nearby residents or office workers" (City of Middletown 2002, p. 13).

Downtown Fort Collins is the city's civic, cultural, and financial center. It is in the downtown that the offices of Larimer County, City of Fort Collins, as well as state and federal government offices are located. Downtown is also the heart of the community's culture. Here is the location of the Lincoln Center, a consummate art and cultural building that hosts live theater, concerts, and other social events. A museum that exhibits the history of early life in Fort Collins, a library, as well as private studios and theaters are also located downtown. Other civic and cultural amenities in the downtown include Old Town Square, Oak Street Plaza, the library, Old Heritage Park, and Lee Martinez Park.

As shown in Table 7.4, "Downtown Fort Collins has no single major attraction, but is home to a variety of unique attractions and events, providing opportunities for social, educational and cultural interaction against an attractive, historic backdrop" (City of Fort Collins 2006, p. 74). The largest draw of the downtown is the festivals that are organized by the Downtown Business Association, which brings in over half a million people to the downtown each year. The Lincoln Center brings in approximately 330,000 people for concerts and performances, in addition to the public library which attracts approximately half a million patrons a year.

Table 7.4 Activities and draw of downtown facilities in Fort Collins, CO

Amenity	Function	Patronage
Fort Collins Museum	A regional center focusing on area history and culture	24,579
Fort Collins Main Library	Library	449,740
Lincoln Center	A 1,500-seat performing arts center, home to the opera, theatrical performances and the chorale, contains three art galleries and conference facilities	329,503
Mulberry Pool	Swimming pool	75,600
Museum of Contemporary Art	Features two art galleries in a renovated 1911 post office	15,000
Old Town Square	Boutiques and retail services, eating and drinking establishments, and professional office space surround a public plaza in a renovated historic setting	NA
Downtown Business Association Events	DBA annually produces over fifty-two promotional event days: Colorado Brewer's Festival, First Night Fort Collins, NewWestFest, afternoon and evening concert series, parades, and other activities	Over 500,000
Fort Collins Municipal Railway Station.	The only original restored streetcar in operation in the western United States	8,000
The Farm at Lee Martinez Park	Depicts life on early 1900s farm; features farm animals, a farm museum, educational programming and horse and pony rides	96,000
Northside Aztlan Community Center	Community, recreation, and group activities	225,000
Public Parks (113 acres)	Within walking distance of Downtown; Lee Martinez, library, Buckingham and Fort Collins Heritage Parks	NA

Source: City of Fort Collins (2006), p. 74.

Resilient Downtowns Are Recognized as Exemplary Places

As shown in Table 7.5, all of the cities with resilient downtowns have received recognition as exemplary places by one or more of the major "placemaking" organizations in the country. These include the American Planning Association, the National Trust for Historic Preservation, the International Downtown Association, and the National Civic League. For example, Chico was recognized as having one of the best California downtowns by the California Chapter of the American Planning Association in 2007. *The California Planning & Development Report* cited the following reasons for the award:

> This Sacramento Valley city may be California's ultimate college town, and that is reflected in the downtown, which lies just across Second Street from the third-oldest campus in the CSU system. Like any good college town, Chico is replete with nightclubs, sports bars, coffee houses, eateries, bookstores and even shops that sell vinyl records. The place literally pulses with energy well into the night. But

you'll also find stores and services that clearly appeal to the college kids' parents, upper-floor professional offices, artist studios and civic institutions. A carefully revamped downtown plaza is only going to get better as it matures, and new housing is on the way. The edge of Bidwell Park—a 4,000-acre jewel that extends for miles from the valley floor into the foothills—is only a couple blocks away.

(Shigley 2007)

In 2008, Santa Barbara was voted second best in mid-sized downtowns in California, second only to Pasadena. *The California Planning and Development Report* noted that "Santa Barbara is a California icon that fits numerous criteria for being a delightful urban place that is both manageable and pleasant with a sense of place and a feeling of vibrancy." Similarly, the American Planning Association's Great Places Award, which is given to communities for their "exemplary character, quality and planning," awarded the City of Greenville two of these awards for the revitalization of the city's core district.

The National Trust for Historic Preservation (NTHP)'s Great Streets Award is given to communities that have demonstrated success in using the organization's four-point approach to rejuvenate their downtowns. Such places show economic vitality, provide a unique sense of place, and promote the cultural and social life of the community. Eight of the resilient downtowns have been recognized by the NTHP with this award: Middletown, Fort Collins, Holland, Greenville, Santa Barbara, Santa Fe, Lafayette, and Charlottesville.

Since 2000, the National Trust for Historic Preservation's Dozen Distinctive Destinations program has also recognized cities and towns that "offer an authentic visitor experience by combining dynamic downtowns, cultural diversity, attractive architecture, cultural landscapes, and a strong commitment to historic preservation, sustainability and revitalization" (National Trust for Historic Preservation 2011). Five of the resilient downtowns won this award.

In 2011, Middletown was listed as having one of the most romantic Main Streets in the country by the National Trust for Historic Preservation. The organization described the city thus: "Middletown's allure includes an artful Main Street brimming with elegant restaurants, an award-winning local chocolatier, and the romantic Inn at Middletown, offering the best of New England Charm" (2011).

The All America City Award is given by the National Civic League to cities that "collaboratively tackle problems and achieve results." It is the oldest community recognition award, having been given to exemplary communities for over sixty years. Holland and Lafayette have both won this prestigious award from the National Civic League.

The Washington-based International Downtown Association (IDA) is a "champion for vital and livable urban centers and strives to inform, influence, and inspire downtown leaders and advocates" (The International Downtown Association 2011, p. 3). The IDA recognizes communities that create healthy and dynamic downtowns. Wilmington won the IDA award in 2007 for the implementation of the city's downtown waterfront plan.

Some of the resilient cities won awards that are not specific to their downtown, but it is safe to say that without a healthy downtown, they would not have won the awards. For example, Fort Collins was named a "Preserve America Community" in 2005 for the city's excellence in historic preservation. The city hosted the first Preserve America grant awards on March 8, 2006 when then First Lady Laura Bush presented the award to the city.

Charlottesville has many accolades to its name. *Arts and Entertainment Television* listed Charlottesville as number six on its "Top 10 Cities to Have It All." In 2004, Bert Sperling and Peter Sander named Charlottesville America's number one city in *Cities Ranked and Rated*. The city was ranked by *Money Magazine* as one of the "Best Places to Live in America." *Explore Magazine* named Charlottesville as the "Best Place to Raise an Outdoor Family," *Travel 50 and Beyond* ranked the city in its top ten list of places to retire, and *Modern Maturity* magazine ranked Charlottesville as one of the "Best College Towns in the Country."

On March 13, 2012 Gallup reported on the Gallup-Healthways Well-Being Index. The index is based on a community satisfaction and optimism survey of 353,492 residents in 190 metropolitan areas in the United States. The survey gauges residents' level of satisfaction of the communities in which they live. Of the top ten metropolitan areas, Greenville-Mauldin-Easley, SC, placed fifth with a score of 74.2 and Fort Collins-Loveland, CO, placed ninth with a score of 70.9. Table 7.5 provides the comprehensive list of recognitions for all fourteen cities. Clearly, these cities and their downtowns are exemplary places.

Design Matters

Cities with resilient downtowns use placemaking principles to design quality public spaces and buildings. The design approaches used by these cities are adaptable to downtowns in other small and medium-size cities and can contribute to improving the quality of place in these districts. In Lynch's *Good City Form* that was referenced earlier, he observed that:

> Although attempts have been made to reduce design to completely explicit systems of search or synthesis, it remains an art, a peculiar mix of rationality and irrationality. Design deals with qualities, with complex connections, and also with ambiguities. City design is the art of creating possibilities for the use, management, and form of settlements or their significant parts. It manipulates patterns in time and space and has as its justification the everyday human experience of those patterns.
>
> (1981, p. 290)

It is up to city leaders in each community to decide how they want to utilize public spaces to enrich the daily life experiences of their residents. How this is done will vary depending on the physical features of the land, the aspirations of city residents, and the vision residents have for their downtowns. What is unmistakable is that good design is an integral part of creating healthy downtowns. Coupled with the appropriate and innovative public policies that we discussed in previous chapters, downtowns can become the quality social gathering places for which they were originally intended.

 Please visit the companion website at http://routledge.com/cw/Burayidi for additional resources.

Table 7.5 Recognitions of resilient downtowns

Community	Award	Year	Recognizing Organization
Middletown, CT	Ranked 11th as Best Place to Live	2011	*Hartford Magazine*
	Top 10 of New England Main Streets	2011	*Boston Globe's ExploreNewEngland.com*
	Most Romantic Downtown	2012	National Trust for Historic Preservation
	Ranked 17th as Best Place to Live	2012	*Connecticut Magazine*
Wilmington, DE	Merit award for implementation of the Wilmington Vision 2020 Plan: A Downtown Waterfront	2007	International Downtown Association
Greenville, SC	Great American Main Street Award	2003	National Trust for Historic Preservation
	One of 10 Great Streets	2009	The American Planning Association Great Places in America program
	America's Best Downtowns	2011	*Forbes*
	The 15 Best Cities for Young Adults	2011	*Forbes*
	The Top 10 Cities to Live	2011	Relocate America
	America's Greatest Main Street	2012	Travel+Leisure
Hendersonville, NC	Marvin Collins Planning Award—City Land Development Code	2009	North Carolina Chapter of the American Planning Association
Charlottesville, VA	Dozen Distinctive Destinations	2007	National Trust for Historic Preservation
	Distinctive Destination	2007	National Trust for Historic Preservation
	Top Ten Charming Towns	2010	TripAdvisor
	Healthiest Place to Live	2010	*Men's Journal Magazine*
	Top Place to Retire	2010	Kiplinger.com
	Most Walkable City in Virginia	2011	Walk Score 2011
	#1 Best Place to Live in America	2011	Yahoo Real Estate/Sperling's Best Places
Mansfield, OH	Great American Main Street Award	2001	National Trust for Historic Preservation
Ripon, WI	Semi-finalist for Great American Main Street award	2011	National Trust for Historic Preservation
	Coolest Small Towns in America	2011	*Budget Travel Magazine*

Location	Award	Year	Source
Holland, MI	All America City	1996	National Civic League
	Great American Main Street	1997	National League of Cities
	Dozen Distinctive Destinations	2002	National Trust for Historic Preservation
	50th Smart Place to Live	2006	Kiplinger.com
	One of the Top Five Places to Retire	2006	A.G. Edwards' Nest Egg Index
	No. 4 Most Affordable Community	2009	Money Magazine
	2nd Happiest Place to Live in America	2010	Gallup-Healthways Well-Being Index
Lafayette, IN	All America City	1995	National Civic League
	Five Star Quality of Life Ranking	2007	Expansion Magazine
	Preserve America Community	2008	Preserve America Foundation
	Great Places Neighborhood Designation	2010	American Planning Association
	Ranked 12th in Best US Small Cities for Business & Career	2010	Forbes Magazine
	America's Top 100 Places to Live	2012	CNNMoney.com
Fort Collins, CO	Dozen Distinctive Destinations	2010	National Trust for Historic Preservation
	Preserve America City	2005	White House
	Best Place to Live	2006 and 2008	Money Magazine
Santa Barbara, CA	Voted No. 2 Best Mid-Sized City Downtown in California	2008	California Chapter of the American Planning Association
	Dozen Distinctive Destinations	2009	National Trust for Historic Preservation
	Trustees Emeritus Award for Excellence in the Stewardship of Historic Sites	2012	National Trust for Historic Preservation
Chico, CA	Best Places to Retire	1998	Kiplingers' Personal Finance magazine
	#13 Best Places to Live	1999	Money.com
	#1 Best Places in America	2000	Forbes Magazine
	Best Places to Retire	2005 and 2006	CNNMoney.com
	Best Places to Retire	2008	US News & World Report
	#3 Best Mid-Sized City Downtown in CA	2008	California Planning & Development Report
Nacogdoches, TX	Texas Treasure Award	2009	Texas Historical Commission
	Best Historic Venue	2009	Texas Monthly Magazine Reader's Choice Awards
	Certified Retirement Community	2010	Texas Department of Agriculture
	Best Destination Management Organization	2010	Texas Monthly Magazine Reader's Choice Awards
	Eight Enticing Low Cost Towns	2011	Where to Retire Magazine
	One of the Friendliest Towns in America	2011	Rand McNally

CHAPTER 8

Economic Distress and Downtown Revitalization

Even with the best of efforts, successful downtown programs can still be derailed by national economic trends. A perennial problem that downtowns must contend with is economic recessions. As subsets of regional and national economies, downtowns are not insulated from supra-local events. The extent to which a downtown is impacted by a recession, however, varies. Although resilient downtowns have felt the symptoms of the recent recession that began in 2007, they have been less adversely impacted by it than other downtowns. Two main reasons explain this. First, resilient downtowns have become multifunctional districts with a myriad of activities besides retail. As a result, these downtowns have been less dependent on one sector of the economy for their economic survival the way that other downtowns and business districts may have been. Second, through design, resilient downtowns have become quality places that continue to attract residents and businesses that find them appealing places to live and do business. Below, we discuss first how an economic recession affects the economies of downtowns and then consider how resilient downtowns have coped with the recession that started in 2007. The discussion sheds light on how other downtowns can adapt to such economic conditions. The chapter concludes with an account from the proprietors of two downtown businesses in Hendersonville that reveal how the private sector handles a recession.

Economic Recessions and Downtowns

The recession that began in 2007 is generally believed to be deeper and longer lasting than many had anticipated. According to the Bureau of Economic Analysis, from the fourth quarter of 2007 to the first quarter of 2009 real gross domestic product (GDP) in the United States decreased at an annual average rate of 3.5 percent, making it the largest decline in national economic output since 1947 when the bureau started keeping records. Figure 8.1 shows the revised annual gross domestic product from 2007 to 2011. The graph shows that the recession began after the third quarter of 2007 and reached its deepest trough in the fourth quarter of 2008.

An economic recession portends several outcomes for downtowns, namely: i) falling property values on which business improvement districts (BIDs) depend for their operations; ii) lower wages and higher unemployment rates affecting consumer disposable incomes; iii) decrease in business orders and production, implying fewer multiplier impacts on the non-basic sector of the economy; iv)

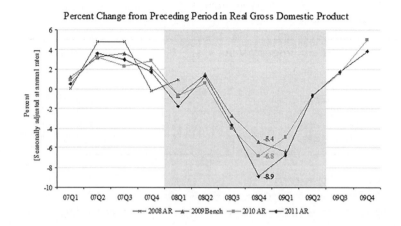

Percent Change from Preceding Period in Real Gross Domestic Product

Figure 8.1 Revised annual gross domestic product from 2007 to 2011. (The shaded area marks the beginning and end of the 2007–2009 recession as determined by the Business Cycle Dating Committee of the National Bureau of Economic Research.)

Source: Short (2013).

stricter lending regulations by banks derailing redevelopment projects and causing delays or outright abandonment of these projects; v) increased vacancy rates of downtown buildings; vi) deferred maintenance of downtown property; and vii) decreased public sector support for downtown programs as a result of decreased government revenues. We consider each of these impacts in greater detail next.

Property Values

BIDs are dependent on property assessment for their operational revenues. In a recessionary period, as demand for real estate drops, property values also decline. As a result, BIDs are unable to raise the same amount of revenue from property taxes as they did before the recession. Thus, recessions have an impact on downtown budgets by decreasing the funds that are available for downtown programs. For example, the City of Wilmington's assessment for the operations of Downtown Visions, its downtown development organization, is 0.2362 for every $100 of assessed value. Given a fixed rate, a decrease in property values means less revenue can be raised from contributing property in the district. Some downtowns may feel this shock more than others. In the city of Holland, Phil Meyer, Director of the city's Department of Community Services, stated that revenues from the city's three assessment programs—the principal shopping district, the parking district, and the snowmelt district—have remained stable. Also, the fund balance in all of the city's downtown programs has remained strong. However, the millage for the downtown development authority declined by approximately 4.9 percent in 2010 and by 4.6 percent in 2011 due to property value decline.

A housing market assessment for Middletown's downtown found that sales of single-family housing peaked in 2005 and for condominium housing in 2006. Similarly, the median price of single-family homes peaked at $247,500 in 2007. According to the report, "Average unit pricing in the downtown was typically 15% to 40% lower than indicated citywide, depending on product type. Pricing also declined more precipitously in the downtown over the last few years than elsewhere in the city" (RKG Associates, Inc. 2010, p. 4).

Table 8.1 Main Street property values from 1988 to 2011 and as a percentage of total city property values

Year	Main Street Property Values	% of City	$/Sq. ft.
2011	$113,199,840	3.9	$61.97
2007	$98,794,643	3.4	$60.55
2002	$63,736,300	3.3	$35.90
1998	$48,809,929	3.5	$32.73
1993	$88,299,400	5.2	$49.57
1988	$48,658,436	5.7	$30.10

Source: City of Middletown (2012).

Even so overall property values on Main Street rebounded after an initial decline. Table 8.1 shows that property values on Main Street increased from a low of about $49 million in 1998 to a high of about $113 million in 2011. The price per square foot of downtown property also increased in this time period as did the share of Main Street's contribution to overall city revenues in property taxes. While property on Main Street is only 0.14 percent of the total land area in the city, it accounted for 4 percent of the total property values in Middletown (City of Middletown 2012).

Vacancy Rates

The contraction of economic activity often means fewer businesses will be looking for space either to locate or to expand. This decrease in demand for space means increased vacancy rates in downtown buildings. Downtowns which already had higher vacancy rates because of business migration to the fringe experience even more vacancy rates during recessionary periods.

Holland's downtown development authority reports that in the last four years, new retail space in the city has been slow to lease, but existing retail and office spaces have remained consistently highly occupied. Also, occasional introduction of new housing units in existing buildings leased quickly. However, no new housing construction has taken place in the downtown in several years. The decrease in demand creates a surplus in rental space. Because of lower demand, real estate investors and developers refrain from building new projects until the economy improves.

The City of Middletown also reports high occupancy rates for its downtown office buildings despite the recession. Table 8.2 shows the three classes of office space in the city's downtown. The data shows Class A office space is fully occupied and both Class B and C office space have at least a 90 percent occupancy rate in the downtown. This is testimony that resilient downtowns continue to attract interest from businesses even in a recessionary period.

Table 8.2 Office space by class in downtown Middletown, 2011.

Class	Number of Buildings	Total Space (sq. ft.)	Available Space (sq. ft.)	Availability Rate	Asking Lease Rate Range
A	5	261,707	0	0.0%	$16.50–25.00
B	13	249,593	22,943	9.2%	$12.00–16.50
C	12	97,810	8,895	9.1%	$9.00–14.00

Source: City of Middletown (2011), p. 1.

Disposable Incomes

Disposable incomes shrink in an economic recession. This happens for several reasons. In a recession, there is low demand for labor as firms employ lean approaches to production that require fewer workers. Those workers who are lucky enough to hold their jobs in a recession may face pay cuts. These survival measures by employers affect the disposable incomes of consumers who respond by decreasing expenditures on goods and services. The economic sector most impacted by this decreased demand is the durable goods sector. While households may be able to do without a new washing machine, they still need to eat and clothe themselves. Figures 8.2 and 8.3 display the nominal and real disposable incomes for the United States from 2000 to 2012. The graphs show that real disposable personal income declined since 2008 and flat lined in 2010.

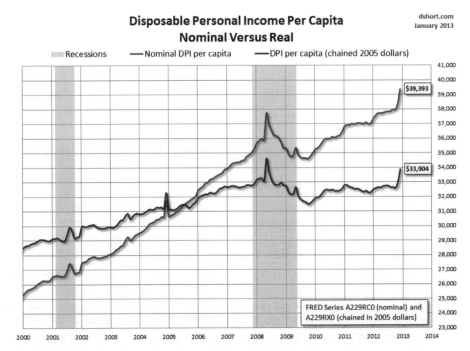

Figure 8.2 Disposable personal income per capita, nominal versus real.

Note
In the original graph the two lines are distinguished by color. "Nominal DPI per capita" is the line that ends above and "DPI per capita (chained 2005 dollars)" is the line that ends below.

Source: Short (2013)

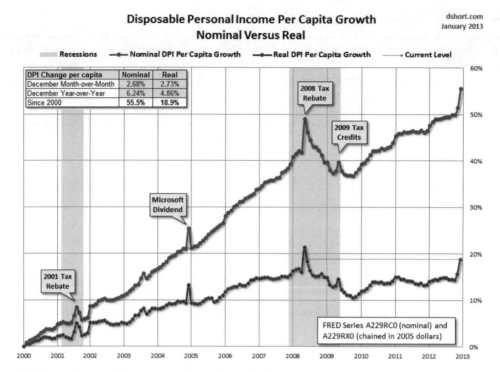

Figure 8.3 Disposable personal income per capita growth, nominal versus real.

Note
In the original graph the two lines are distinguished by color. "Nominal DPI per capita growth" is the top line and "Real DPI per capita growth" is the bottom line.

Source: Short (2013)

Resilient downtowns fared better than other downtowns. A market assessment of downtown Middletown by RKG Associates, Inc., found total consumer expenditure for the downtown market area to be $65.4 million in 2010 with a projected increase to $71.6 million by 2015. Service, hospitality, and electronics are expected to be the major beneficiaries of this increased spending (Milone & MacBroom, Inc. 2011).

Credit Crunch

In a recession, banks tighten their lending policies to decrease risk. They may require higher profit margins from investors as a condition for credit. They may also require large cash reserves of borrowers and charge higher interest rates for credit. These actions put a squeeze on the amount that banks are willing to lend and what businesses are willing to borrow. A tight lending policy by banks affects investment decisions. Property owners who want to refurbish a building for retail, office space, or other uses may postpone borrowing because of these constraints.

Downtown projects in all of the resilient downtowns have been affected by the credit crunch. In Hendersonville, the city's plans to increase the residential population of the downtown through condominium development stalled. Although permits were issued to developers for two condominium projects, developers were unable to proceed with the projects because of the difficulty of obtaining credit from financial institutions.

Prior to the recession, the City of Greenville provided building permits for development of the Peacock Hotel and Spa to be located at East McBee and Spring Street. However, construction of the hotel has been put on hold because the developers were unable to secure financing for the project. In Charlottesville, the Landmark Hotel received a building permit from the city and was under construction when the recession hit and the developer went bankrupt.

Deferred Maintenance and Remodeling

It is not just new projects that become casualties of the recession. Property owners also have difficulty accessing credit for building rehabilitation and remodeling because of high interest rates or stricter lending policies by banks. Many defer maintenance of their properties until better economic times. Several downtown managers reported delays in downtown residential property improvements. Of course, the recession may offer an opportunity for some developers. Shawn Tillman, Senior Urban Planner for the City of Chico, revealed that:

> While budgets have been cut at the city and Downtown Chico Business Association, many private property owners have seen the recession as an opportunity to invest in improvements to their property because construction costs are relatively low. Several important renovations have occurred over the past couple of years in downtown Chico, and other projects are in the pipeline.
> (Personal email to author)

To lighten the burden on property owners and developers, some cities decreased the cost for obtaining building permits. Henderson County, which reviews building permit applications for the City of Hendersonville, decreased the fee for obtaining building permits because of the economic recession. Prior to the recession, commercial permit fees were $7 per $1,000 of project cost, plus a charge of $75. Now the additional $75 is waived.

Sponsorships and Membership Dues

Downtown redevelopment organizations depend on businesses and corporations to sponsor events and programs to decrease the cost of staging these programs. However, in a recession some businesses may decrease the budget that is allocated to advertising and promotion. The resulting effect is that fewer businesses may be able to provide sponsorships for downtown events. Those businesses that continue to support these events may do so at a lower budget, meaning downtown organizations would have to pick up the slack in expenses.

In a recessionary period, downtown organizations are also less able to expand their membership enrollment. Some members may be unable to pay their membership dues or they may not be able to pay their dues on time because of declining revenues and rental incomes. An economic recession may also inhibit the establishment of a business improvement district to fund property upgrades or infrastructure improvements, as cities may have difficulty in getting the support of property owners.

Public Sector Support

Downtown organizations depend on the public sector for some level of support. This usually takes the form of grants, budget appropriations, salary for the downtown manager and other downtown personnel, or tax abatements and subsidies to make downtown projects more feasible. In a period of economic contraction, public sector revenues decrease. At the local level, this happens because property values drop. At the state level, revenues fall because fewer people are shopping, so the state receives less revenue from sales tax. At the federal level, revenues are strained because of reduction in income tax revenue as fewer people are employed. This translates into less revenue for the public sector and its ability to support downtown programs and projects.

California, a state that has been badly hit by the recent recession, offers a good example of how decreased revenues can influence the public sector's support for downtowns. As *The New York Times* reported with respect to the state's budget crisis:

> The departing governor, Arnold Schwarzenegger, has called a special session of the Legislature for Dec. 6 to begin dealing with one part of the problem: a projected $6 billion shortfall in the $126 billion budget passed in October, a record 100 days late. Schwarzenegger's aides said the governor, a Republican who has fought repeatedly with Democrats in pushing through deep spending cuts, will propose another round of reductions to get the state through the end of this fiscal year in June.
>
> (Nagourney 2010)

In January 2011, California's new governor, Jerry Brown, unveiled a budget that called for $12.5 billion in budget cuts, a 10 percent cut in pay for some state employees, and a cut in the state's social service expenditures. In May 2012, the governor announced that the state was faced with a $15.7 billion budget deficit and proposed further cuts in state expenditures. To help rectify the budget deficit, Governor Brown eliminated all redevelopment authorities (RDAs) in the state, a decision that was later upheld in an appeal by the California Supreme Court in December 2011.

Redevelopment authorities were established in California in 1945 to help revitalize blighted urban neighborhoods and to assist in the provision of affordable housing for low-income urban residents. Until their demise in February 2012, nearly 400 RDAs operated in the state with a combined annual budget of about $5 billion. In California, as in many states, the budget for redevelopment authorities comes from tax increment finance revenues:

> Redevelopment agencies gave local governments—usually cities, but sometimes counties—the ability to capture a greater share of property taxes. After an area was declared a redevelopment project area, the share of property taxes that goes to schools and other local agencies was frozen. All of the growth in property taxes from that point until the redevelopment area expired—usually 50 years—went back to the redevelopment agency.
>
> (Taggart 2012)

It is this captured revenue that the governor hopes to unleash to counties and school districts by eliminating the RDAs. By law, in California, public schools must be funded at a guaranteed minimum level. Because of this, the state has had to bridge the gap in school funding that resulted from budget shortfalls of local governments. The end of RDAs has meant that downtown organizations in California have to find new ways to tackle blight and implement other urban projects that were handled by these organizations. In Chico, the city's RDA is credited with several revitalization projects, notably the Chico City Plaza and restoration of the Old Municipal Building. With the elimination of the redevelopment authority, the city now has to re-think how it funds public improvements. In Santa Barbara, Bill Collyer, Executive Director of the city's downtown organization, explains how Santa Barbara is dealing with the elimination of its redevelopment authority:

> Our RDA was to sunset in 2015, so we had begun discussing its non-existence, but we were not prepared to have it immediately cut. As a result, we have had to add some new committees to our organization in order to address the lack of revitalization and identify funding sources to maintain and improve the infrastructure that the RDA created. Among the new committees were a visioning committee and an outreach committee. While both are still in their formative stages, we hope to work with city officials in identifying funding sources for infrastructure maintenance and necessary future revitalization projects. In a nutshell, we are now charged with thinking outside of the box in order to cope with the ramifications of this economically induced loss of funding.
>
> (Personal email to author)

California's example highlights the importance of public sector support for downtown redevelopment programs. When the public sector decreases its support for downtown organizations, new ways have to be found to balance the budgets of these organizations. Making up for this shortfall is even more challenging in a recession.

Weathering an Economic Recession

A recession can seriously disrupt the redevelopment of a downtown. However, in spite of the many obstacles that face small-city downtowns in recessionary periods, an economic downturn does not have to spell doom and gloom for downtowns. As I argued earlier, downtowns, especially the resilient ones, are no longer mono-functional districts. Moreover, many downtowns are now primarily service districts as manufacturing has decentralized to the suburbs and highway locations. An inventory of 206 businesses in downtown Middletown found the following businesses were located in the city's downtown: clothing and clothing accessories, banks, professional scientific and technical services, personal services, food and beverage stores, and food beverages and drinking places (Milone & MacBroom 2011). The list is made up exclusively of professional and consumer service businesses and is representative of the types of businesses that you would find in any small-city downtown.

A number of studies show that the service sector is more immune to recessions than the manufacturing sector, so this bodes well for downtown economies. As Urquhart found out several decades ago:

> The growth of services has been relatively immune to business downturns, with its employment declining in only 1 of 7 postwar recessions. Furthermore, the cyclical fluctuations in the division's employment growth rates are considerably smaller than those of the goods producing sector. The combination of steady growth and relative cyclical insensitivity warrants the conclusion that this division is relatively recession-proof; however, certain qualifying factors are necessary. The rate of growth is reduced during downturns, and some components of this division are more cyclically sensitive than others.
>
> (1981, p. 17)

Figure 8.4 confirms the observations of Urquhart that the service sector has been more resilient to economic downturns than the manufacturing sector. While the manufacturing sector has been much more volatile with huge upswings and downswings over time, the service sector has not experienced such fluctuations. Thus, the impact of a recession on downtowns, which now have a dominance of service sector firms, is expected to be less severe than for other business districts.

Downtowns are part of the national economy and although the recessionary impacts may be far more muted than for other areas of the community, they must take proactive measures to stem the negative consequences of a slow economy. For the most part, during a recession, resilient downtown organizations focus their activities on low-cost but high-impact programming. Here are some of their survival strategies.

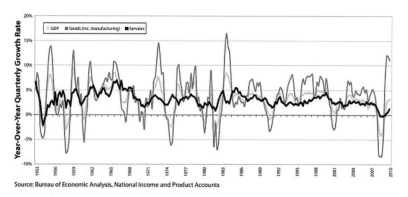

Figure 8.4 Cyclical trends of the service and manufacturing sectors, 1953–2010.

Source: Schnorbus & Watson (2010).

Focus on the Fundamentals

There are three key roles that downtown organizations continue to provide in a recession. These are safety, marketing, and service. The *raison d'être* for many downtown organizations is first and foremost to provide a safe, clean, and friendly environment for their patrons. As we have seen in the case of Wilmington, the downtown organization provides ambassadors who offer walking escorts to customers in the downtown. Downtown Visions also helps businesses refine their marketing strategies. For example, technical assistance is provided to businesses on how to use new media such as Facebook to market their products. The downtown organization also helps businesses to (re)negotiate leases with property owners to ensure that the contracts serve the needs of both tenant and landlord. In doing so, they have helped to decrease business turnover in the downtown.

The City of Middletown employs downtown business district (DBD) guides that help to keep the downtown clean and safe. A staff of two to three part-time guides are hired by the DBD to remove graffiti, maintain the downtown information kiosks, sweep the sidewalks and keep the downtown clean. The guides are also the eyes of the DBD as they interact with downtown shoppers, liaise with police officers in reporting quality-of-life crimes in the downtown such as reporting when street lights are out, and provide directions and assistance to visitors in finding parking.

A recession is also a time for planning and incremental decision making. Phil Meyer of the City of Holland noted that the city's downtown plan was designed not so much to be time sensitive as to be sensitive to triggering activities or development/ redevelopment decisions. Thus, the city continues on a course that is incremental especially in a climate where public and private resources are scarce. As described by Meyer:

> Lack of public and private resources for major capital projects has meant focusing on small details, on making sure we are doing the best we can in terms of maintenance and marketing efforts, on clarifying opportunities, and exploring ideas for future change.
>
> (Personal email to author)

Focusing on these fundamentals places downtowns on a progressive course even in tough economic times. By getting the fundamentals right, downtowns are strategically positioned for growth when the economy improves.

The City of Greenville's Department of Economic Development, which is also the downtown development arm of the city, is charting a similar course by focusing on the fundamentals. The department continues to provide a business-friendly atmosphere for businesses that want to locate in the city, especially in the downtown. According to Mary Douglas Hirsch, Downtown Development Manager for the City of Greenville, when the city receives an inquiry from a prospective business, the economic development staff goes into high gear. They immediately arrange a meeting with the firm to help walk them through the process. If a permit is needed, the code enforcement official provides the business with assistance on how to meet the code. When the business eventually opens in the downtown, the city issues a press release to inform the public of the new business and also holds a ribbon-cutting ceremony, all in an effort to make the business feel welcome. The department also helps new businesses connect with others in the city so that together they can support each other to find solutions to common problems.

Personal Service

Personal attention to the customer is what differentiates downtown merchants from retailers in the mall. In a recessionary period, downtown organizations and merchants accentuate this difference. The relocation of chain stores to the fringe has left many downtowns with family businesses that cater to a niche clientele. Over time, these businesses have developed customer loyalty and a local customer base. Because of these relationships, downtowns may be better situated than suburban retailers to weather an economic recession.

Jennifer Kime of Downtown Mansfield notes that downtown businesses in the city have withstood the recession well, despite the odds. Most of the city's downtown businesses have had their best years during the recession, year after year since 2005. While the outlying suburban areas have seen a decline in retail in the same time frame with restaurants and department stores racing one another to close first, downtown Mansfield has held its own. "It's led to the heightened realization regionally on the importance of protecting our local small business, and there has been a resurgence to support and grow local," Kime said.

Downtown Mansfield, Inc., worked to showcase small businesses and owners by emphasizing their importance in sustaining the community. The downtown organization intended to show the community that these are not faceless businesses, but that they are owned and operated by neighbors. Here is how Kime explains it:

> Our downtown businesses are working together more, supporting one another, growing each other. We are not just a shopping destination; we are a web of community members that grow together. It's one of the real incentives that we offer here. When a business is choosing a location between downtown Mansfield and some random strip mall or faux downtown, if they come here and meet the other business owners it becomes clear to them. While we offer a wealth of unique marketing opportunities, fair prices and unmatched services, our greatest strength is intangible: it's our belief in our community; it's our families that grow up together; it's the legacy of the community; it's history in the making. It's better than a tax incentive any day.
>
> (Personal email to author)

In an interview with the author, Barbara Hughes, owner of Narnia Studios in downtown Hendersonville, put it best: "People spend money where they are happy." On this, the downtown wins the battle over the suburban mall any day!

Build Partnerships

Some of the goals of downtown organizations mesh well with those of other city organizations. Local chambers of commerce want to see a good business environment for their members and seek conditions where local businesses can grow and prosper. Local colleges and universities have community outreach goals and seek opportunities to render service to local organizations. Affiliates of Keep America Beautiful, Inc., seek ways to enhance the quality of public spaces. In hard times and with limited budgets, downtown organizations can link up with these organizations to derive a greater impact from their activities. This is a lesson that resilient downtowns have learned well.

With fewer resources in a recession, downtown organizations can partner with local chambers of commerce for site visits to local businesses. This enables the organizations to stay in touch with individual business owners, show that they care, and most importantly, identify problems that these merchants have and help solve them before they become insurmountable.

The Main Street manager in Nacogdoches worked with the local convention and visitors' bureau to drum up "shop local" campaigns to increase demand for downtown businesses. In Lafayette, Dennis Carson, Director of the city's Economic Development Department, reported that the city built partnerships with other local organizations during the recession to decrease costs. Carson explained, "We try to get more bang for the buck, look for more leverage and broader partnerships" (personal email with author). In Wilmington, the downtown organization worked closely with developers such as the Buccini/Pollin Group, Preservation Initiatives, Pettinaro Enterprises, The Commonwealth Group, and McConnell Johnson to help negotiate purchase and renovation of historic commercial buildings within the business improvement district.

In 2009, the Hendersonville Merchants and Business Association partnered with the local chamber of commerce and other community organizations, namely Downtown Hendersonville, Inc., Flat Rock Merchants Association, Blue Ridge Mall, Fletcher Area Business Association, Highland Square Shopping Center, and Laurel Park Village to implement Shop and Dine. The goal of the program was to get residents to spend money on local businesses rather than outside the county. The merchants raised $10,000 to educate county residents about the advantages of shopping local. Writing about the program Heaslip (2009) noted that "Several business owners reported the Shop and Dine Henderson County campaign was a success, drawing more local traffic into stores for the holiday season and softening the blow of a staggering national economy." Bob Williford, President of the Henderson County Chamber of Commerce, also acknowledged the success of the program: "I think people realize how important it is to support local businesses, who in turn support local charities and nonprofits and provide jobs to our friends and neighbors" (Heaslip 2009).

Market the Quality of the Downtown

In a recession, downtown development organizations may have few, if any, monetary incentives to offer. However, resilient downtowns do not lose the quality environment that they provide for living, work, or play. When carefully built, downtowns can be the place that businesses want to locate, where the creative class wants to live and work, and where people go for their entertainment and civic needs.

While the recession may make it difficult for new projects to proceed, resilient downtowns are still preferred locations because of their existing amenities. Downtown organizations can play up these qualities to their advantage. In Wilmington, although the recession slowed downtown property development and new construction, the downtown continued to be the residential choice for the young and creative class who want to live near the arts, entertainment, and cultural center. Martin Hageman, Executive Director of Downtown Visions, noted that demand exceeds supply for downtown housing units. In his estimation, a thousand more housing units could easily be absorbed by the market even in the recession period. The downtown also continues to be a choice location for businesses. Several new businesses opened in the downtown during the recession. These included service businesses such as Film Bros. Movie Co-Op, Photography Studio on Market, Vultran Creative Marketing Group, Element Design Group, T Mobile Wireless Central, Cool Water Mind & Body Connection, Market Street Chiropractic and Rehabilitation, Virtuous Transitions Hair Boutique, and Salon Studio International. New restaurants and bars locating in the downtown included Shenanigans Irish Pub & Grill, Extreme Pizza, Brew Ha Ha!, The Nomad Jazz Bar, Loma Coffee, Rat Pack Café, Vinoteca 902, 2 Fish Group, and World Café Live. New retail stores were The Bus Stop Corner Store, Paradise Palms, Dimensions & Co. by Ace, The Bike Boutique, NOSO Boutique, and Bloomsberry Flowers, to name but a few.

Resilient downtowns weather the recession well because they are quality places whose demand does not wane in a recessionary period. A good example of this resilience is provided by Charlottesville's downtown pedestrian mall. Business at the mall was not as adversely impacted by the recession as in other business centers in the region because of the quality of place that has been created in the redevelopment of the city's Main Street. As William Lucy, Urban Planning Professor at the University of Virginia and past president of the city's planning commission observed, there were only seven vacancies in the downtown during the recession; three were off the mall. The four that were on the mall were vacant before the recession. The four vacancies occurred because the city resisted the request by a developer to demolish a building that the city considered historic. The stalemate stalled construction and occupancy of the building. Renovation is underway now, as the developer has acquiesced to the city's decision to preserve the building.

As the evidence shows, quality places attract demand. The story of downtown housing shortage is one that was reported in all of the resilient downtowns. Retail businesses also continued to locate in the resilient downtowns despite the recession. This is proof that placemaking is important and that downtowns that pay attention to details in the creation of the built environment may inoculate themselves against business recessions, at least with respect to where people choose to live and where businesses prefer to locate.

Accentuate the Downtown Experience

Downtowns, especially resilient downtowns, have become central social districts that provide an "experience" rather than a single reason for visiting. Historic buildings, retail, museums, dining, and entertainment are all part of the downtown experience. This unique quality of the downtown needs to be emphasized, especially in a recession. Marketing this experience requires little upfront capital outlay but has potential for a huge payoff.

Resilient downtowns are places of socialization and family fun. One may go to the downtown for a yoga class and then take in the museum afterwards. Similarly, a family may go to the farmers' market or art walk and then stop at the corner café for coffee. Free concerts, antique shows, and art walks are all events that increase the social capital of the downtown and help create memories for visitors. An economic recession may provide even more reasons for people to unwind in these districts.

The City of Hendersonville, like many other cities, organizes a concert series. The family-friendly Music on Main Street showcases musicians of all kinds on Friday evenings during the summertime. During these concerts, people can also view a display of classic cars by the Hendersonville Antique Car Club. The city also holds art gallery walks on the first Friday of every month when downtown businesses stay open late. Although sponsorship of these events is low in cost, it can bring significant goodwill to the businesses and companies that underwrite them.

Be a Resource Agent

Downtown organizations can increase their relevance in times of economic recession by being the organization that provides the data and information that is needed for efficient decision making by both the public and the private sectors. For example, developers need data on downtown vacancy rates, city government needs information on property values and business turnover rates, real estate firms need data on rents for downtown buildings and market potential for downtown lofts and condominiums. Downtown organizations can deploy resources to gather, organize, and disseminate this information. In the process, the organization can become an important player in public policy decision making.

For example, Downtown Mansfield, Inc., funded a study to determine whether one-way streets had an effect on property values. The study analyzed property values along 5th Street to Park Avenue and from Diamond to Mulberry and found that the average value of properties on two-way streets was 35 percent higher than those on one-way streets. As a result of the study, Downtown Mansfield, Inc., assisted the city in educating the public about the impacts of one-way streets and in identifying streets that needed to be changed from one-way to two-way.

Lay the Groundwork for Economic Recovery

Finally, downtown development organizations may have difficulty getting shovels in the ground during a recession, but they have to continue to plan for a post-recession recovery. This is what the city of Greenville did during the recession. The city updated the downtown master plan in 2008, which helped the city to identify and prioritize the improvements that needed to be made in the downtown over a ten-year period. The city also prepared a downtown streetscape master plan covering ten miles of streets, providing a template for how to beautify neighborhood and downtown streets. Staff of the city's economic development department also continued to woo potential businesses by attending trade shows such as the one organized by the International Council of Shopping Centers. On such trips, staff members take recruitment packages to share with potential firms and provide demographic and other data that may interest businesses that are considering (re)locating to the city.

Doing Business in a Recession

Thus far we have discussed how a recession affects the redevelopment of a downtown and how downtown organizations have coped. Shouldering an equally significant role in downtown economic revival is the private sector. Downtown shops, restaurants, cafés, and service firms complement the civic, entertainment, and cultural uses that keep downtowns bustling with activity. It is therefore pertinent to understand how the private sector fares in economic tough times. We now turn our attention to the individual downtown businesses for insight.

Downtown Hendersonville provides a useful case study in this respect. The city's downtown is a sixteen-block district that is bookended in the south by the Blue Ridge Performing Arts Center and to the north by the Mast General Store, First Citizens Bank, and Macon Bank. Hendersonville offers small-town warmth and charm where everyone seems to know everyone else and visitors are greeted as though they were long-term residents. The main commercial drag of the downtown is Main Street, a meandering pedestrian-friendly street that was originally designed to be 100 feet wide to enable four horses to turn around with ease. Later, the wide street also aided automobile circulation but posed an impediment to pedestrians. In 1977, Main Street was redesigned to support the goals of returning the downtown to the pedestrian by narrowing it to two lanes, one in each direction. The street is flanked on both sides by angled on-street parking, wide sidewalks, and outdoor seating for restaurants and cafés. Further out to the east and west of Main Street are well-kept historic neighborhoods that contribute to the charm of the downtown. Each of the sixteen blocks has an unbroken street wall of restaurants, cafés, art galleries, professional offices, museums, and upper-floor residential apartments. Even on weekends Main Street bustles with a constant flow of shoppers, diners, and tourists.

Upon arriving in Hendersonville, you may want to check in at the Inn on Church, a bed and breakfast with twenty-one guest rooms. In the morning, you could join other guests for breakfast at the Inn on Church or stroll a block to Main Street where you can have your pick from the many eateries that line the street. For lunch, stop in at Hannah Flanagan's, a popular gathering spot. There you can order a Philly cheeseburger or the Irish-themed bangers and mash—an Irish pork sausage served over fried cabbage and mashed potatoes. To quench your thirst, you can select from more than 100 domestic or imported beers. Alternatively, you may join the lunch crowd at Terra Nova, one of the newest downtown restaurants, and enjoy one of the delicious sandwiches served at the restaurant. If ethnic flavors tickle your taste buds, I recommend the family-owned Lime Leaf Thai Fusion, one of two Asian restaurants that opened in downtown Hendersonville in the midst of the recession. For vegetarians, Never Blue is sure to satisfy your hunger with several selections of

Figure 8.5 Main Street Hendersonville showing outdoor seating, planters, and sidewalk.

epicurean delights. From the lunch menu, you can have your choice of garlic lemon hummus or southern-style boiled peanuts.

If history is your thing, you may want to stop at the Henderson County Heritage Museum or the Mineral and Lapidary Museum located in the basement of the Henderson County Genealogical and Historical Society. You will have a guaranteed lesson on minerals, rocks, and fossil findings. While there, be sure to check out the Fluorescent Display and be informed of how different minerals respond to light.

Model enthusiasts will find Dad's C.A.T.S. a model collector's dream. The store carries models of construction vehicles, tractors, cranes, refuse and die-cast trucks, among others. Your favorite rugs can be restored or hand washed at Carpathian Oriental Rugs. For clothing, you can shop at Mast General Store or at Tribal Trends, which offers ethnic merchandise. Several arts and craft stores satisfy customer needs in paintings, folk, and contemporary art. Wickwire, owned by Shirley Palmer-Hill, is one of many art and craft retail businesses in the downtown and provides original paintings from such renowned painters as Jane Kirkpatrick, Danny Wiley, and Jim Carson. Her website touts a greater mission for Wickwire: "To add to the vibrant, pleasing sights and culture along Main Street."

Downtown Hendersonville also provides a rich selection of professional services. Appraisal, legal, financial, real estate, insurance, accounting, and architectural services are just a few of the firms you will find in the downtown. At the end of the day, you can relax at a salon and spa or catch a meditation class at a yoga studio. And do not forget to drop off your dirty linens for washing at Miller's Laundry.

After this whirlwind tour of the downtown, you may just decide to stay. If you do, you can either rent an upper-floor apartment above one of the downtown businesses, choose a condominium unit downtown, or buy a single-family house in one of the historic neighborhoods of Cold Spring Park, Druid Hills, or Hyman

Heights. You may even be neighbors with North Carolina Senator Tom Apodaca who lives in one of the downtown lofts on Main and 4th Street.

The above narrative paints a vivid picture of downtown Hendersonville's vibrancy. So how do these businesses continue to thrive in spite of the economic recession? I interviewed two downtown business owners, Barbara Hughes, sole proprietor of Narnia Studios, and Richard Crandall, the General Manager of Mast General Store, whose perspectives from our discussions are recounted below.

Narnia Studios, Hendersonville, NC

Barbara Hughes, owner of Narnia Studios (Figure 8.6), is also a lead booster of downtown Hendersonville. For the last seventeen years, Narnia Studios has graced the city's Main Street, providing customers with fresh flowers, candles, plants, wind chimes, fragrances, and an assortment of other products. Narnia Studios also caters for weddings, parties, and other special occasions.

Hughes fell in love with the city following a visit almost two decades ago. She decided to move her business from Florida to downtown Hendersonville in 1994. Hughes was impressed by how the city showed interest in improving conditions in the downtown and how even those with no business interest in the downtown were willing to support improvements in the district. Perhaps because of the size of the community, there is the realization among residents that without a healthy downtown, taxes will have to increase in the rest of the community to make up for revenue shortfall of local government. This collective support for the downtown where everyone chips in to help improve the district impressed Hughes and led her to locate her business in the city. "Things weren't great at the beginning," she says, "but business has since improved."

Figure 8.6 Storefront of Narnia Studios in downtown Hendersonville, NC.

In talking to Hughes, it becomes immediately obvious that she is not just interested in the bottom line of her business but wants to do her part to improve the downtown and the city. It is from this perspective that one can understand why she is taking the lead in promoting the downtown and the city to tourists and the outside world. She has organized numerous downtown promotional events. Among these are "Lover's Lane" on Main where businesses pair up and offer special discounts for people who shop at one venue, the "Gingerbread Cookie Contest" at Christmas time, and the "Mighty Kite Flight". She also initiated "Chalk it Up!," an annual event that brings up to 150 artists to the downtown. The crowds that these events bring to the downtown eat, shop, and get a better feel for the downtown, leading to repeat visits. The boldest of Barbara's local booster programs is her website friendliestcityinamerica.com that proclaims Hendersonville as the friendliest city in America. Hughes hopes the tagline will help bring the city nationwide attention as a friendly place and help draw tourists, investment, and business.

Although I had no appointment to see Hughes when I visited Hendersonville, she welcomed me to her store as though I was an old friend. Her love and affection for the city is infectious. As to how her business is doing in the recession, it almost seemed as if she had to retrieve the answer from memory as she does not think much about the economic conditions. As she put it: "I don't focus on the recession. I know I have to make a living, and therefore I am single-minded about what I need to do." She said that decades of business experience have served her well in all economic conditions. Her previous experience as a business owner in a recession has taught her what pitfalls and mistakes to avoid making. "The way to thrive in a recession is to provide what people need," she said.

Her business has done better every year since she began in downtown Hendersonville over a decade ago. She admits that she has had to adjust to the business cycle to survive and thrive but, "Instead of letting the recession impact me, I altered my business in line with the recession." Here is how she describes her business strategy:

> In this time of a recession I carry mostly American and local-made products. In hard times you appeal to people's sense of patriotism. People feel good when they are buying American-made products. In good times when people don't worry as much about the economy, they buy high-end items such as paintings, but in a recession they can do without such high-end products. Knowing this, I stock up on low-cost items and American products that cost less than $20, and the more I did that the better my business got.

Another reason Narnia Studios is doing well is because of Hughes' devotion to quality service. "The key to a successful business is to know that people spend money where they are happy," she said. That is why she provides her customers with exceptional personal service. This almost guarantees repeat customers who also become good ambassadors for the business:

> We differentiate ourselves from the retail businesses in the malls because we provide personal service to our customers. For example, when an elderly couple come to buy an item but cannot take it to their vehicle, we load it up and

carry it to their trunk for them. Sometimes they tell us to hold their purchase until later in the evening when they can pick it up. They go home and tell personal stories about their buying experience, and this word of mouth wins new customers. When their friends later need a product, we are on the top of their list of places to go.

Perhaps, an additional reason for the success of Narnia Studios is Barbara's adherence to an old-fashioned belief that you should only buy what you can afford. As a result, she is debt-free. She neither has a personal debt nor a business debt. She proudly states that she pays cash for all of what she buys. Both her house and car were purchased outright without credit and she takes pride in owing nothing. This independence has freed her business from the vagaries of the economy. Because she has not borrowed money, interest rate changes and the credit crunch have had little impact on her business.

Mast General Store, Hendersonville, NC

The Mast General Store (Figure 8.7) is considered the anchor of downtown Hendersonville. It is managed by Richard Crandall, a native of New Castle, Indiana. The name of the store is derived from W.W. Mast, a partner with Henry Taylor who opened the store in Valle Crucis, NC, in 1883. In 1913, Mast bought out Henry Taylor and became the sole owner of the business. It was later purchased by John and Faye Cooper in 1980, but the family kept the original name. Mast General Store is a general goods store with seven locations in three states: North Carolina, South Carolina, and Tennessee. The store is employee owned and sells outdoor clothing and gear, books and music, and more than 500 varieties of old-fashioned candy that can be scooped from large display bins in the store.

Figure 8.7 Mast General Store in downtown Hendersonville, NC.

Crandall was a student at Ball State University pursuing a teaching degree when he met his wife at a camp for children with diabetes and physical disabilities in 1958 where they were both counselors. He and his wife came to the mountains on vacation often. Eventually, the couple decided to relocate to the area. Until the demise of Hendersonville Downtown, Inc., Crandall was president of the organization.

The Mast General Store opened in downtown Hendersonville in 1995 and is still the largest retail business in the city's downtown. The store employs thirty-five workers, a quarter of who are part time. Crandall attributes the success of the store to its loyal customers and long-term workers. He hires people who enjoy working with him. Over time, they become like family. Some of them have worked in the store since high school, and after graduating from college, some have come back to work for him. Even in the recession, he has not laid off any workers.

The Mast General Store opened in Hendersonville as the downtown was emptying out, with many retail businesses headed to the malls. It was at this time that the city approached the management of Mast General Store to invite them to consider locating in a building that was for sale in the downtown. The idea and location was in line with the company's philosophy of refurbishing historic buildings for its stores. The company put a lot of money into bringing the building up to code and located its store inside. "Once we started, people found a purpose to shop downtown," Crandall said.

When the recession began, Crandall noted that the store initially had a rough time. However, in the long run, the recession did not impact the store very much. In response to the economic slump, the store had to change its offering to fit customer's shopping habits. This is how he put it:

> We are not so much a luxury store but sell necessities such as camping gear and wear, shoes, and work clothing; these are things that people can't do without. People are not necessarily buying high-end items, but they are still shopping at the store. Our customers are different from those that shop at the chain department stores. Chain store customers want to get as much with their money as they can. Our customers are middle-class shoppers many of whom are middle-aged, retired, or elderly.

So despite the hard times, the Mast Department Store is doing well. There is a constant flow of customers in and out of the store, business remains brisk, and employees stay busy all day long responding to customer needs.

Conclusion

Undoubtedly, a recession can strike a major blow on downtown by reducing funds available for downtown programs. It can also adversely impact the fortunes of businesses that are located in the downtown. As we have seen, resilient downtowns withstand a recession better than other business districts because they are desirable places for business and residence. Nonetheless, retailers have had to adjust their business practices in the recession due to lower disposable incomes of consumers. They do so by increasing the stock of lower-end products and necessities. They also stock up on American and locally made products to appeal to customers' sense of patriotism. Additionally, quality service becomes paramount in a recession.

One notable characteristic of many of the downtown businesses is that they are "other-regarding" and have a larger view of their business than simply making profit. As Barbara Hughes of Hendersonville stated, "I don't feel like something is owed to me, but that I owe something to the community, so I look for ways to give back." It is this symbiotic relationship between community and business that keeps these downtowns thriving.

 Please visit the companion website at http://routledge.com/cw/Burayidi for additional resources.

CHAPTER 9

Downtown Alive!

The resilient downtowns discussed in this book all vary in their physical structure, in the history of their formation, and in the catalytic events that precipitated their decline and eventual renewal. Some of the downtowns such as Wilmington and Santa Fe are as old as the European settlement of the new world. Others like Fort Collins and Chico are relatively new. Many of the downtowns such as Hendersonville, Lafayette, Charlottesville, and Greenville were planned settlements, while some like Holland and Middletown developed organically. Despite these differences, the downtowns all share one commonality: they have all undergone rebirth and are now lively places.

In the previous chapters, I have recounted what I considered to be the contributory factors to the resilience of the downtowns in these cities. In my discussions with civic leaders and downtown managers, I also asked for their viewpoints on why their downtowns are resilient. In this chapter, we will hear from the players of this renewal, those civic and downtown managers who have been in the thick of it all. What do they consider to be the reasons behind the health of their downtowns? After paying audience to them, we will revisit the key factors in downtown resilience and construct a scorecard so other communities can determine the resilience index for their downtowns.

Voices of Resilience

Some of the civic leaders in the communities attribute their downtown resurgence to the public–private partnerships that worked together to resuscitate the downtowns. Dennis Carson of Lafayette, Matt Robenalt of Fort Collins, Patty Fitzpatrick of Holland, and Mary Douglas of Greenville see their downtown's revitalization from this perspective. In Lafayette, government leaders, financiers, and private investors collaborated in the redevelopment of the city's downtown. In Fort Collins, there was the realization from the public and private sectors that the whole was greater than the sum of the individual actors. Hence, the public and private sectors joined forces to maximize the outcome of their actions. In Holland, an understanding among civic leaders that the downtown reflected on the entire community brought people together to restore its image. In Greenville, there is a strong relationship between the various downtown actors. As the initial catalytic projects they collaborated on succeeded, this led to further collaboration between the public and private sectors on other projects. Here are the reasons for the downtowns' successes in their own voices:

We have the confidence of local government leaders, the financial institutions, and private investors. All three are critical to having a good healthy downtown, and all have worked together for a number of years to make the downtown healthy.

(Dennis Carson, Director, Economic Development Department,
City of Lafayette)

Fort Collins has a resilient downtown because public and private interests learned they are more successful working together to achieve strong "community benefit" than they are making decisions that only benefit an individual interest.

(Matt Robenalt, Executive Director, Downtown Development Authority,
City of Fort Collins)

Holland has a resilient downtown because we have always been aware that downtown symbolizes the community's character and vision. Downtown represents the community's uniqueness, rich heritage, and evolving diversity. For decades we have worked toward securing comprehensive public-private partnerships, historic preservation in the context of economic development, and strove towards innovative, creative ways to plan for downtown's development.

(Patty Fitzpatrick, Downtown Manager, City of Holland)

Downtown Wilmington is resilient because of the many partnerships we've developed with the public, private and non-profit sectors. As a small community we build relationships and get to know each other well.

(Martin Hageman, Executive Director,
Wilmington Downtown Visions)

Greenville has a resilient downtown because of the public and private sectors working together. The history of strong public–private partnerships is evident throughout downtown Greenville with numerous projects such as the Hyatt Regency/Greenville Commons, the Peace Center for the Performing Arts, the BI-LO Center, Falls Park, RiverPlace, Fluor Field, and many more. In Greenville, both sectors rely on each other to make things happen, and it is this collaborative spirit which enables downtown Greenville to grow and prosper.

(Mary Douglas Hirsch, Downtown Development Manager,
City of Greenville)

Jim Tolbert, Meredith Williams, and Jennifer Kime each attribute their downtown's renewal to the variety of uses that attract people to the downtown and the growing number of people that are choosing to live downtown. Because downtowns provide one-stop shopping, they appeal to customers' need for convenience.

Charlottesville has a resilient downtown because of the dynamic mix of businesses and entertainment and the growing resident population.

(Jim Tolbert, Director, Neighborhood Development Services,
City of Charlottesville)

Chico has a resilient downtown because it is regularly visited by residents of Chico and the surrounding communities, as well as students from the adjacent California State University, Chico, and nearby Chico High School campuses who enjoy its unique shopping opportunities, use services at City Hall and the Post Office, seek entertainment at restaurants, bars, and theaters, and socialize in the central plaza, at the farmers' markets, and other outdoor events.

(Meredith Williams, Associate Planner and lead author of the Downtown Element in the City of Chico 2030 General Plan)

Downtown Mansfield is strongly supported by the community. There is a strong sense of importance in our downtown. The community both reinvests in our downtown and spends time in recreational activities downtown. One of the things that differentiates our downtown from other downtowns our size is that we've remained an active working downtown throughout. In many communities our size, there is a period of time when banking, legal, and government offices moved out of their downtown. That has not happened in our community.

(Jennifer Kime, Director of Downtown Mansfield, Inc.)

For Sarah O'Brien and Bill Collyer, downtown Nacogdoches and Santa Barbara are special places with unique features and characteristics. In Nacogdoches, it is the careful preservation of the city's heritage resources that make the downtown a special attraction to residents and visitors. In Santa Barbara, it is both the heritage resources and the rich arts and cultural setting of the city's downtown that have contributed to its renewal.

Nacogdoches has a resilient downtown because we have embraced our historic past while preparing for our future.

(Sarah E. O'Brien, Main Street Manager, City of Nacogdoches)

Downtown Santa Barbara is resilient because our downtown organization is a strong entity, and our relationship with the county cultural arts commission helps us to tell our story. Our downtown is rich in culture and history, and the players involved are motivated to enhance and maintain the aspects of our downtown that are important to keeping the downtown vital.

(Bill Collyer, Executive Director, Santa Barbara Downtown Organization)

Persistent long-term investment in the downtown is also required for success, suggesting there are no quick fixes to downtown redevelopment. Staying the course and not veering from the long-term vision even in the midst of difficulties and government turnovers is crucial. This is the one attribute that Craig Tebon credits for downtown Ripon's success:

Downtown Ripon is resilient because we don't give up. I don't believe in winning the war. There are several battles that must be won and these successes add up to make a difference. Incremental processes are most important to downtown success.

(Craig Tebon, Executive Director, Ripon Main Street, Inc.)

Paul Casey and W. Ferguson also attribute the success of their downtowns to location and the work that civic leaders put into making the downtowns preferred "third places" for residents.

> Downtown Hendersonville is resilient because the community has made consistent and significant investments in the downtown infrastructure and the business environment. Since downtown revitalization began in the 1970s there has been a repeated focus on Main Street. We have also been beneficiaries of luck. We are in a highly attractive geographic location that is easily accessible to large population centers. A lot of our downtown resilience has been due to the rising interest in tourism and Hendersonville was strategically well placed to benefit from this trend.
>
> (W. Bowman Ferguson, City Manager, City of Hendersonville, NC)

> We were successful to a large extent because of our location. It helps to have a good climate and a picturesque setting that attracts people, but in the long run you have to have a vision and stick to the vision. Our downtown success story took us forty years in the making. You can't change your long-term vision from one year to the other. Also communities need to be creative and innovative with parking as we have in Santa Barbara, but shouldn't make it central to the redevelopment of the downtown. Our mantra has been "Bodies on State Street," meaning we do everything we can to put people on State Street, whether this means opening businesses late to cater to customers or holding a weekly farmers market downtown. We also know the arts bring people downtown, so we hold a First Thursday gallery walk downtown and have revitalized Granada Theater so people come downtown for their entertainment needs.
>
> (Paul Casey, Assistant City Administrator, City of Santa Barbara)

From these voices we can summarize the requirements for downtown resilience as follows: a sustained vision and commitment from city leadership to see it through, collaboration between the public and private sector organizations, utilization of historic preservation as a tool for economic development, and the creation of a multifunctional downtown.

Downtown Resilience

The rationale given by the civic leaders and downtown managers for the resilience of their downtowns supports the discussions in the previous chapters. Resilience is the ability of an organization to bounce back from an incapacitating shock. This disrupts the systemic structure of the organization by changing its normal functioning and operation. Consequently, the organization must restructure itself and adapt to the change in order to survive. Hill et al. (2008, p. 3) define resilience as the "extent to which a regional or national economy that has experienced an external shock is able to return to its previous level and/or growth rate of output, employment or population." Organizations that make successful adaptations thrive. Those that fail to adapt to the new circumstances are likely to face continuous decline. Such is the case with downtowns.

Since the beginning of the twentieth century, downtown economies have been disrupted by economic recessions, deindustrialization, globalization, and decentralization of economic activity to the suburbs. Resilient downtowns successfully recovered from these extenuating circumstances and became even better prepared for future disruptions. In other words, they have been adaptable to change. Dawley et al. (2010) made the distinction between "adaptation" and "adaptability." When a downtown adapts to a disturbance, it is able to snap back to its formal condition and trend of growth. Adaptability, however, positions a downtown to take a new and different trajectory and to develop the capacity to deal with future uncertainties.

Downtowns that are resilient are dynamic, multifunctional districts with retail, residential, entertainment, civic, and cultural activities. They are not dependent on a single economic activity such as retail, but several economic activities. Diversified economies are more "adaptable because they act as a 'shock absorber,' dissipating negative effects across an array of economic activities and places rather than concentrating and reinforcing them, and so helping to speed up any recovery therein" (Dawley et al. 2010, p. 657). To be adaptable downtowns must develop the capacity to respond to change.

Table 9.1 summarizes the qualities of resilient downtowns and provides a scorecard for determining downtown resilience. The scorecard provides a self-assessment tool for cities so they can determine their downtown resilience index. The resilience index is a measure of a community's ability to regain its normal functioning and growth trend after an exogenous disturbance. The index is on a scale of 0 to 10, with 0 being least resilient and 10 being most resilient. The indicators in Table 9.1 are also meant to generate discussions in communities, especially because some of the measures of resilience are subjective, requiring deliberation among residents in deciding whether their downtowns meet the requirement or not. The discussions will also help communities identify the particular areas that they may be deficient in and how they can take corrective measures to ameliorate them.

To determine the resilience of a downtown, a community must tally its score on the ten items to obtain its resilience index. A score of seven and above will rank a downtown as high resilient. A score of four to six will rank a downtown as moderately resilient. A score of less than four indicates that the downtown has poor resilience. The factors that comprise the resilience index are elaborated below.

Qualities of Resilient Downtowns

Table 9.1 lists ten qualities that are required of a resilient downtown. The factors can be categorized into three groups: i) the traditional Main Street redevelopment approach; ii) the expanded and "en-RICHED" approach to downtown revitalization that is advocated in this book; and iii) the institutional framework for implementation of downtown redevelopment strategies.

Table 9.1 Downtown resilience scorecard

	Factor		Score = 1	Score = 0
The traditional Main Street approach	Retail development		About 8% of all retail businesses in the city are located in the downtown.	Less than 8% of all retail businesses in the city are located in the downtown.
Expanded and "en-RICHED" downtown redevelopment strategy	Residential population (R)		At least 5% of the city's population is resident in the downtown.	Less than 5% of the city's population is resident in the downtown.
	Immigrants (I)		Civic leaders in the community welcome diversity and immigrants. As evidence, at least 2% of the city's population is foreign-born.	Civic leaders in the community are not welcoming of diversity and immigrants. As evidence less than 2% of the city's population is foreign-born.
	Civic and cultural facilities (C)		More than half of all civic and cultural facilities in the city are located in the downtown and near downtown neighborhoods.	Less than half of all civic and cultural facilities in the city are located in the downtown and near downtown neighborhoods.
	Designated historic/heritage property (HE)		At least one-tenth of the designated historic property on the National Register of Historic Places is located in the downtown.	Less than one-tenth of the designated historic property on the National Register of Historic Places is located in the downtown.
	Design (D)	Design guidelines	City has design guidelines for downtown.	City has no design guidelines for downtown.
		Pedestrian friendliness	Design of downtown makes it easy for pedestrians to get around.	Difficult for pedestrians to get around the downtown.
		Downtown gathering place	Community has a public gathering place that is highly patronized.	No gathering place in the downtown or the gathering place is not well patronized.
Institutional framework for implementation of downtown programs	Civic leadership		Strong support for downtown redevelopment by civic leaders.	Support for downtown redevelopment is ambivalent with no declaratory support for downtown redevelopment.
	Downtown Development Authority		The city has a downtown Development Authority/ Organization.	City does not have a Downtown Development Authority/Organization.

The Traditional Main Street Approach

The focus of the traditional Main Street redevelopment approach is retail promotion. Retail is important to the health of a downtown. That is why the goal of the National Main Street's four-point strategy has been the commercial revitalization of Main

Street. Cities must continue to pursue this strategy to ensure that retail activity remains a vital part of a revitalized downtown. Four approaches have typically been used to promote retail. These are i) business attraction, ii) business retention, iii) business expansion, and iv) business incubation strategies. Each city will differ on which of the strategies or combination of strategies to pursue. Economic conditions may influence the choice of strategy. In an economic recession, it is more difficult to pursue the business attraction strategy as cities have fewer resources to provide (re)location incentives to firms. Decreased consumer demand also means existing businesses may have difficulty expanding. Therefore, policies and programs to retain existing businesses in the downtown and perhaps support the incubation of new retail outlets may be the logical option.

Table 9.2 shows the number of businesses that are located in the case-study cities and in their downtowns. All of the cities have a healthy number of businesses in their downtowns, ranging from fifty in Nacogdoches to almost 1,250 in Santa Barbara. Proportionally, 40 percent of all businesses in Greenville are located in the downtown; in Chico it is 22 percent; and in Nacogdoches, it is 17 percent. Wilmington has the lowest percentage of businesses that are located in the city's downtown, followed by Hendersonville and Holland. The average for all cities is 8 percent. Thus, cities that want to maintain a vital retail sector in their downtowns should aim at having at least 8 percent of their retail activity in the downtown.

Table 9.2 Number and percentage of businesses in each city that are located in the downtown

Community	Number of Businesses in Community	Number of Businesses in Downtown	Percentage of Businesses in Downtown
Middletown, CT	3,794	221	5.8%
Wilmington, DE	22,364	341	1.5%
Greenville, SC	3,000	1,200	40.0%
Hendersonville, NC	5,095	197	3.9%
Charlottesville, VA	3,000	250	8.3%
Mansfield, OH	5,672	600	10.6%
Ripon, WI	394	125	31.7%
Holland, MI	6,113	250	4.1%
Lafayette, IN	3,500	500	14.3%
Fort Collins, CO	16,261	1,000	6.1%
Santa Barbara, CA	5,000	1,249	24.9%
Chico, CA	2,050	450	21.9%
Nacogdoches, TX	290	50	17.2%
Santa Fe, NM	5,000	350–450	8.0%
All Cities	**81,533**	**6,833**	**8.3%**

Source: Data obtained from a survey of downtown managers of resilient downtowns by author.

Expanded and "en-RICHED" downtown redevelopment strategy

In addition to retail, an expanded downtown redevelopment approach would utilize the "en-RICHED" approach to downtown revitalization. This strategy aims at increasing the residential population of the downtown (R), attracting recent immigrants to downtown and near downtown neighborhoods (I), retaining and increasing the traditional role of the downtown as the city's civic and cultural center (C), using historic preservation and heritage tourism to boost the economy of the downtown (HE), and enhancing quality of place in the downtown through innovative placemaking and design (D). This "en-RICHED" approach is explained next.

Increasing Downtown Residential Population (R)

It is important that communities have a visible residential population in their downtowns as this ensures a lively downtown and provides the customer base for downtown retail. The housing that is provided downtown should meet the needs of the different demographic segments that are attracted to downtown living including empty nesters, single professionals, and co-habiting couples. Greenville's downtown, for example, is capturing only 10 percent of the demand for urban living so the city's downtown strategic plan identified the problem and outlined the response as follows:

> Over the next ten years, the potential exists for approximately 1,400 residential units in downtown. The cost of downtown land, new construction and parking may require joint public/private investment to achieve a diverse mix of residential products in downtown. Creating housing affordable to households earning $35,000 to $75,000 may be difficult in the downtown setting, yet these residents (many of which are young) are a vital ingredient to a vibrant downtown. Price write-downs, public sector ownership of key sites, public parking development and other incentives may need to be considered. Without a significant downtown population, downtown runs the risk of simply being a culture and employment center, which will also further limit its retail potential.
> (Sasaki Associates, Inc. 2008, p. 19)

Each city will have to examine the existing and potential demand for downtown residential housing in deciding the types of housing to provide and how to meet this demand. Table 9.3 shows the number of housing units that are located in the resilient downtowns. Hendersonville (15.9%), Holland (15.5%), and Nacogdoches (27.8%) have the highest proportion of housing units in their downtowns. Correspondingly, these cities also have the highest percentage of downtown residents. By contrast, Santa Fe (0.9%), Lafayette (1.7%), and Ripon (1.9%) have the lowest percentage of housing units and the lowest percentage of residential population in their downtowns. On average, 5 percent of housing units and 4.6 percent of the population in these cities reside in the downtown (see Tables 9.3 and 9.4).

Cities that want to cultivate a strong residential population in their downtowns

Table 9.3 Proportion of housing units in a city that are located in the downtown, 2010

City	Housing Units in City	Housing Units in the Downtown	Percentage of Housing Units in the Downtown
Middletown, CT	21,223	872	4.1%
Wilmington, DE	32,820	1,057	3.2%
Greenville, SC	29,418	840	2.9%
Hendersonville, NC	7,744	1,232	15.9%
Charlottesville, VA	19,189	1,623	8.5%
Mansfield, OH	22,022	1,285	5.8%
Ripon, WI	3,306	220	6.7%
Holland, MI	13,212	2,054	15.5%
Lafayette, IN	31,260	542	1.7%
Fort Collins, CO	60,503	1,550	2.6%
Santa Barbara, CA	37,820	1,746	4.6%
Chico, CA	37,050	2,190	5.9%
Nacogdoches, TX	13,635	3,796	27.8%
Santa Fe, NM	37,200	339	0.9%
All Cities	**26,172**	**1,305**	**5.0%**

Source: U.S. Census: General Housing Characteristics, Summary File 1, 2010 Demographic Profile Data. American FactFinder. United States Census Bureau.

Table 9.4 Downtown Residential Population 2010

City	2010 Population		
	City Population	Downtown Population	Percentage of City Population Resident Downtown
Middletown, CT	47,648	1,540	3.2%
Wilmington, DE	70,851	1,365	1.9%
Greenville, SC	58,409	954	1.6%
Hendersonville, NC	13,137	2,240	17.1%
Charlottesville, VA	43,475	2,783	6.4%
Mansfield, OH	47,648	2,428	5.1%
Ripon, WI	7,733	272	3.5%
Holland, MI	33,051	6,958	21.1%
Lafayette, IN	67,140	806	1.2%
Fort Collins, CO	143,986	2,487	1.7%
Santa Barbara, CA	88,410	3,266	3.7%
Chico, CA	86,187	4,801	5.6%
Nacogdoches, TX	32,996	7,352	22.3%
Santa Fe, NM	67,947	336	0.5%
All Cities	**808,618**	**37,588**	**4.6%**

Source: U.S. Census: Profile of General Population and Housing Characteristics, 2010 Demographic Profile Data. American FactFinder. United States Census Bureau.

should aspire to have a minimum of 5 percent of the total city population residing in the downtown. Though not all of the resilient downtowns meet this threshold requirement, the cities that fall below this criterion have acknowledged housing shortage as a problem and are working to ameliorate it. As we have seen in our earlier discussions, both Santa Barbara and Santa Fe have policies and programs to increase the supply of affordable housing in their downtowns. As the Santa Fe plan states:

> A comprehensive policy approach to downtown Santa Fe housing—especially affordable housing—needs to complement and expand upon the city's existing affordable housing initiatives. Santa Fe's newly enacted "Santa Fe Homes" ordinance requires that 30% of all new housing be priced to be affordable to people earning between 50% and 100% of the city's median income.
> (City of Santa Fe 2007, p. 19)

The city outlined several strategies to achieve this goal including a waiver of development fees, and density bonuses. All of the other cities that fall below this minimum threshold are implementing policies to increase their downtown housing stock and residential population.

Immigrants (I)

In Chapter 4 we saw how important it is for a city to be open and accepting of people of diverse backgrounds. We used the foreign-born population as a proxy for measuring a community's openness. This factor is important to downtown resilience because many, if not most, new immigrants to a city reside in the downtown or near downtown neighborhoods, injecting new life into these places. The size of the foreign-born population in the cities ranged from a low of 2 percent in Mansfield to a high of 25 percent in Santa Barbara. Because of the different locational characteristics of cities, we will use the lowest band of 2 percent as the minimum proportion of foreign residents that cities pursuing a policy of openness and diversity should aspire toward.

New immigrants provide one way for cities to boost their downtown and near downtown residential population. While downtown housing in communities that have been successful in revitalizing their downtowns may be out of reach for new immigrants, cities that are starting a program of downtown revitalization will likely have neighborhoods in or near the downtown where housing costs are relatively cheap compared to the outer areas. Such neighborhoods can provide the housing that new immigrants need. The North End neighborhood in Middletown, CT, is archetypal of a near downtown neighborhood that has attracted immigrants for centuries. The city's urban renewal plan acknowledged this role of the neighborhood:

> Within the larger history of Middletown, the North End has played a special role. It is, as it always has been, an active living area within the city center, characterized by a lively mixture of people and uses. The North End has often served as a reception area and first neighborhood for groups of new arrivals.
> (City of Middletown Redevelopment Agency 1992, p. 11)

The North End was one of the first neighborhoods in Middletown to be settled by Puritans from the Massachusetts Bay colony in 1650. The first settlers built a meeting house at the north end of present-day Main Street, thus giving the neighborhood its name. Since then the North End has been the neighborhood of choice for new immigrants to the city starting with the Irish in the nineteenth century, so that by 1880 about a third of North End residents were Irish. As new immigrants gain a foothold and are assimilated into the community, they move out to better neighborhoods only to be replaced by a successive wave of newer immigrants. Thus, the Irish in the North End were replaced by immigrants from Europe. Prominent among these were Italians, Poles, Germans, Jews, and Swedes. Today, the North End continues to attract new immigrants to the city and is a multicultural and multiethnic hub in the City of Middletown. Though recent immigrants to the city are of non-European origins, the story is the same.

Table 9.5 shows the population of the North End grew from 1,304 residents to 1,540 residents between 2000 and 2010 and that the population in the neighborhood became more diverse in the decade. For example, whereas 9.9 percent of Middletown's population was foreign-born in 2010, as many as a fifth of North End residents were so classified. There were also more minorities in the North End neighborhood than for the city as a whole. A quarter of the North End neighborhood was African American, and almost the same proportion was Hispanic. Asians made up 4 percent of the neighborhood population in 2010. Also, while the population of Whites was declining in the neighborhood between 2000 and 2010, the proportion of minorities grew.

Another characteristic of the North End is that unlike south Main Street, the North End was not affected by the urban renewal program that destroyed many historic landmarks in the city. Thus, many of the neighborhoods historic commercial, residential, and religious buildings remain. Redevelopment of the neighborhood seeks to preserve these historic elements. Because of its diverse population, there are an assortment of ethnic restaurants and businesses in the North End including Chinese, Tibetan, Vietnamese, Italian, and Mexican restaurants. As Larry McHugh, president of the Middlesex County Chamber of commerce remarked with respect

Table 9.5 Demographics of North End Residents and City of Middletown, CT. 2000–2010

	North End (Census Tract 5416)		City of Middletown, CT	
	2000	2010	2000	2010
Population	1,304	1,540	43,167	47,648
White	61.7%	57.3%	80.0%	75.8%
Hispanic	13.6%	23.4%	5.3%	8.3%
Black	22.9%	25.0%	12.3%	12.8%
Asian	4.2%	4.1%	2.7%	4.9%
Percentage foreign-born	7.8%	22%	9.6%	9.9%

Source: U.S. Census: Profile of General Population and Housing Characteristics, 2000 and 2010 Demographic Profile Data. American FactFinder. United States Census Bureau.

to the neighborhood, "When you go into our restaurants, they are all destinations. People come from all over to go there. That also generates excitement for people about what's going on in Middletown" (Beals 2012).

Of course, the quality of housing and neighborhood amenities in the North End is not as good as it is in other parts of the city, accounting for the lower cost of housing and its attraction to immigrants. However, the North End Action Team (NEAT), a grass-roots resident-led organization is working to improve conditions for residents. NEAT meets once a month to discuss concerns of the neighborhood and take action to remediate neighborhood problems. Mayor Daniel Drew even proclaimed April 21, 2012 as North End Pride Day in honor of the work that the organization is doing to enhance the quality of life for residents in the North End. The diversity of population and activities in the North End contributes to the vitality of Middletown's downtown and is one way that new immigrants enhance the dynamics and cultural tapestry of a community.

Civic and Cultural Uses (C)

At the time of settlement, most if not all civic and cultural facilities were centrally located in the downtown. These facilities included courthouses, museums, performing arts centers, post offices, police stations, county and municipal government buildings, and libraries. This is for good reason. As the City of Fort Collins explains:

> A concentration of administrative offices, finance, insurance, education, business and professional services should continue to have a strong presence in downtown. Taken together, these establishments create opportunities for employment. These employees in turn provide an important pool of customers for Downtown services, shops and restaurants.
>
> (City of Fort Collins 1989, p. 2)

Civic and cultural facilities bring people to the downtown. As people come to places of entertainment or to take care of their civic needs, they patronize downtown businesses and provide the customer base for downtown retailers. Over the last two decades or so, some communities have seen a decentralization of these amenities to locations outside of the downtown. In many cases, this is because of the need for expansive land, which may be difficult to assemble in the downtown. In other cases, it is because of the need to update the buildings to meet safety and ADA requirements. Regardless, the relocation of these buildings outside the downtown can inflict hardship on downtown retail businesses as fewer people now have reason to go to the downtown.

When a city has fewer than half of its civic and cultural facilities in the downtown or near downtown neighborhoods, it has likely reached a tipping point. Local, county, state, and federal governments often have control over the location of these facilities. When these facilities are relocated outside of the downtown, it sends a negative signal to the private sector; it is an indication that the public sector has given up on the downtown. This can result in an exodus of private firms and businesses out of the downtown.

Historic Preservation and Heritage Tourism (HE)

Historic preservation is an important element of downtown resilience for several reasons. The preservation of historic property helps to define the character of the downtown. Second, historic preservation can boost a community's tourism potential. By attracting heritage tourists to the downtown, historic preservation can help boost the daytime population of the downtown. With that said, historic preservation ordinances differ. Some landmarks commissions have a strictly advisory role, while others have final say. In some cities, the decision of commissions can be over-ruled by the planning commission or city council. One study found 41 percent of landmarks commissions need the consent of a property owner before they can designate the property as historic (Robins 2005).

Weak preservation ordinances allow a landmarks commission to only delay the destruction or alteration of a historic property, after which the property owners can proceed as they please. Some commissions have enforcement powers, but their decisions are subject to approval by the planning commission or city council. In 2004, the *Denver Post* reported the case of a historic property in Fort Collins where Dick and Diane Rule owned an early twentieth-century farmhouse with a barn at 4824 S. Lemay Ave. The couple applied to the city for a permit to tear down the structures, but the city's Landmarks Preservation Commission denied them the demolition permit because the property was historic. However, the Fort Collins City Council voted 5–0 to allow the Rules to demolish the property (*Denver Post* 2004).

One of the problems with enforcing historic preservation ordinances is that designated historic properties confer public benefits but impose private costs. Property owners are the ones who have to bear the higher cost of modifications that must meet historic regulatory standards. This often occurs without adequate public subsidy. To address this problem, some communities have established preservation foundations. These foundations enter into contractual agreements with owners of historic property to create preservation easements that decrease the cost to the owners of historic properties. The Historic Santa Fe Foundation is one such example.

The Historic Santa Fe Foundation was established in 1961 to help protect the heritage and culture of the city. The mission of the foundation is "to own, preserve and protect historic properties and resources of Santa Fe and its environs and to provide historic preservation education." The foundation owns eight properties in the city including the James L. Johnson House at 545 Canyon Road, the Garcia House at 524 Alto Road, and the Felipe B. Delgado House at 124 West Palace Avenue. The foundation is credited with saving the Oliver P. Hovey House, built in 1851, from destruction by purchasing and restoring it to its old glory.

One other medium that the Historic Santa Fe Foundation and others like it utilize to protect historic property are historic preservation easements. A preservation easement is defined by the Historic Santa Fe Foundation as: "a legally enforceable, voluntary agreement between the owner of an historic property and the Historic Santa Fe Foundation (HSFF) under which the owner retains possession of the property while the HSFF assumes responsibility for its preservation." Owners of historic preservation easements qualify for federal income tax deductions under Internal Revenue Code 170(h), as well as estate and property tax breaks from county government. Once the easement is established, the owner of such property must first obtain approval from the easement manager before any alteration or addition to the property is made.

Historic preservation ordinances enable a city to work with property owners to educate and prevent alterations that impact the historic character of a building. Coupled with preservation easements and design guidelines, such an ordinance can help protect historic property and establish a strong character for the downtown.

But a strong historic preservation ordinance is meaningless unless a community actually designates historic property for protection. Therefore, going hand in hand with having a historic preservation ordinance is the need to designate the community's heritage resources for protection. The proportion of a community's designated historic property that lies within the downtown or near downtown neighborhoods will establish the degree to which a downtown can benefit from heritage tourism.

As we have seen in Chapter 6, in the fourteen cities with resilient downtowns, an average of one-fifth and a minimum of one-tenth of their historic structures that are on the National Register of Historic Places are in the downtown. By this standard, and given that much of a community's historic buildings were located in or near the downtown, it stands to reason that if more than 90 percent of a city's properties that are on the National Register of Historic Places are outside the downtown, then the city may have already lost much of its heritage through demolition. Cities with a large proportion of their designated historic buildings located in or near downtown stand to benefit greatly from heritage tourism. The concentration of these buildings also helps to establish the unique character of the downtown.

Design (D)

In addition to having strategies for increasing the downtown population, cities must also ensure that a quality downtown is created in the redevelopment of buildings and public places. Three design factors are critical to downtown resilience: i) provision of design guidelines; ii) ensuring that the downtown is pedestrian friendly; and iii) providing a gathering place downtown.

DESIGN GUIDELINES

Design guidelines provide standards and procedures to ensure that new development in the downtown is in line with the community's history, culture, and heritage. The guidelines provide the public sector, property owners, and developers with direction on how to remodel, preserve, or pursue new construction in the downtown. Design guidelines help preserve city landmarks and historic integrity, and identify elements in buildings that need to be maintained or enhanced. They can be used to ensure aesthetically pleasing street facades and to encourage landscaping designs that are desirable for parking lots and parking structures. Design guidelines can also be used to regulate the massing of buildings and the bricking of sidewalks and pedestrian crossings to ensure safety. When design guidelines are closely followed, they ensure safety, livability, and quality improvements to the downtown. In addition to controlling private development, design guidelines can also be used to enrich the public sphere by regulating signage, street furniture, and lighting.

These guidelines are often included as part of a city's zoning and land use control ordinances. In Charlottesville, Jim Tolbert, Director of the city's Neighborhood Development Services, attributes part of the success of the downtown to the rewriting of the city's development code:

> We made a decision in 2000 to take a look at our community and decide what we want to be. So we rewrote the code to reflect what we want and how it can encourage developers to invest in the downtown. Once we rewrote the code and the design guidelines we got out of the way.
>
> (Personal interview with author)

Cities with design guidelines typically appoint a design review board to be responsible for assessing the quality of development applications to determine if they meet the recommended standards before building permits are issued by the city.

PEDESTRIAN FRIENDLINESS

Desirable downtowns are pedestrian friendly. Even when a downtown has all the amenities residents want, people must feel safe navigating the streets before they will visit. Pedestrian-friendly designs have the following features: wide sidewalks, slower traffic speeds, demarcated cross-walks, easy wayfinding, and less emphasis on parking and the automobile.

One impediment to pedestrian navigation of the downtown is one-way streets. In the 1970s, many cities changed their streets from two-way to one-way to aid traffic flow. This has had the effect of encouraging speeds "through the downtown" rather than "to the downtown." The faster traffic also decreased the chance for

Figure 9.1 A sidewalk and street planting in downtown Greenville, showing an example of quality redevelopment streetscape.

drivers to notice street-level activity such as retail stores in the downtown. As the City of Mansfield's downtown strategic redevelopment plan noted, one-way streets in the city "have increased vehicular capacity and reduced congestion in the central business district. At the same time one-way traffic reduces the visibility from vehicles to retail storefronts by half, creating a potentially adverse impact on retail sales" (Mansfield Alliance et al. 2003, p. 31). More importantly, faster speeds decrease the pedestrian experience of the downtown because of safety concerns. In 2001, a study was done by Vollmer Associates for the Hyannis Main Street Business Improvement District in Cape Cod, Massachusetts. The firm studied twenty-two cities that converted their streets from one-way to two-way streets and found that as a result of the change in traffic flow, the number of businesses located in the downtown increased. Furthermore, there was an increase in pedestrian friendliness and an improvement in overall "livability" and "sense of community." The report concluded that:

> The objectives of improving the pedestrian environment were largely achieved by lowering the traffic speeds in the desired areas as well as slightly increased pedestrian clearance times at the intersections. Pedestrian and vehicular collisions and their related costs both showed improvement following the conversion.
>
> (Vollmer Associates 2001, p. 14)

The sidewalk and overall street ambience can also enhance the pedestrian experience of the downtown. For example, heavily used sidewalks improve downtown security. As people walk along the street, they keep an eye on activities in the neighborhood and deter crime. To be utilized, the sidewalks should be wide enough to accommodate pedestrians. A standard minimum width of 5 feet that is wide enough for two people passing each other or for a couple to walk side by side is ideal. In addition to wide sidewalks, the existence of traffic-calming techniques such as canopied trees along the sides of the street, raised pedestrian crossings, or textured crosswalks help make the downtown a more pleasant and enjoyable experience.

PROVISION FOR A COMMUNITY GATHERING PLACE

Downtowns play both symbolic and functional roles. The symbolic role of the downtown is just as important as its functional role. Part of downtown's appeal is that it symbolizes unity and togetherness. Downtown is where the holiday parades and political rallies are held. It is the place where community residents gather in good times to celebrate and rejoice and in bad times to comfort each other. To play this role effectively, the downtown must have a gathering place. Communities without a downtown gathering spot are places without a center. Take the case of Littleton, Colorado, for example. At the time of the Columbine Massacre in 1999 when two teenagers shot and killed several of their classmates, the community needed a place to hold a memorial service for those who were killed. Lacking such a gathering place, residents held the memorial service in the parking lot of the suburban West Bowles Shopping Center. It was the only venue large enough to accommodate Littleton residents for the event. Unfortunately, Littleton is not alone. There are many communities around the country where the shopping mall has assumed the role of the communities' gathering place. But shopping malls lack the qualities of downtowns. They are usually not located at the center of the city, their buildings have no ties to the communities' history, and they are not viewed by residents as having the unifying attributes of the downtown.

Resilient downtowns have a public gathering place. This gathering place may be open or enclosed, but for the gathering place to function well, it must invoke both spontaneous and formal use. It should also be a place where people of all ages, classes, and races feel comfortable to go. It should provide an opportunity for both active and passive engagement and relaxation. If the gathering place is not actively used, it becomes a haven for drug dealers, prostitution, and other social deviance.

At a minimum, three placemaking factors—design guidelines, a community gathering place, and pedestrian maneuverability—are required to ensure a quality downtown. Next, a community must assume responsibility for or create the institutions that will provide stewardship for the downtown vision.

The Institutional Framework

Good stewardship of the downtown vision requires good leadership and a downtown redevelopment agency to administer the long-term execution of the vision. Here is why these are important.

Civic Leadership

For a downtown to adapt and be successful in its redevelopment efforts it must have a long-term vision that is supported by the city's leadership. Civic leadership is particularly important in times of economic disruption to coordinate the response from the public, private, and non-profit sectors. Civic leaders help define the values of a community, its vision, what it cherishes, and establish its budgetary priorities. Civic leadership is thus an important ingredient in the revitalization of a downtown. If civic leaders are supportive of the downtown, they can rally community support to ensure its recovery. Alternatively, if civic leaders in a community do not see the importance of a healthy and strong downtown, then it will not become a part of the public conversation. Look around in your travels. Communities with declining downtowns are those that lack strong civic leaders, which likely reflect the communities' low self-image and a lack of "pride of place."

All of the communities that have resilient downtowns have strong and supportive civic leaders who are conscious of the downtown's image in their community. As a result, they took the leadership role in rallying public support for its renewal. In these communities an identifiable person or group of people took the lead in organizing, funding, and providing the cheerleader role to get the revitalization of the downtown started.

In Santa Barbara, the dominant force behind the preservation movement was Pearl Chase. It was her rallying cry for protecting the city's heritage that led Santa Barbara to adopt a historic preservation ordinance. In Fort Collins, it was George

Mitchell who in 1984 organized the community to oppose the widening of U.S. Route 287 that went through the downtown, and subsequently led efforts to restore Old Town. In Holland, it was Edgar and Elsa Prince, leading industrialists and philanthropists, whose tireless leadership and generosity helped to resuscitate the city's declining downtown. While each of these figures is deserving of entire chapters, let us pause to consider the pivotal role Edgar and Elsa Prince have played in the revitalization of Holland's downtown.

Edgar and his wife Elsa were both born in Holland. Edgar's father, Peter Prince, was the owner of a produce company. Elsa's parents owned Zwiep's Seed Store and Ebelink's Florist. She received a degree in education and sociology from Calvin College in Grand Rapids, MI. Edgar attended the University of Michigan where he earned a degree in engineering in 1953. Thereafter, he was hired as an engineer at Buss Machine Works, a die cast machine manufacturing company, where he rose to become chief engineer. In 1965, he and a few of his colleagues broke away to form their own company. Later known as the Prince Manufacturing Corporation, the firm diversified its production line to include other related automobile products such as metal fabrication, sheet metal forming, finishing, design, metal stamping, as well as powder, liquid, and coating services. By 1990, Prince Corporation employed as many as 1,500 people (The New Netherland Institute 2012).

The rejuvenation of downtown Holland had many starts and fizzles beginning shortly after the fire of 1871 that gutted most of the downtown. In the 1970s, a plan was suggested to turn 8th Street into a pedestrian mall, but concern over the price tag of $3.2 million and the impact that a pedestrian mall would have on the city's Tulip Time celebration made it unworkable. While the proposal never materialized, it resulted in a streetscape improvement project that was funded by the city at a cost of $100,000. In the 1980s there was a proposal to build a 254,000 square foot enclosed shopping mall along 7th Street at an estimated cost of $26 million. The City and the Holland Economic Development Corporation (HEDCOR) both contributed to the purchase of land for the building of the mall, but the idea was opposed by downtown merchants because the construction of the mall would have required demolition of many historical buildings. Thereafter the land was given to Holland Development Corporation, who ultimately sold it to Riverview Development Limited Partnership, now the Riverview Group.

The proposed mall was eventually built outside the downtown and became a competitor to downtown retail businesses. Concern over the state of the downtown and the impact that the new mall would have on downtown led the city to form a Main Street Committee in 1984 for the purpose of revitalizing downtown. It was at this point that Edgar's wife, Elsa, got involved as a member of the Main Street Committee. It was Elsa who got her husband involved in the city's downtown revitalization. Here, Elsa explains the reason for their involvement in the redevelopment of the downtown:

> We were really concerned about the future of downtown and the possibility that boarded-up buildings might someday appear on Eighth Street. There were already signs that downtown was hurting. There seemed to be an eyesore in every block. And when you let things go, you attract problems. I credit

my awareness of what can happen when the core of a city is gone to my sociology classes. Unless you keep the core of the city vital, which historically is downtown, you will have an area that fails. … We felt a sense of urgency to keep and maintain the heritage that was established.

(Lozon 1994, p. 102)

Besides their concern for the state of the downtown as philanthropists, Edgar and Elsa Prince also had a personal interest in the downtown. In order for them to sell Holland to their employees, they also needed to sell the downtown where most civic and cultural activities are located. As said by Phil Meyer, Director of Holland's Department of Community and Neighborhood Services, "Potential employees wanted to go to where the action is, and in the case of Holland that was in the city's downtown. However, the downtown was struggling and on the decline as many retailers were moving out to the suburbs."

The Princes got involved in the downtown redevelopment process in part because they wanted it to provide a welcoming and quality environment for their workers. Among the many projects that Edgar and Elsa helped bring to fruition in downtown Holland were the Tower Clock building, the Evergreen Commons senior center, the renovation of 8th Street, the Holland Museum, Freedom Village retirement home, and the Knickerbocker Theater. Edgar is also credited for underwriting one of Holland's signature projects, the Snowmelt system. He had installed a snowmelt system in the driveway of his house and at the loading dock of Prince Corporation and thought it would be a good idea for the city to have such a system in the downtown. The price tag of the snowmelt system was quite high for the city. At a cost of half a million dollars, property owners and the city found this a bitter pill to swallow. To help finance the project, Edgar contributed half of the project cost. He is quoted as saying:

Having something unique, like Snowmelt, helps to set downtown apart. I was convinced it was a good idea and that Holland should have it. But having a good idea was not enough. You had to get people to buy into it. We couldn't have sold the Snowmelt idea without making the offer of the matching $250,000 donation.

(Lozon 1994, p. 86)

Edgar's legacy continues to live on even after his death. He founded Lumir Group, LLC, as a downtown development arm of the Prince Corporation. The firm continues to be a leader in the restoration and redevelopment of historic property in downtown Holland. Edgar and Elsa also established the Edgar & Elsa Prince Foundation, which continues to fund community development activities in the city. The Riverview Development Limited Partnership was also founded in 1988 with the assistance of Edgar Prince. The major goal of this limited liability partnership is to use private investment to assist in the redevelopment of the downtown. Riverview Group continues to play a major role in the redevelopment of downtown Holland. The Princes' leadership is what helped to turn downtown Holland around. It speaks to the importance of civic leadership in downtown's renewal.

Downtown Development Authority

In addition to supportive leadership, it is important to have an organization whose sole responsibility is to coordinate the various downtown redevelopment agencies and to champion the long-term redevelopment of the downtown. There are four models for this organization. These are: i) the business improvement district (BID) organizational model; ii) a separate BID organization and a downtown development authority (DDA) model; iii) an independent downtown development authority that usurps the functions of the BID organization; and iv) the city agency model of downtown redevelopment. Each of these models has its advantages and disadvantages. Let's consider each and what I regard to be the ideal organizational model.

Business Improvement Districts, or BIDs, are formed by local businesses and property owners for the purpose of improving conditions in their jurisdictions. In this model, property owners and businesses band together and use a self-imposed property tax to finance infrastructure improvements and services. This augments services that the public sector provides in the business district. There are a number of objectives of BIDs, but common to all of them is the need to ensure a safe and clean environment for their patrons. The advantage of BIDs as a downtown development organization is that they are privately run and funded. Members decide on the structure of the organization and the projects on which they spend their funds. The shortcoming of this model is that BIDs typically do not have the personnel and the capacity for long-term planning. Because BIDs are member-driven organizations, most are involved in short-term remedial activities, not long-term programmatic decisions. That indeed was the reason for discontinuing Downtown Hendersonville, Inc., the City of Hendersonville's downtown redevelopment organization, in 2010.

The City Council dissolved the organization and moved its duties in-house. According to City Manager W. Bowman Ferguson, the city wanted the downtown organization to focus its attention on long-range planning issues as opposed to marketing and events. The downtown organization also felt that because the downtown had become so successful, there was no need for long-term planning. The city did not share this view.

In the second model, a DDA is formed to complement the work of the BID if one already exists. In Fort Collins, the city has both a downtown development authority and a BID. Wilmington has Downtown Visions, which also houses the Main Street program and the Wilmington Renaissance Corporation (WRC), a privately funded organization whose goal is to strengthen economic development and enhance investment in the city's downtown. In these cities, two organizations take on the responsibility for downtown redevelopment. In the case of Fort Collins, funding for the DDA comes from a tax increment finance district that was created by the city. The problem with this organizational model is that the funds for the DDA are tenuous and unsustainable in the long term. Most states place a limit on the life of tax increment districts (TID) such that the TID has to be retired after a given length of time. With that being the case, the DDA has no independent sources of funding unless it is part of a local government budget line item.

Some communities such as Holland, Ripon, and Santa Barbara utilize the third organizational model, which combines the functions of both the BID and DDA. Such an organization may have different names such as Main Street, Inc., or simply the Santa Barbara Downtown Organization. In this organizational structure, the DDA benefits from revenue derived from the self-assessed property tax and at the same time can receive funding from the public sector for its operations. This structure enables the organization to employ permanent full-time workers who can engage in both short-term and long-range planning. Because of this arrangement, such an organizational structure is able to respond to both the immediate needs of its members and also undertake long-term planning for the redevelopment of the downtown.

A fourth variant of the downtown development organization is the city agency model. In this case, a city department, typically an economic development or neighborhood development department, takes on responsibility for the redevelopment of the downtown. Downtown redevelopment thus becomes part of a line department. If the DDA is located within city government, then it is subject to the vagaries of local politics. The budget can be increased or decreased, and the entire organization can be dissolved, all depending on the politics of the day. The best downtown organizational arrangement is thus to merge the BID and DDA into an independent organization, which is located outside city government.

Table 9.6 shows the different organizational structure of the downtown redevelopment authority in the fourteen cities. Seven of the cities have an independent downtown redevelopment authority, five have their downtown redevelopment agency embedded within a city government department, and two have both a BID and a downtown redevelopment agency.

Paths to Resilience

As we have seen there is no "one formula fits all" approach to downtown redevelopment. All of the resilient downtowns have taken different paths to revitalize their downtowns. For some, redevelopment efforts were started by the private sector. For others it was initiated by the public sector. For some communities, downtown revitalization efforts were a reaction to an external event, as was the case with the widening of U.S. Route 287 in Fort Collins. For others, such as Santa Barbara, the initial impetus for downtown redevelopment was internal to the community: the need to preserve the city's historic heritage. In Hendersonville, it was a desire to protect declining property values that led to a collective effort to redevelop the downtown.

The lesson for cities contemplating the redevelopment of their downtowns is first to get organized. Downtown redevelopment is a process. It is not a sprint event but a marathon. The cities that are now recording successes in the redevelopment of their downtowns have been at it for decades. The essence of the process is that a community must articulate a vision for the downtown, nurture buy-in from residents for the vision, and then stick to this vision for the long haul.

The vision should include a physical component developed possibly through a charrette process to generate discussion and community support. Next, incremental but measurable steps should be taken in moving the community toward the vision. Tangible outcomes, even if small, help to build public confidence in the

Table 9.6 Downtown redevelopment organizational structures

City	Downtown Development Organization	Type	Year of Formation of Downtown Redevelopment Agency
Middletown, CT	Downtown Business District	Independent DDA	2001
Wilmington, DE	Downtown Visions (BID) Wilmington Renaissance Corporation (WRC)	BID Organization and DDA	1994
Greenville, SC	Economic Development Department of City of Greenville	City Agency	1997 2008
Hendersonville, NC	Main Street/Economic Development	City Agency	1970 1986
Charlottesville, VA	Department of Neighborhood Services	City Agency	1970
Mansfield, OH	Downtown Mansfield Downtown, Inc.	Independent DDA	1984
Ripon, WI	Ripon Main Street, Inc.	Independent DDA	1988
Holland, MI	Main Street/Downtown Development Authority	Independent DDA	1979
Lafayette, IN	Economic Development Department	City Agency	1958
Fort Collins, CO	Downtown Development Authority Downtown Business Association	Independent DDA and BID organization	1981 1982
Santa Barbara, CA	Santa Barbara Downtown Organization	Independent DDA	1967
Chico, CA	Downtown Chico Business Association	Independent DDA	1975
Nacogdoches, TX	Nacogdoches Downtown Business Association	Independent DDA	1983
Santa Fe, NM	Economic Development	City Agency	2008

redevelopment of the downtown. The DDA in Holland did this by taking leadership in replacing a roof on a downtown building that was blown away by a strong wind. Other cities such as Greenville and Ripon started with streetscaping improvements to the downtown. Such a visible transformation of the downtown yields community support for the process and for the downtown organization.

Cities also need to pay attention to detail in the redevelopment of the downtown. Hence, placemaking matters. A quality downtown shapes behavior. Quality begets quality. It motivates private developers to invest in the downtown and attracts residents and other retail businesses. That is why design guidelines are important in helping to influence the nature of redevelopment in the downtown. With a clear vision, tenacity of purpose, and the fortitude of civic leadership, downtowns can rise again to play the central role that they were designed to perform.

 Please visit the companion website at http://routledge.com/cw/Burayidi for additional resources.

Bibliography

1 Bringing Downtowns Back to Life

AARP The Magazine (2003, April 1). The 15 best places to reinvent your life. p. 54.

Associated Press (2012, March 6). Tornado damage may spell the end of tiny towns. *The Star Press*, p. 1B.

Bardstown Mainstreet. (n.d.). Downtown Bardstown vision plan. Retrieved September 10, 2012, http://www.bardstownmainstreet.com.

Birch, E. (2005, November). *Who Lives Downtown*. Living Cities Census Series, The Brookings Institution. Retrieved September 10, 2012, http://www.brookings.edu/metro/pubs/20051115_Birch.pdf.

Bloom, S. (2006). The new pioneers. *Wilson Quarterly*, 30(3), 60–68.

Brandon, E. (2010, February 6). Ways baby boomers will reinvent retirement. *US News*. Retrieved September 10, 2012, http://money.usnews.com/money/retirement/articles/2010/ 02/16/10-ways-baby-boomers-will-reinvent-retirement.

Breen, A. & Rigby, D. (2005). *Intown Living: A different American dream*. Westport, CT: Praeger Publishers.

Brenckle, L. (2009, October 27). In 2000 suit, Linda Thompson claims gas station spill lead to fear of filling up. *Pennlive.com*. Retrieved August 31, 2010, http://www.pennlive.com/midstate/index.ssf/2009/10/in_2000_suit_linda_thompson_cl.html.

Briner, V. (2008, February 9). Feds say current courthouse site is best. *Pennlive.com*. Retrieved August 31, 2010, http://www.pennlive.com/midstate/index.ssf/2008/02/courthouse.html.

Carcamo, C. (2009, January 30). 4th Street's empty shops reflect immigrants' empty wallets. *The Orange County Register*. Retrieved September 10, 2010, http://www2.ocregister.com/articles/street-shop-fourth-2295033-immigrants-business.

Castelli, K. (2007, July 13). Specter questions courthouse site. *Pennlive.com*. Retrieved August 31, 2010, http://blog.pennlive.com/patriotnews/2007/07/247915congress_has_the_final_ authori.html.

Christie, L. (2006, June 15). Cities are hot again: After years of urban flight, Americans are finding the appeal of places like Philadelphia, Nashville and Seattle. *CNNMoney.com*. Retrieved September 1, 2010, http://money.cnn.com/2006/06/15/real_estate /return_to_cities/index.htm.

Cochran, B. (2011, October 27). New poll reveals midlifers will retire close to home: Living near family far outweighs living near other retirees. *Lifegoesstrong.com*. Retrieved September 10, 2012, http://home.lifegoesstrong.com/article/new-poll-reveals-midlifers-will-retire-close-home.

Cromartie, J. & Nelson, P. (2009). Baby boom migration and its impact on rural America. *Economic Research Report* No. (ERR-79) 36 pp, August.

Dane, S. (1997). *Main Street Success Stories*. Washington, DC: National Trust for Historic Preservation.

Davis, L. (2004, February). Finding room for history in the desert: can Tempe afford — or afford not to — keep its oldest houses. *The Next American City*. Retrieved September 9, 2011, http://www.americancity.org.

Ewing, W. (2004). Migrating to recovery: The role of immigration in urban renewal. *Immigration Policy Brief*. Retrieved July 2006, http://www.immigrationpolicy.org/sites/default/files/docs/Brief7%20-%20Migrating%20to%20Recovery.pdf.

Ezell, K. (2006). *Retire Downtown: The lifestyle destination for active retirees and emptynesters*. Kansas City, MO: McMeel Publishing.

Grabow, S., Ryan, B., & Ziegelbauer, R. (2005). The importance of government facilities in downtowns: An analysis of business establishments in Wisconsin's county seats. *Let's Talk Business: Ideas for Expanding Retail and Services in Your Community*, 12 (111).

Graham, R. (2003). Trail tourism: Promotion of the Katy Trail in Missouri. *American Trails*. Retrieved May 2011, http://www.americantrails.org/d/economics/KatyTourism.html.

Herman, R.M. (2010). Will a dying city finally turn to immigrants? *New Geography*. Retrieved September 11, 2012, http://www.newgeography.com/content/001472-will-a-dying-city-finally-turn-immigrants.

Hiller, H. & Pennington, D. (n.d.) Downtowns and small towns. *1000 Friends of Florida*. Retrieved September 11, 2012, http://www.1000friendsofflorida.org/Panhandle/Downtowns&Small%20Towns/D&S.asp.

HyettPalma & Indiana Association of Cities and Towns. (2007). Lafayette downtown action agenda update 2007. Retrieved September 11, 2012, http://www.hyettpalma.com/about-us.php.

Fairlie, R. (2011, March). Kauffman index of entrepreneurial activity 1996–2010. *The Kauffman Foundation*. Retrieved September 11, 2012, http://www.kauffman.org/uploadedFiles/KIEA_2011_report.pdf#page=4.

Langdon, P. (2003). Public buildings keep town centers alive. *Planning Commissioners Journal*, 49, 10–16.

Lee, J. (2010, March 17). Korean immigrants moving to small towns. *The Korean Times*. Retrieved September 11, 2012, http://www.indypressny.org/nycma/voices/416/ news/news_4/.

Luciew, J. (2007, June 20). GSA to unveil shortlist of sites for U.S. courthouse in Harrisburg. *Pennlive.com*. Retrieved August 31, 2010, http://blog.pennlive.com/patriotnews/2007/06/gsa_set_to_unveil_short_list_o.html.

Luciew, J. (2007, June 21). Feds eye 2 sites for courthouse. *Pennlive.com*. Retrieved August 31, 2010, http://blog.pennlive.com/patriotnews/2007/06/down_to_two_officials_look_ at.html.

Luciew, J. (2007, August 22). Reed warns of federal ploy in courthouse battle. *Pennlive.com*. Retrieved August 31, 2010, http://blog.pennlive.com/patriotnews/2007/08/reed_warns_of_ new federal_ploy.html.

Luciew, J. (2007, August 28). City Council joins federal courthouse debate. *Pennlive.com*. Retrieved August 31, 2010, http://blog.pennlive.com/patriotnews/2007/08/city_council_ joins_federal_cou.html.

Luciew, J. (2008, July 24). Reed plans to "wait out" GSA on courthouse site. *Pennlive.com*. Retrieved August 31, 2010, http://www.pennlive.com/midstate/index.ssf/2008/07/reed_plans_to_wait_out_ gsa_on.html.

Luciew, J. (2010, January 7). GSA buildings commissioner views potential federal courthouse sites in Harrisburg, speaks with mayor and judges. *Pennlive.com*. Retrieved August 31, 2010, http://www.pennlive.com/midstate/index.ssf/2010/01/gsa_buildings_commissioner _vie.html.

Lucy, W. (2010). *Foreclosing the Dream: How America's housing crisis is reshaping our cities and suburbs.* Chicago, IL: American Planning Association Planners Press.

Lynch, B.F. (2008, August 19). Downtown revitalization. *Blog from the Office of the City Manager, Lowell, MA.* Retrieved September 11, 2012, http://lowellma. wordpress.com/2008/08/19/downtown-revitalization/.

Mandala Research, LLC. (2009, October 21). New study reveals popularity of U.S. cultural and heritage travel. News Release. Washington, DC.

National Association of Realtors. (2011, April 4). NAR study finds Americans prefer smart growth communities. Retrieved September 11, 2012, http://www. realtor.org/news-releases/2011/04/nar-study-finds-americans-prefer-smart-growth-communities.

Nau, J. (2005, September 21). Marketing your past: the future of tourism. *Governor's 2005 Colorado Tourism Conference, Denver, Colorado.* Retrieved September 11, 2012, http://www.achp.gov/PATOOLKIT/docs/material/speeches/Speech%20 -%20ACHP%20Chair%20Nau,}=%20%20Colorado%20Preservation%20 Institute,%20February%202005.pdf.

Min, Pyong Gap and Kim, C. (2010). Growth of the US Korean population and changes in their settlement patterns, 1990–2008. Research Report No. 2, Research Center for Korean Community, Queens College of the University of New York.

Motoko, R. (2006, March 16). Picket fence to skyline view: Big builders come to town. *The New York Times.* Retrieved September 11, 2012, http://www.nytimes. com/2006 /03/16/garden/16turf.html?pagewanted=all.

Patriot News (2008, February 10). Courthouse plan disappoints residents. Retrieved August 21, 2010, http://www.pennlive.com/midstate/index.ssf/2008/ 02/Courthouse_plan_disappoints_re.html.

Pennlive.com. (2008, May 5). Midtown Harrisburg to get 5-story building. Retrieved August 31, 2010, http://www.pennlive.com/midstate/index.ssf/2008/05/midtown_ to_get_5story_building.html.

Pennlive.com. (2008, May 17). GSA spent $197,000 on PR for Courthouse. Retrieved August 31, 2010, http://www.pennlive.com/midstate/index.ssf/2008/05/_the_ federal_agency_ planning.html.

Pennlive.com. (2009, October 28). Harrisburg mayoral candidate Linda Thompson says questions about her nonprofit group are offlimits. Retrieved August 31, 2010, http://www.pennlive.com/midstate/index.ssf/2009/10/harrisburg_mayoral_ candidate_l_3.html.

Robertson, K. (1999). Can small-city downtowns remain viable? *Journal of the American Planning Association,* 65, 270–283.

Robertson, K. (2001). Downtown development principles for small cities. In Burayidi, M.A. (ed.) *Downtowns: Revitalizing the centers of small urban communities.* New York, NY: Routledge, pp. 9–22.

Robertson, K. (2004). The Main Street Approach to downtown development: An examination of the four-point program. *Journal of the Architectural and Planning Research,* 21, 55–73.

Rypkema, D. (2003). The importance of downtown in the 21st century. *American Planning Association Journal,* 69 (1), 9–15.

Sheffield, R. (2008, August 18). Rite site Harrisburg celebrates its first year. *Pennlive. com.* Retrieved August 31, 2010, http://www.pennlive.com/midstate/index. ssf/2008 /08/right_site_harrisburg_celebrat.html.

Sims, D. (2008, October 17). Strategies for rebuilding Cleveland: What can be learned from other cities. *The Plain Dealer.* Retrieved September 11, 2012, http:// blog.cleveland.com/metro/2008/10/strategies_for_rebuiding_cleve.html.

Slabaugh, S. (2012, August 24). Growing strong: Combined, Ball Brothers and George and Frances Ball foundations rank 8th in value in state. *The Star Press*, p. 1A.

Smith, K. (1999, December 1–5). Ultimate work planning: The high performance organizational tool for the next decade. *Main Street News*.

Thompson, C. (2010, April 26). Midtown Harrisburg site chosen for federal courthouse. *Pennlive.com*. Retrieved September 11, 2012, http://www.pennlive.com/midstate /index.ssf/2010/04/midtown_harrisburg_site_chosen.html.

United States Department of Homeland Security. (2009, August). *2008 Yearbook of Immigration Statistics*. Retrieved September 11, 2012, http://www.dhs.gov/xlibrary/assets/statistics/yearbook/2008/ois_yb_2008.pdf.

2 Historical and Regional Context of the Resilient Downtowns

Bailey, L. & Barber, J. (1998). *Hendersonville and Henderson County: A pictorial history*. Norfolk, VA: Donning Co.

City of Fort Collins. (1991). Fort Collins history and architecture. *Fort Collins Museum & Discovery Science Center and the Poudre River Public Library District*. Retrieved August 31, 2012, http://history.fcgov.com/archive/contexts/introduction.php.

City of Greenville. (2012). History of Greenville. Retrieved September 11, 2012, http://www.greenvillesc.gov/Culture/History/HistoryofGreenville.aspx.

City of Middletown. (n.d.). *Middletown, CT: It's All Here!* Middletown, CT. Retrieved October 11, 2012, http://www.middletownplanning.com/documents/MiddletownGuide08.pdf.

City of Middletown. (1955). *General Plan for the City of Middletown, CT*. Adopted by the Commission on the City Plan, June 16, 1955. Middletown, CT.

City of Santa Barbara. (2000). City of Santa Barbara Chronology. Retrieved August 31, 2012, http://www.santabarbaraca.gov/Resident/Community/Heritage/Chronology.htm.

Dabney, M. (1951). Jefferson's Albemarle: History of Albemarle County, Virginia, 1727–1819. Doctoral dissertation. Norfolk, VA: University of Virginia.

Edney, K. (1997). *Kermit Edney Remembers Where Fitz Left Off*. Alexander, NC: WorldComm.

Ericson. J. (2003). The *Nacogdoches (Texas) story: An informal history*. Berwyn Heights, MD: Heritage Books, Inc.

Huff, A.V. (1995). *Greenville: The history of the city and county in the South Carolina Piedmont*. Columbia, SC: University of South Carolina Press.

Johnson, W. (1988). *Charlottesville 2020: A thirty year vision balancing development and preservation on West Main Street and the mall*. Charlottesville, VA: University of Virginia Press.

Martin, F. & Woods, P.A. (1994). *Greater Lafayette: A pictorial history*. St. Louis, MO: G Bradley Publishing.

Miller, G.H. & Pedrick, S.M. (1964). *A History of Ripon Wisconsin*. Ripon, WI: Ripon Historical Society.

Moon, D. (2003). *Life and Times of a City of Fortune*. Charleston, SC: Arcadia Publishing.

Noble, D.G. (2008). *Santa Fe: History of an ancient city*. Santa Fe, NM: School of American Research Press.

United States Department of the Interior (1976). *National Register of Historic Places Inventory Nomination Form: Downtown Lafayette Historic District, Lafayette, IN*. Retrieved June 10, 2012, http://www.lafayette.in.gov/egov/docs/1234376344_94299.pdf.

Vande Water, R.P. (2002). *Holland: The tulip town (MI)*. Chicago, IL: Arcadia Publishing.

Van Reken, D. (1977). *A Brief History of Holland, Michigan*. Holland, MI: Author.

Warner, E.A. (1990). *A Pictorial History of Middletown (Connecticut)*. Middletown, CT: Great Middletown Preservation.

Whittemore, H. (1884). *History of Middlesex County: The town & city of Middletown*. New York, NY: Beers Co.

Wilmington Renaissance Corporation. (2008). *A Partnership for Progress: Strategic Plan 2009–2012*. Wilmington, DE: Wilmington Renaissance Corporation.

Wilmington Renaissance Corporation. (2012). *Mission and Vision*. Wilmington, DE. Retrieved November 5, 2012, http://www.downtownwilmington.com/mission-vision.

3 Cultivating Downtown Living

Anderson Economic Group. (2008). *Ottawa County, MI Housing Needs Assessment*. Grand Haven, MI: Anderson Economic Group.

Baker, J.M. (2011). The path to a world-class city: A decade of accomplishments. Retrieved November 15, 2011, http://www.wilmingtonde.gov/docs/102/Baker-Administration-Accomplishments.pdf.

Beckmann, B. (2007). Three redevelopments in downtown Holland to create 45 new jobs. *Michigan Economic Development Corporation*. Retrieved September 8, 2012, http://www.michiganadvantage.org/Press-Releases/Three-Redevelopments-in-Downtown-Holland-to-Create-45-New-Jobs/.

City of Greenville. (2012). City of Greenville living: Newcomers. Retrieved February 21, 2012, http://www.greenvillesc.gov/Living/newcomers.aspx.

City of Holland. (2010). The center of centers: Expectations for property redevelopment in the heart of Holland's central neighborhood. Retrieved August 31, 2012, http://www.cityofholland.com/sites/default/files/fileattachments/Center%20of%20Centers.pdf.

City of Santa Barbara. (2009). Municipal code, title 28: The zoning ordinance. Retrieved August 31, 2012, http://www.santabarbaraca.gov/Documents/Municipal_Code/03_Individual_Titles/SBMC_TITLE_28_The_Zoning_Ordinance.pdf.

City of Wilmington. (2009). Market street upstairs fund regulations and forms. Upstairs Funding Review Committee, City of Wilmington Office of Economic Development, Wilmington, DE.

City of Wilmington. (2011). Façade and upstairs improvement program. Retrieved August 31, 2012, http://www.downtownvisions.org/_files/docs/facadeupstairsbklet_small-version.pdf.

City of Wilmington & Mullin & Lonergan Associates, Inc. (2010). FY 2011–2015 five-year strategic plan & FY 2011 annual action plan. Retrieved August 31, 2012, http://www.wilmingtonde.gov/docs/97/FY2011-2015-Consolidated-Plan-DRAFT072210.pdf.

Corley, T. (2009). The best affordable places to retire in the USA. *The Best Places to Retire*. Retrieved August 31, 2012, http://bestplacestoretire.wjsites.com/the-best-affordable-places-to-retire-in-the-us.htm.

Downtown Mansfield, Inc. (2009). *Westinghouse District Development Project*. Mansfield, OH: City of Mansfield, OH.

Downtown Mansfield, Inc. (2010). *Neighborhood Development*. Retrieved May 1, 2012, http://www.downtownmansfield.com/index.php/neighborhood-development.html.

First Avenue, Kinzelman Kline & Gossman, & Mansfield Alliance. (2003). *Mansfield Downtown and the Miracle Mile: Strategic Redevelopment Plan*. Mansfield, OH: Author.

Holland Sentinel. (2009, July 22). Our view—"Mixed-use" could help break our dependence on the automobile. Retrieved November 7, 2012, http://www.hollandsentinel.com/opinions/x639772241/Our-view-Mixed-use-could-help-break-our-dependence-on-the-automobile.

Kloosterman, S. (2009, November 22). 3 dilemmas empty schools present. *The Holland Sentinel*. Retrieved November 7, 2012, http://www.hollandsentinel.com/news/x441551139/3-dilemmas-empty-schools-present.

Lucy, W.H. (2002). *Charlottesville's Downtown Revitalization*. Charlottesville, VA: City of Charlottesville.

Mansfield Alliance. (2003). *The Mansfield Alliance Strategic Redevelopment Plan*. Mansfield, OH: Kinzelman Kline Gossman Design and Planning, Cincinnati, OH.

Manwell, A. (2011, October 9). E.E. Fell School becomes Midtown Village. *The Holland Sentinel*. Retrieved February 14, 2012, http://www.hollandsentinel.com/news/x1581990785/E-E-Fell-School-becomes-Midtown-Village.

Meekins, B.J., Wood, K.F., & Guterbock, T.M. (2000). *City of Charlottesville Neighborhood Planning Needs Survey 2000*. Charlottesville, VA: Center for Survey Research, University of Virginia.

Milone & MacBroom, Inc., & Vanasse Hangen Brustlin, Inc. (2011). Downtown gateway study: Middletown, Connecticut. Retrieved September 17, 2012, http://www.middletownplanning.com/documents/DowntownGatewayFINALREPORT_2011.pdf.

MLive.com. (2007, September 26). Vacant Holland factory targeted for lofts. Retrieved April 4, 2012, http://blog.mlive.com/grpress/2007/09/vacant_holland_factory_targete.html.

Nathans, A. (2011, December 4). Settling down after retirement: Retirees must consider many factors when deciding living situation. *The News Journal*. Retrieved August 31, 2012, http://www.delawareonline.com/article/20111204/BUSINESS/112040323/Settling-down-after-retirement.

National Park Service. (2006). Foord Massey Furniture Company. Retrieved September 12, 2011, http://pdfhost.focus.nps.gov/docs/NRHP/Text/06000145.pdf.

Peck, N. (2011, October 11). Midtown Village opens after 6 years. *MiBiz.com*. Retrieved February 14, 2012, http://www.mibiz.com/news/design-build/19001-midtown-village-opens-after-6-years.html.

Peikert Group Architects, LLP. (2003). Feasibility study of downtown affordable housing project. Retrieved June 2, 2011, http://www.santabarbaraca.gov/NR/rdonlyres/49700A97-5714-41C5-B04C-B1C9A003C155/0/EPS_Study.pdf.

Randolph McKetty & Associates. (2005). Affordable housing opportunity assessment. Retrieved February 12, 2012, http://www.greenvillehousingfund.org/images/uploads/OppAssessment.pdf.

Roland, K. (2006, fall). Leaders look to market-rate housing to foster Wilmington's revitalization. *Cascade: A Community Development Publication*, no. 63. Federal Reserve Bank of Philadelphia, PA.

Saints Andrew and Matthew. (2010). Shipley artist lofts. Retrieved September 12, 2012, http://www.ssam.org/shipleyLofts.htm.

Santa Barbara City Council Subcommittee on Homelessness and Community Relations. (2011). Strategies to address community issues related to homelessness in the City of Santa Barbara. Retrieved September 18, 2012, http://www.santabarbaraca.gov/Documents/Other_Committees/Homelessness_and_Community_Relations/Current/03_Staff_Reports/2009-02-09_Strategies_to_Address_Community_Issues_Related_to_Homelessness_in_the_City_of_Santa_Barbara.pdf.

Sasaki Associates. (2008). Downtown Greenville Master Plan. Retrieved March 26, 2012, http://www.greenvillesc.gov/PlanningZoning/forms/DowntownMasterPlan FinalReport.pdf.

Schmidtchen, K. (2008, May 7). The new expansion of luxury townhomes and condos in Santa Barbara CA. *Santa Barbara Real Estate Voice*. Retrieved December 12, 2011, http://santabarbararealestatevoice.com/2008/05/07/the-new-expansion-of-luxury-townhomes-and-condos-in-santa-barbara-ca/.

Sebens, S. (2011). City wants downtown growth, but are regulations inhibiting it? *StarNewsOnline.com*. Retrieved February 3, 2012, http://www.starnewsonline. com/article/20110326/ARTICLES/110329772.

Teffer, A. (2008, September 7). Lofty goal: Scrapyard Lofts owners hope to have building ready by October. *The Holland Sentinel*. Retrieved April 4, 2012, http://www.hollandsentinel.com/news/x392064346/Lofty-goal-Scrapyard-Lofts-owners-hope-to-have-building-ready-by-October.

The Vincent Group. (2006). Downtown living: Is there demand for additional residential development in the Wilmington CBD? A report prepared for the Wilmington Renaissance Corporation. Wilmington, DE: Author.

Welsh, N. (2009, July 27). Can't get there from here: dueling over density continues; no end in sight. *Santa Barbara Independent*. Retrieved September 12, 2012, http://www.independent.com/news/2009/jul/27/cant-get-there-here/.

Wilmington Renaissance Corporation. (2008). *A Partnership for Progress: Strategic Plan 2009–2012*. Wilmington, DE: Wilmington Renaissance Corporation.

4 Courting New Immigrants

Christina Cultural Arts Center. (2012). About Christina Cultural Arts Center, Wilmington, DE. Retrieved October 24, 2012, http://www.ccacde.org/about_ccac.php.

City of Charlottesville. (2011). City notes. November/December. Charlottesville, VA.

City of Chico. (2009). Public art program. Retrieved September 25, 2012, http://www.chico.ca.us/arts_commission/public_art_program_homepage.asp.

City of Chico. (2011). Diversity action plan 2011. Retrieved September 25, 2012, http://www.ci.chico.ca.us/econdev/documents/FinalDiversityActionPlan.pdf.

City of Greenville. (2003). Vision update: 15 year countdown. Retrieved May 16, 2012, http://www.greenvilleforward.com/Download/Reports/Vision%20 2025%202010-01.pdf.

City of Middletown. (2012a). Affirmative action and equal employment opportunity statement. Office of the Mayor, City of Middletown, CT 06457.

City of Middletown. (2012b). *Downtown Middletown: In the Middle of It All!* Middletown, CT: Trevor Davis Commercial Real Estate.

City of Nacogdoches. (2012). Boards and commissions. Retrieved May 1, 2012, http://www.ci.nacogdoches.tx.us/pdf/boardhandbook.pdf.

Clarke, K. (2012). Workforce management selected as 2012 top business recipient. *DiversityBusiness.com*. Retrieved September 25, 2012, http://www.workforcemgt.com/view_news.php?newsid=8.

Cormier, R. (2010, September 23). Wilmington fringe starts Wednesday: Pulp culture. *Delaware Online: A Gannett Company*. Retrieved May 18, 2012, http://blogs.delawareonline.com/pulpculture/2010/09/23/wilmington-fringe-starts-wednesday/.

ICG Europe Limited. (2009). ICG Europe Limited presented Diversity Award to Willard McRae 10/28/2009. Retrieved May 1, 2012, http://icgeuropeltd.com/aboutus/news_8ba980d649c840759c160cd12de0b2d5.asp.htm.

In Wilmington. (2012). Fringe Wilmington. Retrieved September 25, 2012, http://inwilmington de.com/events/FringeWilmington.

Islamic Society of Central Virginia. (n.d.). Charlottesville Masjid & Islamic Community Center (MICC) Project. *Islamic Society of Central Virginia (ISCV)*. Retrieved September 25, 2012, http://www.charlottesvillemasjid.org/masjid_proj.pdf.

Izyumov, A., Nahata, B., Price, M., Narang, R., & Kirby, A. (2000). Attracting immigrants to an urban area: Literature review and findings. *C.E. & S. Foundation*. Retrieved September 25, 2012, http://www.workforcemgt.com/view_news.php?newsid=8.

Knight Foundation. (2010). Knight soul of the community 2010: Why people love where they live and why it matters. Retrieved April 20, 2012, http://www.soulofthecommunity.org/sites/default/files/OVERALL.pdf.

Lakeshore Ethnic Diversity Alliance. (2011). 2011 Spring Community Institute. Holland, MI. Retrieved October 20, 2012, http://www.ethnicdiversity.org/whatwedo/workshops/2011-spring-community-institute.

Longworth, R.C. (2008). *Caught in the Middle: America's heartland in the age of globalism*. New York, NY: Bloomsbury.

Nixon, A.A. (1994). Diversity plan ratified in Middletown. *Hartford Courant*. Retrieved May 10, 2012, http://articles.courant.com/1994-11-22/news/9411220571_1_school-board-region-s-school-state-funding.

Painter, G. & Yu, Z. (2005). Leaving gateway metropolitan areas: Immigrants and the housing market. Unpublished paper. Lusk Center for Real Estate. Los Angeles, CA: University of Southern California.

Pugliese, M. (2010, May 12). Oddfellows Playhouse celebrates 35 years. *The Middletown Eye*. Retrieved October 19, 2012, http://middletowneyenews.blogspot.com/2010/05/oddfellows-playhouse-celebrates-35.html.

Santa Barbara County Arts Commission. (2009). Project Archive: Arts Commission Accomplishments for 2008–2009. City of Santa Barbara, CA. Retrieved October 24, 2012, http://www.sbartscommission.org/about/projects_archive.html.

Santa Barbara Hispanic Chamber of Commerce. (2009). Welcome to the SBHCC. Retrieved May 5, 2012, http://sbhcc.org/.

Satchell, S. (2008, September 3). New Islamic center coming to Charlottesville. *Newsplex.com*. Retrieved September 25, 2012, http://www.newsplex.com/news/headlines/27832899.html.

Tenia, M. (2009). Charlottesville mayor unveils plan for workplace diversity. *Newsplex.com*. Retrieved May 14, 2012, http://www.newsplex.com/home/headlines/42327307.html.

The Novak Consulting Group. (2012). Hendersonville City Council retreat, February 2012. Retrieved September 25, 2012, http://cityofhendersonville.org/Modules/ShowDocument.aspx?documentid=4934.

West Michigan Chamber Coalition. (2007). Strategies for a culturally competent region. *Diversity Management Strategists, LLC*. Retrieved September 25, 2012, http://diversity.wnj.com/wp-content/uploads/2007/12/strategiesforaculturallycompetentregion110607.pdf.

5 Downtowns as Civic and Cultural Centers

Board of County Commissioners. (2006). Regular meeting of November 28. Santa Fe County, Santa Fe, NM.

Butler, P. (2010, May 21). State's plans for new courthouse will devastate Nevada City, mayor says. *Nevada City Advocate*. Retrieved October 10, 2011, http://www.nevadacityadvocate.com/nevada-city/3448.html.

California Courts. (2008). SB 1407: Landmark law finances unprecedented courthouse rebuilding program. Retrieved November 7, 2011, http://www.courts.ca.gov/2027.htm.

Campos, P. (2008, March 9). Public inpu's built into courthouse plan. *The New Mexican*. Retrieved May 15, 2010, http://www.santafenewmexican.com/Opinion/Many-downtown-buildings-exceed-height-limits.

Cartier, C. (2008). Courthouse debate continues to swirl. *Hollister Free Lance*. Retrieved March 16, 2011, http://www.freelancenews.com/news/239048-courthouse-debate-continues-to-swirl.

Dawson, W. (2009, February 15). Courthouse "Moving Bug" meeting strong resistance in Greene County & Greensboro. *The Herald-Journal Advocate*. Retrieved November 4, 2010, http://www.avoc.info/info/article.php?article=3986.

Ferenchik, M. (1996, July 14). Mansfield rides its carousel to dizzying success. *The Repository*, Canton Ohio.

Foley, N. (2010). Orchestrating experience: The context and design of Charlottesville's pedestrian mall. *Magazine of Albemarle County History*, 68, 111–132.

Futty, J. (1988, December 3). Carousel fate up to council today. *News Journal*, p. 5-A.

Futty, J. (1991, August 25). Government funds opened the door. *Carousel Journal*, p. 3.

Grimm, J.A. (2005, January 20). County looks to relocate court. *The Santa Fe New Mexican*, pp. A-1, B-4.

Grimm, J.A. (2010, December 15). Gas leak running up cost of court complex. *The Santa Fe New Mexican*. A-1. Retrieved March 7, 2011, http://www.santafenewmexican.com/localnews/Gas-leak-running-up-cost-of-court-complex.

Gurr, S. (2010). Future of Habersham Courthouse debated: Many oppose the proposed site outside of downtown Clarksville. *Gainesville Times*. Retrieved March 16, 2010, http://www.gainesvilletimes.com/archives/28964/.

Haywood, P. (2007, September 5). County to roll out courthouse designs. *The Santa Fe New Mexican*. Retrieved March 7, 2011, http://business.highbeam.com/2849/article-1G1-177146065/county-roll-out-courthouse-designs.

Haywood, P. (2010, January 15). Courthouse cleanup: A daunting task; costly downtown pollution cleanup to take years. *The Santa Fe New Mexican*. Retrieved March 7, 2011, http://www.thefreelibrary.com/COURTHOUSE+CLEANUP%3B+A+DAUNTING+TASK%3B+COSTLY+DOWNTOWN+POLLUTION...-a0216635182.

Herman, S.M. (2010). *The Downtown Pedestrian Mall in Charlottesville: A pedestrian mall born out of urban renewal*. Charlottesville, VA: Lawrence Halprin Associates and Harland Bartholomew & Associates.

Hollister Freelance. (2008, March 24). Courthouse debate continues to swirl. Retrieved May 8, 2010, http://www.freelancenews.com/printer/article.asp?c=239048.

Hunt, G. (1996, April 19). Cities benefit from Main Street. *News Journal*, Business 7B.

Hutto, K. (2007). The Charlottesville Pavilion: Offering entertainment in a unique atmosphere. *Chamber Quarterly Report*, 3 (3), 9.

Judicial Council of California. (2009). Fact sheet: Improving trial court facilities: Butte—New North Butte County Courthouse. Retrieved September 25, 2012, http://www.courts.ca.gov/documents/butte_fact_sheet.pdf.

Lawrence Halprin & Associates. (n.d.). CBD Masterplan Report, 2. Prepared for the City of Charlottesville, Charlottesville, VA.

Lucy, W.H. (1998). Planning commissioners' problems, policies and strategies. Unpublished manuscript. Charlottesville, VA: University of Virginia.

Lucy, W.H. (2002). *Downtown Revitalization: Charlottesville*. Charlottesville, VA: City of Charlottesville.

Nevada City Advocate. (2011, May 18). State's plans for new courthouse will devastate Nevada City, mayor says. Retrieved August 8, 2011, http://www.nevadacityadvocate.com/mobile/nevada-city/3448.html.

Ogletree, L. (2009, February 9). Letter to the editor. *Herald-Journal*. Retrieved July 15, 2010, http://www.avoc.info/info/article.php?article=3986.

Pew Charitable Trusts. (2010). Bringing downtown back to life: Programs that create viable local economies. Retrieved September 25, 2012, http://www.pewpartnership.org/pdf/What%27s%20Out%20There2.pdf.

Santa Barbara County. (2011). Legislative platform. Retrieved September 25, 2012, http://www.countyofsb.org/uploadedFiles/ceo/legis/2011%20Legislative%20Platform.pdf.

Sasaki Associates, Inc. (2008). Downtown Greenville Master Plan. Retrieved September 25, 2012, http://www.greenvillesc.gov/PlanningZoning/forms/DowntownMasterPlan FinalReport.pdf.

Schaut, S. (2010). *Historic Mansfield: A bicentennial history*. San Antonio, TX: Historical Publishing Network.

Seiter, P. (1996, October 31). *Great American Main Street Entry*. Holland, MI: City of Holland, MI.

Seiter, P. (2011). Response to downtown survey questionnaire from author. Muncie, IN.

Sharpe, T. (2008, August 6). Pieces of the past. *The Santa Fe New Mexican*. Retrieved March 7, 2011, http://www.thefreelibrary.com/PIECES+OF+THE+PAST.-a0187579064.

Sumo, V. (2007, fall). Downtown is dead: Long live downtown. *Region Focus*. Federal Reserve Bank of Richmond, Richmond, VA, pp. 16–17.

Superior Court of California & County of Santa Barbara. (2010). Project feasibility report. *Administrative Office of the Courts, Office of Court Construction and Management*. Retrieved September 25, 2012, http://www.courts.ca.gov/documents/santabarbara_ pfr.pdf.

The Capitol Connection. (2008). Legislation introduced to Improve California Courthouses. Vol. 10 (1), 8. Retrieved March 11, 2011, http://www.courts.ca.gov/documents/capcon-spr08.pdf.

The New York Times. (2009). Build it so they'll come. [Opinion Pages: Room for Debate]. Retrieved January 5, 2012, http://roomfordebate.blogs.nytimes.com/2009/02/27/pedestrian-malls-back-to-the-future/.

Thomas, J.B. (2011). Availability and affordability of homes for families with children in Charlottesville, VA. PLAC 5440-Affordable Housing, University of Virginia, Charlottesville, VA.

Yellig, J. (2006). Downtown mall: Charlottesville's public square. *The Daily Progress*. Retrieved January 17, 2012, http://www2.dailyprogress.com/news/cdp-newslocal/2006/jun/25/downtown_mall_charlottesvilles_public_square-ar-99161/.

6 Historic Preservation and Heritage Tourism

BBC Research and Consulting and Clarion Associates. (2005). The economic benefits of historic preservation in Colorado, 2005 Update. Retrieved October 4, 2012, http://oahp.historycolorado.org/crforms-edumat/pdfs/1620.pdf.

Bowen, S. (2011). Tourism boom for downtown started more than 20 years ago. *StarNewsOnline.com*. Retrieved May 28, 2011, http://www.starnewsonline.com/article/20110528/ARTICLES/110529683.

Brown, G.C. (1978). *The Genesis of the Wisconsin Republican Party, 1854*. Madison, WI: University of Wisconsin Press.

CIC Research, Inc., and Lauren Schlau Consulting. (2008). Santa Barbara County Visitors Survey and Economic Impact Study. *Santa Barbara Conference and Visitors Bureau and Film Commission*. Retrieved October 4, 2012, http://www.santabarbaraca.com/includes/media/docs/Visitor-Survey-and-Economic-Impact.pdf.

City of Charlottesville. (2012). Historic preservation and design planning. Retrieved October 3, 2012, http://www.charlottesville.org/Index.aspx?page=2369.

City of Fort Collins. (1981). *Design Guidelines for Historic Old Town Fort Collins*. Fort Collins, CO: Downing/Leach & Associates, Boulder, CO.

City of Fort Collins. (2006). Fort Collins downtown strategic plan. *Community Planning & Environmental Services*. Retrieved October 4, 2012, http://www.fcgov.com/advanceplanning/pdf/dsp-doc.pdf.

City of Fort Collins. (2007). *Apparitions of the Past: The ghost signs of Fort Collins, historical context*. Larimer County, CO: Advance Planning Department.

City of Fort Collins. (2011). Coca Cola sign Rehabilitation Project 2009-M2-007: Fieldwork treatment report. Fort Collins: City of Fort Collins, Co.

City of Middletown. (2002). Middletown design: A framework for development. The Middletown Design Review and Preservation Board, The Department of Planning, Conservation, and Development, July 2002. Retrieved October 2, 2012, http://www.middletownplanning.com/documents/guidelines.pdf.

City of Middletown. (2005). *Inventory of Historical and Architectural Resources*, vol. IV. The Greater Middletown Preservation Trust. Middletown, CT: City of Middletown, CT.

City of Middletown. (n.d.) Section 39D – Downtown Village District. *Zoning Code*. Department of Planning, Conservation, and Development, City of Middletown, CT. Retrieved October 10, 2012, http://www.middletownplanning.com/.

City of Nacogdoches. (1991). *Design Guidelines for Nacogdoches, TX*. Boulder, CO: Winter & Company.

City of Nacogdoches. (2012). Code of ordinances, section 50–32. Nacogdoches, TX. Retrieved March 8, 2012, http://library.municode.com/index.aspx?clientId=10966.

City of Ripon. (1969). Little White Schoolhouse: Birthplace of the Republican Party. National Register of Historic Places Inventory Nomination Form, United States Department of the Interior, National Park Service. Retrieved October 4, 2012, http://pdfhost.focus.nps.gov/docs/NHLS/Text/73000079.pdf.

City of Santa Fe Planning and Land Use Department. (2005). Santa Fe general plan update (draft), 2005–2025 (City of Santa Fe, 2004). *Santa Barbara Lower Rivera Historical Study*. Retrieved October 4, 2012, http://www.santabarbaraca.gov/Resident/Community/Heritage/accessed.

City of Wilmington. (2003). A *City-wide Plan of Land Use: A component of the Comprehensive Development Plan for Wilmington, Delaware*. Wilmington, DE: Department of Planning.

City of Wilmington. (2009). Substitute No. 1 to Ordinance No. 09-007: An ordinance to amend Chapter 5 of the Wilmington City code relating to public nuisance properties. Retrieved February 22, 2012, http://www.ci.wilmington.de.us/docs/317/3111Rev1.pdf.

City of Wilmington. (2011a). Vacant property registration fee program, Wilmington DE. Retrieved November 20, 2011, http://www.ci.wilmington.de.us/government/vacantproperties.

City of Wilmington. (2011b). Wilmington's innovative vacant property registration fee program celebrates nine years of reducing abandoned and vacant properties. Retrieved October 3, 2012, http://www.ci.wilmington.de.us/news/news.php?newsID=210.

Clarion Associates. (2005). *The Economic Benefits of Historic Preservation in Colorado, 2005 Update*. Denver, CO: Colorado Historical Society, BBC Research and Consulting.

Days, M.L. (1984). *A Visit to Santa Barbara's Historical Architectural Highlights*. City Community Development Department. Santa Barbara, CA: Author.

Downtown Visions. (2011). *Façade and Upstairs Improvement Programs*. Wilmington, DE: Main Street Wilmington.

Historic Landmarks Commission and City Council. (2009). *El Pueblo Viejo Design Guidelines*, third edition. Santa Barbara, CA: Author.

Hutto, K. (2007, September). The Charlottesville Pavilion: Offering entertainment in a unique atmosphere. *Chamber Quarterly Report*, 3 (3), 9.

J.H. Beers & C. (1884). *The History of Middlesex County 1635–1885, NY*. New York. Transcribed by Janece Streig. Retrieved January 5, 2012, http://dunhamwilcox.net/town_hist/middletown_history5.html.

Loomis, J. & McTernan, J.E.S. (2010). *Results of a Survey of Summer Non-Resident Visitors to Selected Fort Collins Area Attractions*. Fort Collins, CO: Department of Agricultural and Resource Economics. Colorado State University, Fort Collins, CO.

Maloney, A.M. (2009). The Delaware historic preservation program: Restoring history and communities. *Delaware Division of Historic and Cultural Affairs*. Retrieved October 4, 2012, http://history.delaware.gov/pdfs/maloneyReport.pdf.

McWatters, L.D. (2007). The city different? Historic preservation and the Santa Fe Plaza. *The Public Historian,* 29 (4), 87–90.

Nacogdoches Convention & Visitors Bureau. (n.d.). Historic Nacogdoches: The legacy of Diedrich Rulfs. Retrieved October 3, 2012, http://www.visitnacogdoches.org/pdf/Rulfsbrochure.pdf.

Preservation Delaware. (2012). Delaware Preservation Fund. Retrieved October 4, 2012, http://preservationde.org/delaware-preservation-fund/.

Purdom, G. (2011, February 3). HUD grant to turn threatened Indiana house into affordable apartments. Preservation. *The Magazine of the National Trust for Historic Preservation*. Retrieved October 4, 2012, http://www.preservationnation.org/magazine/2011/story-of-the-day/hud-grant-indiana-house.html.

Santa Fe Convention and Visitors Bureau. (2010). *Santa Fe Convention and Visitors Bureau Phone and Email Study*. Albuquerque, NM: Southwest Planning and Marketing & CR & Associates.

Slabaugh, S. (2011a, November 6). Blight Watch: Historic Jackson Street home to be saved. *The Muncie Starpress*. Retrieved September 20, 2012, http://www.thestarpress.com/article/20111107/NEWS01/111070312/BLIGHT-WATCH-Historic-Jackson-Street-home-saved.

Slabaugh, S. (2011b, December 11). Blight Watch: Agreement reached on unsafe properties in historic districts. *The Muncie Starpress*. Retrieved September 20, 2012, http://www.thestarpress.com/article/20111205/NEWS01/112050311/BLIGHT-WATCH-Agreement-reached-unsafe-properties-historic-districts.

The Greater Middletown Preservation Trust. (1979). *Historical and Architectural Resources*, Vol.1. City of Middletown, CT: The Greater Middletown Preservation Trust.

Thomas Jefferson Planning District Commission. (2012). Heritage tourism toolkit, online. Retrieved October 4, 2012, http://www.tjpdc.org/workforce/tjV_heritage Tourism.asp.

Tourism Development International. (2007). Greenville, South Carolina: Tourism Product Development Concept. Retrieved October 4, 2012, http://www.greenvillecvb.com/!UserFiles/docs/Tourism_Rpt_11x17.pdf.

7 Designing Resilient Downtowns

Art and Artifacts. (2010). Inside Santa Fe. 11 (1), 39–96.

Cerin, E., Duncan, M. J., du Toit, L., Leslie, E., Owen, N., Sugiyama, T., & Winkler, E. (2010). Relationship of land use mix with walking for transport: Do land uses and geographical scale matter? *Journal of Urban Health: Bulletin of the New York Academy of Medicine*, 87 (5), 782–795.

City of Fort Collins. (1989). Downtown plan: An element of the comprehensive plan. Retrieved June 8, 2011, http://www.fcgov.com/advanceplanning/pdf/downtown-plan-doc.pdf.

City of Fort Collins. (2006). *Fort Collins Downtown Strategic Plan*. Fort Collins, CO: Downtown Development Authority.

City of Greenville. (2010). Downtown facts & figures. Retrieved October 5, 2012, http://www.greenvillesc.gov/EconDev/forms/DowntownFacts.pdf.

City of Lafayette–West Lafayette. (n.d). *Graphics Standard Manual: Downtown districts*. Lafayette, IN: Author.

City of Middletown. (2002). *Middletown Design: A framework for development*. Middletown, CT: Middletown Design Review and Preservation Board.

City of Ripon. (2007). *Go Ripon! Draft downtown Ripon Strategic Plan November 26, 2007*. Madison, WI: Vandewalle & Associates, Inc.

City of Santa Fe. (2007). Santa Fe downtown vision plan. Retrieved May 17, 2010 http://www.santafenm.gov/DocumentView.aspx?DID=1408.

City of Santa Fe. (2010). Visual Arts: Santa Fe—the biggest little art city in the world. *Sante Fe: The Official Santa Fe Visitors Guide*. Santa Fe, NM: Santa Fe Communication and Visitors Bureau.

City of Wilmington. (2003). A city-wide plan of land use. Retrieved March 30, 2011, http://76.12.60.78/Planning/Citywide-Plan-of-Land-Use.pdf.

Estrada, L.E. (2008, October 11). Mission: Santa Barbara, Alta California 1782. [Web log comment]. Retrieved October 4, 2012, http://www.travelblog.org/North-America/United-States/California/Santa-Barbara/blog-335942.html.

Ettenson, R. & Ettenson K. (2010). *Inside Santa Fe*. Santa Fe, NM: Vacation Publications.

Forsyth, A. & Krizek, K. (2011). Urban design: Is there a distinctive view from the bicycle? *Journal of Urban Design*, 16 (4), 531–549.

Hirsch, M.D. (2011). Response to downtown development questionnaire from author, Muncie, IN.

Jacobs, J. (1961). *The Death and Life of Great American Cities*. New York: Random House.

Lynch, K. (1960). *The Image of the City*. Cambridge, MA: The MIT Press.

Lynch, K. (1981). *Good Urban Form*. Cambridge, MA: The MIT Press.

Mitchell, J. & Reynis, L. (2004). The economic importance of the arts and cultural industries in Santa Fe County. The University of New Mexico Bureau of Business and Economic Research. Retrieved October 5, 2010, http://bber.unm.edu/pubs/SFC.ArtsPt2.pdf.

Morales, L. (2012, March 13). Provo-Orem, Utah leads U.S. in city optimism. *Gallup Wellbeing*. Retrieved October 5, 2012, http://www.gallup.com/poll/153206/Provo-Orem-Utah-Leads-Metro-Areas-City-Optimism.aspx.

Mullin Associates, Inc. (1996). Downtown market area plan: Middletown, CT. Retrieved October 5, 2012, http://www.middletownplanning.com/documents/DOWNTOWNMULLINREPORT1996.pdf.

National Trust for Historic Preservation. (2011). Most romantic main streets. Retrieved October 5, 2012, http://www.preservationnation.org/main-street/main-street-now/most-romantic-main-streets.html.

Project for Public Spaces. (2009). What is placemaking? Retrieved August 31, 2012, http://www.pps.org/reference/what_is_placemaking/.

Ripon Historic Preservation Commission. (2008). Historic downtown design manual: Guidelines for Ripon's central business district. Retrieved October 5, 2012, http://www.riponmainst.com/riponmainst/Renovation/Downtown%20Ripon%20Design%20Manual%20%282010%29.pdf.

Seiter, P. (2011, June). Response to downtown development questionnaire administered by author to Downtown Managers.

Shigley, P. (2007). California's best and worst mid-sized city downtowns. *California Planning and Development Report*. Retrieved January 31, 2012, http://www.cp-dr.com/node/1782.

Sumo, V. (2007, fall). Downtown is dead: Long live downtown. *Region Focus. The Federal Reserve Bank of Richmond*, Richmond, VA, pp. 12–17.

The International Downtown Association (2011). *Facebook*. Retrieved November 1, 2011, http://www.facebook.com/pages/International-Downtown-Association/217227978398939?id=217227978398939&sk=info.

The Vincent Group. (2006, July). Downtown living: Is there demand for additional residential development in the Wilmington CBD? Prepared for the Wilmington Renaissance Corporation, Wilmington, DE.

Vahl, H. (2010). Gateway signs expected to improve city navigation. Retrieved October 5, 2012, http://www.middletownpress.com/articles/2010/01/18/news/doc4b53dba.

Wilmington Renaissance Corporation. (2009). *A Partnership for Progress: Strategic Plan, 2009–2012*. Wilmington, DE: Wilmington Renaissance Corporation.

8 Economic Distress and Downtown Revitalization

City of Middletown. (2011). *Downtown Middletown: In the Middle of It All!* Middletown, CT: Trevor Davis Commercial Real Estate.

City of Middletown. (2012). Main Street and Grand List Values: 1998–2011. City of Middletown, Department of Planning, Conservation, and Development.

Heaslip, J. (2009, January 4). Merchants report campaign success. *Hendersonville Times-News*. Retrieved October 5, 2012, http://www.narniastudios.com/narnia_in_the_news.html.

Milone & MacBroom, Inc. (2011). Final Report: Downtown Gateway Study Middletown, Connecticut. Retrieved October 5, 2012, http://www.middletownplanning.com/documents/DowntownGatewayFINALREPORT_2011.pdf.

Nagourney, A. (2010, November 18). For California, another day, another deficit. *The New York Times*. Retrieved October 5, 2012, http://www.staradvertiser.com/news/20101118_For_California_another_day_another_deficit.html?id=108871364.

RKG Associates, Inc. (2010). *Downtown Housing Market Study, Middletown, CT*. Dover, NH: Author.

Sasaki Associates, Inc. (2008). Downtown Greenville Master Plan. Retrieved October 5, 2012, http://www.greenvillesc.gov/PlanningZoning/forms/DowntownMasterPlanFinalReport.pdf.

Schnorbus, R.H. & Watson, A. (2010). The service sector and the "great recession"—a fifth district perspective. *The Federal Reserve Bank of Virginia*. Retrieved October 5, 2012, http://www.richmondfed.org/publications/research/economic_brief/2010/pdf/eb_10-12.pdf.

Short, D. (2013). Real disposable income per capita: up only 0.2% since February 2012. *Advisorperspectives.com*. Retrieved February 1, 2013, http://advisorperspectives.com/dshort/updates/DPI-Monthly-Update.php.

Taggart, K. (2012). Explainer: The end of redevelopment agencies. *California Watch*. Retrieved October 5, 2012, http://californiawatch.org/dailyreport/explainer-end-redevelopment-agencies-1462.

The Economist. (2011). *America's Economy: Distress Signal*. Retrieved July 29, 2012, http://www.economist.com/blogs/freeexchange/2011/07/americas-economy.

Urquhart, M.I. (1981, October). The services industry: Is it recession-proof? *Monthly Labor Review*, 12–18.

9 Downtown Alive!

Beals, S.R. (2012, May 10). Middletown's North end seeing growth, change. *Hartford Courant.com*. Retrieved October 19, 2012, http://articles.courant.com/2012-05-10/community/hc-middletown-north-end-0506-20120510_1_community-health-center-building-wharfside-commons-mark-masselli/2.

Birch, E.L. (2005). Who lives downtown. *The Brooking Institution*. Retrieved October 5, 2012, http://www.brookings.edu/research/reports/2005/11/downtownredevelopment-birch.

City of Fort Collins. (1989). *Downtown Plan*. Fort Collins, CO: Author.

City of Mansfield. (2012). Main Street quick start survey. Retrieved October 5, 2012, http://surveys.verticalresponse.com/a/show/312351/257b7663e0/0.

City of Middletown Redevelopment Agency. (1992). *North End/CBD Urban Renewal Plan*. City of Middletown, CT.

City of Santa Fe. (2007). Downtown Santa Fe Vision Plan (Draft Report). *Steering Committee, Santa Fe, NM*. Retrieved October 5, 2012, http://www.santafenm.gov/DocumentView.aspx?DID=1408.

Dawley, S., Pike, A., & Tomaney, J. (2010). Towards the resilient region? *Local Economy*, 25 (8), 650–667.

Denver Post. (2004, July 27). Fort Collins couple wins fight to raze barn, house, B1.

Downtown Mansfield, Inc. (2007). *Downtown Mansfield Appraised Values Study*. Mansfield, OH: Author.

Heyer, Gruel & Associates. (2009). Preserving community character: recommendations for a historic commission. Township of South Orange Village, Essex County. *Acroterion, LLC, Historic Preservation Consulting*. Retrieved October 5, 2012, http://www.south orange.org/historicpreservation/HistoricFiles/HistoryPreservationPlan_72309.pdf.

Hill, E.W., Wial, H., & Wolman, H. (2008). Exploring regional resilience, working paper 2008–04. *Institute of Urban and Regional Development & McArhur Foundation Research Network on Building Resilient Regions*. University of California Berkeley: Author.

Hopper, T. (2012, January 8). Taking a u-turn on the one-way street. *National Post*. Retrieved January 8, 2012, http://news.nationalpost.com/2012/01/08/taking-a-u-turn-on-the-one-way-street/.

Lindstrom, T. (2012). Business owners want two-way street. *Your News Now*. Retrieved October 5, 2012, http://ithaca-cortland.ynn.com/content/top_stories/586402/business-owners-want-two-way-street/?ap=1&MP4.

Lozon, M. (1994). *Vision on Main Street. Lumir Corporation*. Holland, MI: Author.

Mansfield Alliance, Fifth Avenues, and Kinzelman, Kline & Gossman. (2003, March). *Mansfield Downtown and the Miracle Mile: Strategic Development Plan*. Mansfield, OH: Author.

Martz. L. (2012). Reaction mixed on two-way: Some worry about safety, possible drop in customers. *Mansfield News Journal*. Retrieved May 24, 2012, http://www.mansfieldnewsjournal.com/article/20120524/NEWS01/205240302/Reaction-mixed-two-way.

Metropolitan Planning Commission. (2012). Chatham County historic preservation ordinance. Retrieved October 5, 2012, http://www.thempc.org/documents/CCHPC/CHATHAM%20COUNTY%20HISTORIC%20PRESERVATION%20ORDINANCE%20REVISED%202-27-09.pdf.

Robins, A. (2005). The case for preservation easements: When municipal ordinances fail to protect historic properties. *Thompson & Columbus, Inc.* Retrieved October 5, 2012, http://www.sfheritage.org/wp-content/uploads/2011/03/Robbins-ReportWEB.pdf.

Sasaki Associates, Inc. (2008). *Downtown Greenville Master Plan*. Greenville, SC: City of Greenville.

The New Netherland Institute. (2012). Prince, Edgar D. (1931–1995). Cultural Education Center, Albany, NY. Retrieved August 19, 2011, http://www.nnp.org/nni/Publications/Dutch-American/prince.htm.

Vollmer Associates. (2001). Downtown Hyannis Traffic Circulation Study, Vol. I of II. Prepared for the Town of Barnstable, Boston, MA. Retrieved May 8, 2011, http://www.capecodcommission.org/resources/transportation/2001_HYNS_CIRC_STDY_1of2.pdf.

Index

Locators in *italics* refer to figures or tables.